RAW CHRISTIANITY THE WAY
JESUS CHRIST
EXPECTS ALL TO KNOW IT!

For the Christian, the non-Christian even the Skeptic!

TONY GALANTE

PRESS

Raw Christianity The way Jesus Christ Expects All to Know it!
For the Christian, the non-Christian even the Skeptic!
by Tony Galante

Printed in the United States of America

ISBN 9781628714807

www.xulonpress.com

—⦿—

THE AUTHOR / Tony Galante is a graduate of Lancaster Bible College, where he earned a Bachelor of Science in Biblical Studies. He also attended Luther Rice Seminary. He has pastored two churches and has been a rescue mission chaplain. He was also a very successful fundraiser with the U.S. Chamber of Commerce, based in Washington D.C. God has blessed and called him to be very successful evangelistically by preaching the Good News of the Gospel of Christ to groups as large as 1,500 persons and as small as one person. He is very truth-driven and not driven by unbiblical theological opinion. It is estimated that he has given the gospel on an individual basis to as many as 30,000 persons and many of these from non-Biblical faiths. This is in addition to his preaching at Christian churches.

DEDICATION

—⁓⁓—

It is to my wife Karen, with love
and joy that I dedicate this book

TABLE OF CONTENTS

PREFACE

───◈◈◈───

There once was a boy who was fortunate to be raised in a multi-cultural home, who was taught to enjoy the gifts of other cultures. His father knew five languages and his grandmother, who was close to her grandson, knew seven languages. The boy's mother knew three languages and also had an understanding of the culture with these languages. The boy's father and grandfather were more of a pioneering type.

Along with this multi-cultural home came the concept, understanding and love for the only true God. When this boy was in the fifth grade and studying his social studies textbook, he was reading about World War II. It was at this time that he asked his dad "Who started World War II? Was it Germany or Japan?" He gave the boy the answer that the Germans were responsible for the start of the war. But to the boy's surprise, his father told him that all history books do not give the same account of history. The books in Europe were different than the American books. For instance, the Germans blame the English for the start of the war and during that time the French also gave the English the blame. Of course, these were books written right after the war and they may be different today. But it showed the boy in his youth that the authors of these history books did not write from a perspective of truth but through their opinion. They did not write based on the total truth as all need to see it! The young boy was amazed at this!

Another time in this boy's life, at the age of about six years old, the U.S. got involved in a space exploration race. This was months before Alan Shepherd and John Glenn went up into space. There was so much science fiction on TV, such as Flash Gordon and Superman, etc., all pointing to going to Mars, etc. As a six-year-old, the boy asked his mother who was the spaceman going up this time and she said John Glenn. So, the boy said, "is he going to Mars?" She replied, "no honey, he will go into space and circle the earth." The boy replied to his mother, "No Mars." Then the mother said, "no honey, we haven't even gone to the moon yet!" At that point, the six-year-old felt betrayed and deceived by all the ridiculousness and hoopla that he saw on TV about going to Mars. "You mean no one even got to the moon yet?" The year was 1962. This young boy was so amazed about the childishness of the adult TV media, and their going so far out to fantasize about going to Mars, and yet the Americans were just starting to truly enter into only circling the earth's space atmosphere.

There was another thing that the youth learned at an early age and that was if there were no true solid foundational guidelines, things in man's hands can get pretty muddy. Such as if you tell one person that you stubbed your toe, and that person tells another person, and so on. By the time this is told to 100 people the last person would be saying something such as "Oh really, you mean he (she) fractured their head?" This is what can be called "the broken toe to broken head" phenomenon and is due to over-generalizing. This has also happened by the embellishments of stories of the generations. The reason for this is that these stories are man-made and not protected by God as the Holy Bible is protected by God. This is because the Scriptures in the Bible are from God and not by the will of man. But the immense confusion about the Holy Bible is due to man because of not reading it or studying it from God's perspective. Yet all men are responsible to God first and foremost, not to man. God cares not of a man's fame or popularity if that focus is not on God, rather than man's will in putting his spin on what the current day populism or accepting trend is. This is why this book was written. Because many in their comfort zone would prefer to go along with the populous even though it is not God's true way. So the person who thinks they know God needs to read this book for their own sake and their loved ones. This book is also written for the one who is seeking the true God, along with the young and mature Christian, to get the most important master teachings or doctrines to give them a greater spiritual power and strength in Christ, because unfortunately, many are not getting these real important truths today.

Finally, this book is written to the person who is misinformed that the Holy Bible of Christianity contradicts itself or that it is based on getting your money or that Jesus Christ was just some religious figure just like all the other religions. One more thing: it is also written to the person that thinks that there is no God, and perhaps that person's eyes can be opened by God. This book will show the reader the True foundational truths of Christianity that everyone is responsible for and no one is allowed to ignore. This book was written to show the reader, whoever they may be, in a form and style not to confuse or intimidate, but by writing the full name of the book referred to in the Bible along with its chapter address and verse(s). Some of the referenced Bible verses may be repeated or used in more than one master teaching or doctrine, to familiarize the reader that one verse may be used to teach more than one master truth or doctrine. There are many Bible verses presented in this book, but I encourage you to get a Bible or to go into your own Bible to look up the verses that are only addressed and not printed in this book. This book is designed this way so that you open your Bible and read these verses yourself from God's true Holy and Only Book! Oh, incidentally, the young boy I told you about was me!

INTRODUCTION

GOD'S STRUCTURE FOR TRUE CHRISTIANITY AND REAL SPIRITUAL LIFE

———ⲟⲟⲟ———

There is a definite structure, path, and focus to all things in life. It is the correct structure and path that gives us the ability to have the best possible quality of life. Focus, on the other hand, if done properly, brings forth the motivation for properly experiencing an ongoing quality of life.

If structure is not understood properly, it cannot bring about the other two advantages to life such as path and focus. All things have structure. For instance, in nature there are four basic elements. They are air, fire, water and earth. All living things are made up of these basic elemental parts here on earth. If a plant would have no water, it would shrivel up and die and the same would happen to the plant if one of the other elemental parts were missing. Think of this in terms of your body's needs. You need protein, fat, carbohydrates and vitamins and minerals. Your body has a need for all these things. But, if you just feed your body four of these things without a fifth type of nutrient, your health would eventually suffer and break down to the point of death. So all of these structural nutrients are important for life and its overall quality.

How odd would it be if you purchased a new automobile and it had no brakes in it at all? You and your loved ones would be in great danger from the very first time you or they would drive it. Let's suppose you had your kitchen renovated and remodeled and the building contractor took it for granted that you would have the sink put in yourself because you may have told him that your brother was a plumber in town. Then, from your point of view, you may have thought that the contractor who was renovating your kitchen would naturally put in a sink that you said you liked. You see there was an inadequate, concrete, poor conviction, poor conversation and poor agreement and the physical structure of a sink missing, one of the most important elements of any true kitchen on any scale.

How well do you think your path would be to making a simple recipe like baking bread without water for mixing the other ingredients? The simple truth is it would not happen. The focus to this current recipe would be an inconvenience to making the bread or not even starting at all. In the end there is not much of a quality to the experience. As you can see, structure is very important to life and in life, because if a proper structure is missing, there is no life. Your body has bones to give it structure. Try moving your home without boxes and proper wrapping of items. Something is bound to scratch or break. If structure is missing, there is no quality of life. And if some of the needed structures are missing, there is a lack of life.

In the spiritual world there are also structures, paths and focus that the True God has for mankind to understand. For instance, in the Biblical book (John 3:5-7), Jesus talks about two births: one of water and the other of spirit. The birth by water is the natural birth. But why did Jesus use the word by "water"? The reason is that our bodies are made up of a large majority of water, around 70%. And without water there is no human physical life. Jesus then mentions that the other birth is spiritual and it is the second birth. The spiritual birth is one that must be accepted as the work of God if we are to receive everlasting spiritual life. Jesus also says in (John 14:6), speaking of Himself, "...I am the way, and the truth, and the life; no one comes to the Father but through Me." Here you have three different modes or methods that are interconnected, and correct structures, paths and true focus of how to receive, understand and live in the blessing of everlasting life. Then in (John 14:7), Jesus Christ, the Son of the living God, explains that if a person comprehends, recognizes, believes and identifies that He, Jesus Christ the Son, has come through God the Father and the Son is equal to the Father, they have known God the Father. We could only know this because God's Word, the Bible, claims that the Father is equal to the Son and that the Son is equal to the Father. This is because we must understand the master teachings or doctrines as they were originally taught by the Old Testament Prophets, by Jesus Christ Himself, and those men chosen by Christ called the Apostles. These master or original teachings that are properly called doctrines show us the true structural parameters, paths and focus in a very important essential way that all Christians need to have a knowledge of, and understanding, in order to spiritually grow strong. This knowledge and understanding will give the Christian believer insight to discern if something they hear or read is from the viewpoint of the True God. These master teachings or doctrines will protect you and your loved ones if they are taught them and if they believe them.

In today's church there are many pastors, priests, teachers, etc. who will speak or write only their opinion. And yet they may give you their feelings of psychology or being politically proper and philosophizing good information. But it may not be the master teaching or the doctrines of the Bible. You may, in fact, be deceived from a humanistic approach. Another thing is that you may have or may not have heard or have only been taught about the Bible stories. Bible stories are always good. Everyone seems to know about David and Goliath, Samson and Delilah and Jonah in the belly of the great fish. But without the original master teachings, called doctrines, to understand the true meaning and depths of how these true events are pointing to Jesus Christ and His salvation for us, this could not truly be understood except for having a knowledge of the doctrines. Most people will take these stories in the Old Testament of the Old Testament Prophets as good stories to teach children to have courage and to do the right thing, without knowing the most important things pointing to the coming of the Messiah (Christ). It is imperative that a true spiritual person learns the master teachings, again called the doctrines. The natural man thinks senses and feels through his natural insight and perception by seeing, tasting, smelling, hearing and touch. The spiritual person lives by faith—and this is not blind faith in any way, as some think or have been taught. This way of thinking is based on human authority. But true faith is based on real, evidential facts as in the New Testament book of Hebrews (11:1-40). In other words, the true Christian faith is based on certainty and in no way fantasy or human idea. This means that there truly is a definite healthy framework of doctrine for Christians. Not with "myths" or tales and "speculation". Again, by doctrine it is the teaching as from the Biblical Prophets, Jesus Christ and the Apostles that He chose. The Apostle Paul, who is responsible for writing most of the New Testament, gives a warning in (1 Timothy 1:3) to Christian teachers to teach the sound master teachings (doctrines) and that the Christian faith is not to teach and promote "strange doctrines". By strange teaching or doctrines, he means things like speculations, foolishness and outright lies, which have no place in Christianity. It is only sound, logical and valid doctrine that will nourish the Christian believer (1 Timothy 4:6).

The Apostle Paul also tells us this:

> Pay close attention to yourself and to your teaching; persevere in these things, for as you do this you will ensure salvation both for yourself and for those who hear you. 1 Timothy 4:16

As you can see from this verse, Paul is warning the person teaching the master teaching or doctrine that what they say and what others believe from them has eternal significance for the salvation of the teacher and hearer. So who can this teacher be? They can be a pastor, professor, priest, father, mother or even a first time acquaintance, etc. And who can the hearer be? A non-Christian, a child or an adult of any sort including some pastors, priests, professors, fathers, mothers, etc. Why? The reason is that if any minister of any type of faith or denomination doesn't teach sound doctrine from the Word of God, then he is in grave danger! This is not my idea; this is according to the Apostle Paul who is telling us this by God's Word. The Apostle Paul says that it is the minister's responsibility to hold strong and stay on course with what the Bible tells us in it's original teaching, so that he is encouraged in the valid and binding doctrine of true biblical faith, and to contradict and disapprove any fallacy being taught (Titus 1:9). All Christians are also responsible in this way. The problem is that many ministers and so-called Christians think that anything that appears or feels spiritual is from God. This, as you can see, is far from the truth! The Bible in its original teachings (doctrines) is the spiritual truth and all other forms contrary to God's Word are lies and false. The Apostle Paul says another thing is that all Christians are to be ready and prepared with the right original teachings (doctrines) for their true purpose, which is each person's individual ministry in service (Ephesians 4:4-13). The ultimate goal is that all true Christians are to grow to the fullest knowledge and life in Jesus Christ the Lord. Then in verse 14, Paul tells us of this outcome: that we are not like children anymore, who are naive and don't know if we are going in a right or wrong direction, or even a possibility of getting drawn in some type of deceptive trick and cunning twist of the original master teachings of Biblical Scripture.

The goal of this book is to give every Christian, and sincere person who is not sure about what true Christianity is all about, a firm and strong grip of the original doctrines or teaching with the same view, conviction and scope of the elements of the true faith as Jesus Christ, and His hand-picked Apostles, and His Old Testament Prophets declared.

Here are just some doctrinal truths or teachings covered in this book.

1) Who is the true God, His nature and His characteristics?

2) Why is the Bible so important and what is meant by it, being God's inspired Word?

3) Why is Jesus Christ and His work so important?

4) Who and why is the Holy Spirit important?

5) What does Salvation really mean?

6) Where did man come from and what is his true condition?

7) What is sin and what are its results?

8) Are there really good angels?

9) Is there really a devil?

10) Are there bad angels?

11) Who is the true church?

12) What does the Bible really tell us of future events to come?

Here is a comparison example of those in the natural life and those in the true spiritual realm:

Natural	Spiritual
Parents	One God, the fullness in three persons and invisible, the Father, planner and giver of life
Protector	Jesus Christ, God the Son in the flesh with the Father and Holy Spirit
Comforter	God the Holy Spirit. Guiding and convicting man of sin and indwelling man with the Father and the Son.
Parent's instructions	The Bible, God's Word to man
In the care of others like doctors, teachers, nannies	Good Angels
Brothers and sisters, older or younger	The Church

Disobeying parents, breaking the law	Sin
Parents blood transfusion or any life saving	Salvation
Head terrorist	The devil and hateful instigator (Satan)
Sub terrorists	The bad angels (demons)
Any good thing you love like health, life, riches, marriage, etc.	Future events such as blessings, rewards and life everlasting in and with Jesus Christ

These are only examples and very weak comparisons. For instance, parent's instructions may not truly be perfect and best for the child, but God's Word the Bible is perfect, because He is the only perfect being. Also, if your parents save your life by being able to give you a blood transfusion or mouth-to-mouth resuscitation, you may recover, but you will not physically live forever. But God's plan of salvation, only through Jesus Christ, gives a believer everlasting life. Again the goal of this book is to explain the loving plan and adventure the only true God has for you!

1

OBSTACLES TO THE TRUTH

The Holy Bible is to be the only source of teaching about God. Even more so than life and nature itself! Why, you ask? The reason is that all of humanity is flawed collectively as well as individually in various ways. The main reason why nature today is so flawed is due to sin. We have all been born with a sin nature. This sin nature occurred in the time of Adam and Eve. Adam and Eve rejected God by not trusting their Creator's words of warning to them.

Yes, it is a truth that God created them in perfection and gave them a free will as a gift of His love to them. This great human gift that all of us have, even today, is in fact the greatest of all the human gifts we have from God. Just think of the possible wonderful experiences Adam and Eve have witnessed because of their unmarred free will. This is one of the reasons so many seek after the past — for the history and the genius of their ancestor's free will — to this day.

But it is sin that has marred the entire creation, all because one and only one condition was given to Adam and Eve. This condition was loyalty in the form of worship to God. The loyalty that was and is due to Him by the human race, His greatest creation! The first created male and female, Adam and Eve. Because of their sin we were all born with a nature to sin. Their failure is our failure. Therefore we were all born into a state of human failure. The Bible says it this way:

...for all have sinned and fall short of the glory of God. Romans 3:23

This verse is basic. It tells us that we are all sinners in the eyes of God. We all sin against God and our fellow man.

All humanity suffers in so many ways! We suffer spiritually, physically, mentally, emotionally, financially, etc., because of our own sins and those who have sinned against us.

Then there are some who suffer because, if we may say it this way, nature gave them a raw deal. In the Gospel of John (9:1-3), we see Jesus Christ's disciples asking Him who was at fault due to sin in the blindness of a man that was born blind. Jesus replied by telling them that the blindness was for the work of God to be seen in his life. I have experienced a child of mine who was born with underdeveloped lungs. He needed a respirator for a total of twenty-one days. At that time it was a truly dangerous time for the child. I was even told that the day after his birth he was not better, but worse. However, after thirty days, he was released from the hospital and grew to be a good student and also a good athlete. Praise God, our prayers were answered! I also know of a different situation of a child whose father was a Nazi soldier. As his wife was giving birth to her son, he ordered the nurses to immediately remove all symbols and things related to God because he didn't want his child to see God in any way at his birth. Well, this may sound like a coincidence, but the child was born blind. So what does this all mean? Many of us take the day to day blessings for granted in this life. So because of this, we easily get to the point of forgetting the most important blessing, the blessing of eternal life that God has been the total provider of. God gave man the greatest natural gift, the gift of free will. He is also the giver of the greatest spiritual gift, the gift of everlasting life! This gift of everlasting life is only acceptable and provided through His only Son Jesus Christ.

But there are those that look to nature and say this is enough to know who God is. Some even say there is no God because their senses do not detect a God. They don't see one, hear one, and can't touch Him, etc. This is faulty reasoning and logic in itself. There are thousands of things we have not seen with the naked eye, but that simply doesn't mean they don't exist. If a person is hard of hearing and they cannot hear a bird singing outside their window, that doesn't mean that the bird is not truly singing, does it? Denying the truth doesn't change the absoluteness of the truth! In fact, it reveals that a person is self-disliked due to the fact of their disbelief of the truth.

Then there is a matter of completeness of truth. For one to believe only in the Old Testament today makes them miss the completeness of spiritual truth. One must also understand and believe the New Testament to understand the complete truth. Even though the New Testament may give the greater part of truth, the Old Testament is needed to understand the history on the coming Savior and Messiah. You need to understand the Old Testament to understand the fulfillment of other true prophecies that were only fulfilled by the Son of God, who is also called the Spirit of Prophecy, and He is Jesus Christ.

We must also know that nothing else is to be added to the Holy Bible. This is so there is no possibility of giving it a distinctive slant on any of its teachings from God and to prevent any corruption of its truth in any possible way. By this I mean that there are to be no other so-called testaments added (or even catechisms) as a source of belief, for the simple reason that these are man-made with the intent to slant the truth of God's Holy Word. There are many books, tools and notes that are good sources to bring about better understanding of the loving truth of who God truly is, but these sources are never to replace the Bible as so many think it is ok to do today. In fact, many people even read other things about the Bible more than the Bible itself! This puts the major teachings of God's Word on the back burner where they should never be placed.

There are so many bibles today with good notes placed within them. The problem with this is that it is the author's point of view. This is ok in good teaching, but they go as far as placing their own name in front of the Word of God that is the Holy Bible. I'm not saying that many of these teachers are not due respect for their work, but the placement of one's name before the word or words "Bible or Holy Bible" is a form of arrogance that is not biblical. This should never be. The Bible can have notes, lessons, and maps, etc., as teaching aids, but placing the name of some fallible person in front of the Holy Bible is not giving God all the glory. This is a form of one-upmanship, as well as a modern form of marketing and concealed arrogance. This attitude tries to promote that this author is closer to God than another person. This modern form of marketing the Bible takes away from the exclusiveness of the Word of God. The Bible is for all humanity, to be read and understood. It is not to be treated as some common marketing tactic. These are stumbling blocks to the true faith in Christ.

The Bible teaches us the Gospel, which is the Good News message. This Good News Gospel can only be understood by one understanding the major truths of the Bible. These major truths are called Doctrines. The word doctrine has a much greater power and weight in meaning than the word teaching. The reason for this is that the facts of a teaching can be changed but doctrines are absolute facts, revealed to mankind through God's Holy Word, the Bible. For example, at one time the world was considered flat. Today, however, we have many proofs that the world is round. Therefore, the old fact is considered a total falsehood today. Doctrines, however, are revealed to us through the Bible, and because the Bible is God's supreme facts as well as His truth, they are immutable or unchangeable. Because the Bible is God's truth, one needs to understand that all three persons in the Godhead — the Father, the Son and the Holy Spirit — are always in total unison and in agreement and have been participants in the writing of the Biblical Scriptures.

The goal of the author is to point to these major truths in an unadulterated way. This is without man's pride, desire or denominational distinctions. Man needs to look at God's Holy Bible as from God and not as some common manmade book. It needs to be preached, thought, and lived by, without man's pride and personal feelings involved in any way. By this I mean that man should put his own slants, likes, dislikes or desires aside when preaching or teaching the Word of God. The Holy Bible needs to be proclaimed only by God's likes, dislikes and desires. This is truly the Good News of God's blessed freedom declared to us in the Bible. It is the blessed truth that can free any man, woman or child looking forward to a blissful, everlasting life in Heaven. The hub of this Good News Gospel centers all on the greatest miracle of all time! What is this miracle you ask? It is that God, in bodily form as Jesus Christ, destroyed the power of death by the shedding of His blood and gave eternal life by the power of His resurrection. No one in all the past, present or future has ever performed such a greatness of a miracle, nor ever will as Jesus Christ the Son of God, for He is God incarnate (in bodily form).

Because of the nature of man, he seems to think that he must systematize his theology to the fullest and if it is disagreed upon, he needs to go to the Bible and check his understanding of God. This must be done in the full context of the Bible. After that is done, if his theology still goes against the doctrine(s) of the Scripture, then that part of his personal understanding of God or theology must be discarded as out of Bible context of God's Word. It must be viewed as being false and he must rethink to understand the Truth.

Every human has a need to worship. This is because God the Creator has instilled this need of worship in our very being! The reason this need to worship God is instilled in us is because the human race was made in His image; by this I mean we are the greatest of all His created creatures. Another reason is that God is not a God who wants to distance Himself from us. He wants us to live very close to Him and to have very close communication with Him. This is the reason our prayers to Him are so important, as well as His word to us in the Holy Bible. We are not perfect, but God is perfect; therefore, God's Word is His priceless gift to all mankind.

All people look for the truth of life if we look inside ourselves. We all want to help ourselves and others; this is just part of humanity. We all know and feel safe with the right boundaries in life. Part of our humanity is seeing others reach their greatest potential even if we do not have that potential ourselves. Everyone, in love with humanity and not having a calloused heart, has a desire to give to one going through misfortune. Everyone is in need of a strong intelligent leader to protect them for a life of progress. We are all in need of kindness and goodness and one to help us in our time of helplessness. These things are all in the character of God the Creator. He also created all of us to follow after His character. Man, unfortunately in his self-love and pride, many times feels that it is ok to push away the Doctrines or master teachings of God and teach about God his own way. This is a great disaster and extremely dangerous because it leads men astray. This pride of man's own idea of God is a false teaching and effects the individual, their family, society and the world. This is why I am writing this book and will be bringing forth the Major Teaching of God called the Doctrine of the Word of God.

Modern men, including many Pastors, Priests and teachers, would like you to think that the Doctrine of the Scriptures is out of date or insignificant. But without an understanding of these Major Doctrines (teachings), any person who willfully rejects any one of them and believes they are unimportant is by their pride nullifying any possibility of eternal life. Why? Because eternal life is God's work toward us and we can do nothing to obtain it or receive it our way. Eternal life must be received God's way, and in no way by man's flawed imaginations.

Finally, if you are a new Christian or even a person in high status in the church, these doctrines are a biblical must. They are a must because it is by these major biblical doctrines that one can receive by faith the gift of eternal life, only through Jesus Christ the Lord. If you are a non-Christian the same applies to you also. What needs to be understood is that the current trend within many churches today is for the sermons to be popular, upbeat, emotionally pleasing and psychologically encouraging. The subjects are mostly about marriage, family, kindness, goodness and even money. These are good topics, but they are not the primary teaching of the Bible. In fact, these are supposed to be the things that come to our understanding after you have accepted Christ and truly understand the doctrines of the Bible. We have to be careful because sometimes, these subjects are not even from the Bible, but from non-biblical, dangerous sources.

It is not enough for a church to claim that they are "Bible believing" today. Unfortunately, there is a good share of denominational and non-denominational churches where the ministers are highly educated but are as biblically and spiritually dead as driftwood. Don't get me wrong, I am a very strong promoter in formal bible education as long as it is based on the foundational doctrinal teachings of the Bible and not the pride, fear or politics of man. This is the purpose of this book! It is to give you the Biblical Factual Foundational Doctrines (teachings) and point you to book, chapter and verse so you can see them for yourself. This is so you can understand and believe in God His way, not my way. It is by understanding these things that you can truly understand God's freedom, love, strength, encouragement and assurance in your life.

2

THE MANY OBSTACLES AND DISTRACTIONS TO THE TRUE FAITH IN GOD

—⸎—

There are many obstacles to a true and proper faith in God. You may ask, "why?" The main reason is because we allow these obstacles and distractions to be placed on us. We also make some of them ourselves. Consider how so many people are preoccupied with so many things that have little or no value in their life in comparison to knowing the God of the universe. Many times, there are strong passions that the world mercilessly uses to persuade us, thus driving us into a state of compulsion. This gives us the tunnel vision effect for life, where only one thing is important. Then there are obstacles like being overly responsible for things that we should not be responsible for. Too much responsibility in the wrong areas of our life can build a great drama, but in the end, it only snags us and can totally shut us down to the important things of life.

There is a growing trend in America and in some parts of the world where we look, think and feel that so many things are obsolete and out of date. With this way of thinking comes the mentality that because of this older way, which is not really old but relevant even for today, has a modern tag placed on it that has little value. All because it is not stylish or current. Today we live in a time where we are encouraged to think and feel comfortable with the choices we make in the little things, as well as for the most important things. Along with this we are very confident with ourselves, immoveable, willful and unyielding in our human spirit. Why must we be this way, when we could have a fuller intelligence and be able to have a proper compliance for our eternal benefit in knowing who the Loving One, True God is.

There are also situations that are working hard to hinder and even block us from going in the direction of God's plan for each one's life that He has for us here on earth. Evolution is taught in schools and universes with no choice of believing in a greater being than us. A being that had an intelligent design in creating the universe, as well as all the minute combinations of things we see in all creation. By true creation I mean that all things were creatively made out of nothing.

Another obstacle to a true and definite faith is that some see this matter as obtuse, dull, slow-witted and downright stupid. But if you really look at this way of thinking in comparison to an all powerful, all knowing, and all present being that many call God, it seems that the person who doesn't want to believe a living, true, all-powerful being as God, is in fact the one that is truly obtuse, dull and slow of wit and not understanding of life. There are people who think that the life they have is an occasion for them to wait, because they think in their own logic that they have plenty of life and time to live before they need to look at this God stuff! But no one knows how long they will live or how long their spouse or children may live. They think time is on their side. They may assume that there is a God and that He is a God of love. And He is! But what they may not know or comprehend is that He is also a just God, and true faith comes from Him, and He demands in His wisdom that we need to love and believe in Him, His way only. Because if it is our individual way, we are greatly misguided, lost and in a state of peril.

Another hindrance to true and definite faith is how people see their circumstances of life or events. They view their circumstances or certain things that happen to them in life as leading to consequences or how their life has gone. But God is

29

stable in His love and justice, mercy and care. He is immutable. This means He is unchanging. Some may think that they are okay and safe in revolting against the need for them to understand the true God. This is self destructive and faulty logic, because God is just, and yet He finds our rebellion displeasing and depraved no matter how minute. He loves mankind but He is very offended by our sin. Yet He (God) supplies the way out through His Son, Jesus Christ.

There are followers and even leaders in this day and age that have accepted many individual fantasies and fallacies about God. They are on their own odyssey and their own quest or voyage. They think that the odyssey they choose must be good for themselves, family, and mankind. The worst part of this way of thinking and acting is that they think this pleases God. It is this kind of thinking that hinders them away from God in that God has a special plan for them. The problem with this faulty thinking is that it is in direct opposition to God's Special revealed plan, given by His direct inspiration, revealed only by His Word the Holy Bible. Just picture going before the Creator and He tells you that you invested your whole life on your own quest, no matter how good it seemed to you or those in your life at the time. Then He reveals the plan He had for your life—if you had only taken the time to listen. How sad that would be.

There is a hindrance of a type that seems out of the norm in this modern time. Some feel that it's just plain offbeat to bother with this religious, old book the Bible. Some see it as just a big bunch of religious stuff or think of it as strange, or even eccentric and peculiar to believe in this Christian stuff. Others may believe they are too sophisticated or knowledgeable and getting involved with this "seeking God" stuff is just plain rude to their taste, and too down to earth for their lifestyle. Jesus Christ, who came from the riches of heaven to this earth, didn't think that way. As a matter of fact, He said that the concern of a rich man could keep him away from getting eternal life.

Some people feel they cannot handle the unpleasantness of their past acts. This is because they see this as attacking who they are and may make others see them as revolting or offensive. The fact is, however, that God knows all about everyone's past and nothing surprises Him. This kind of person needs to understand that in spite of all they have ever done, God still loves them! They are rejecting the way to freedom from themselves and their past when they think this way.

The next hindrance is a belief or feeling by some that to go to God is to have a cushion or crutch for the hard times of life. They are too proud of themselves and want to go it alone. For this person, this is a way of thinking that seems to put a crack in their self-sufficiency and pride. Others see having a relationship to God as a need for balance for their life, but still have an idea that God may tilt the balance away from them. They fear the outgrowth of the harmony they desperately need. This comes about because of living by their sight, for an outcome of their own agenda, rather then God changing their direction and course to a greater abundance of life.

In today's society, due to the knowledge explosion, it is no surprise that many in this world will hinder themselves by thinking that the God of the Bible and the understanding of His Son are old, distant and ancient. They feel they are justified in their thinking and that true Christianity is to be abandoned. So why is this, you may ask? It is because of the lack of understanding for the wonderful promises of God's Word. There are warnings in the Word of God about the future, such as the Second coming of Christ and how one must be prepared for this day. But in our day and age, we are in an age of procrastination for true stability. Upper progression is the thriving thought for today. If it is not new, then it is not good. This may be true in many areas of life, but not in the area of an all-powerful, eternal God who has extended Himself in glorifying Himself, by sending His Son to give those who accept His Son the gift of everlasting life. This by no means is to be taken lightly. Nor are we to add or subtract from His way in any way. One of the biggest problems in life is that man, due to his pride, wants to do things his way. Yet God tells us in His Word, by His teaching, that man's way doesn't count. We are all commanded to do things His way. It is also very unfortunate that many try to sway us to their way of thinking by adding or subtracting from what God has for each individual as well as all mankind.

One of the most deceptive hindrances to a true faith in God is that there is a jumbled variety of other so-called faiths mixed together to make a person think and feel that they are safe and covering all grounds. Unfortunately, this is a mentality that fears to offend anyone in these so-called belief systems. But there is no true consideration of what the True God says and how offensive it is to Him. The problem is that many think of proper Christianity as very offensive, even though the Christian is not trying to be offensive, but is only living according to the Word of God. The Jesus Christ in the Bible states:

Jesus said to him, "I am the way,
and the truth, and the life; no one
comes to the Father but through Me." John 14:6

Then there is a highly, emotionally subjective hindrance. One may look for a sign, symbol, or signal to discern which way to go in making a decision between two or three options rather than choosing the best choice, which is based on God's true logic found in His Word the Bible. One needs to understand that there are many experiential situations that can and will take place in every belief (as well as non-belief) system on earth. This is where the Biblical Scriptures come in and one needs to know if the experience is of God, or some type of subjective emotional experience or some form of spiritual deception. In this day and age we are living in there are so many distractions. They pull us away from giving us a true understanding of ourselves, and this is because of one's attraction and desire for entertainment. Unfortunately there are some who have such incorrect and strong ideas of what true Christianity is today. Who is to blame for this? The media has a great deal to do with this way of thinking. They see Christianity as unfavorable, threatening and even sinister.

A person who truly loves their family needs to look and understand Christianity for the Master Teachings or Doctrines and how it gives one true freedom and not bondage. The person that does this will be truly surprised at how the Christian faith, in the true biblical sense, will clearly be liberating. Some people will be so concerned for their mental and physical wellbeing that they will go to the spa or gym to workout and do things that only take care of the external part of themselves. This is great, but they don't consider the Spiritual side, which in the end will make them a complete failure because they never consider the Creator of their total being. Because of this lack of love and understanding for the Creator they will spend an eternity in Hell.

Then there is a hindrance that is so destructive that a person coming to the true faith may think and believe that it is okay to have a mind of one-sidedness or bias. This type of person may say something such as, "Well I'm a [then state a certain group or denomination]." This is truly not the Christian way. The Christian way is to call themselves as they truly are, a Biblical Christian. A Christian is a disciple or a learner of Christ by His Word. The true Biblical Christian is not to think that he or she is better then any other true Christian biblical group. Some think that because their church is more traditional, it must be better. Others think because their church is considered on the modern scale, they must be better. According to what the Bible says, this has no bearing at all of what is best. What the Bible does state emphatically is that the only way to God is by His Word and nothing else matters. There is no room for unfairness toward others and prejudice in the Kingdom of God.

The next hindrances are the "sit-still hindrances". This is where some may think all of this is okay for you, but not for me. I'll just observe, sit back and be a spectator of this Christian stuff. These are the people who think that being an onlooker will show them all they need. This is the lazy, weak, mild uncommitted way. This person is the person of deluded comfort and will not go beyond what they see, instead of learning about the Good News of God's loving truth in making the most intelligent choices they can make in their lifetime.

There are also some who allow themselves to be hindered by thinking that this "spiritual stuff" may put some religious burden or duty on them. They are afraid to think that True Christianity is a better way of life then they are living. They do not want to consider that this may actually be a better way of life to live in spiritual freedom and live with fewer burdens because of it.

Openmindedness can be a good and healthy thing at times, but one can be so openminded, tolerant, impartial and liberal that they can open their mind up to the whims of pure foolishness just for the sake of keeping those around them happy. The conclusion of this way of thinking is that this person couldn't truly know if something or someone were good for them. It is this type of superficiality that can give a person an extreme feeling and belief that they need to be liked by all and not hurt anyone's feelings. This is at the cost of their eternal life! They do this by rejecting the true God and what He says in His Word. God's word shows them that they can have everlasting life by accepting His way, which is through His Son Jesus Christ and is provided for all mankind.

These are just some of the hindrances that many individuals are responsible for, by allowing themselves to be affected in their thinking by being deluded to the point of eternal regret.

3

THREE KINDS OF FAITH

—~~~—

Whether you're a Christian or not, this is a topic that everyone needs to know and understand. Within this topic of faith, there are three very important parts. First, every person has and exercises faith of some sort. We all believe in some person or system whether true or false, good or bad. Some examples of the people we believe in are doctors, accountants, parents, teachers, ministers, mechanics, our government leaders and the list goes on. Second, faith has a direction within a person or religious system. The direction can be in what kind of doctor, such as a surgeon or a non-invasive doctor or a psychologist, in comparison to a doctor who is a nerve specialist. As for government there are your basic Republicans or Democrats, Libertarians or Independents. As to religious systems, you have your basics. There are Protestants such as Baptists, Methodists, Presbyterians, and Lutherans, etc. Then of course there are many others such as Roman Catholics, Jews, Muslims, Hindus and Buddhists, etc.

Third is the part of faith that one is responsible for to the highest degree. By that I mean that there is some type of book or written code for that particular faith. For the Christian faith, for instance, it is the complete cannon of the Scriptures such as the Old and New Testaments (the Holy Bible) nothing more or less. Then there is the hierarchy of faith. The first level is experiential faith based on emotions. Another name for this kind of faith is blind faith. Let's look at faith based on emotions or blind faith. This is the weakest of all the kinds of faith. This kind of faith comes from mindless reaction or ones feelings. Unfortunately, this kind of faith can come from one being deceived by a false leader that speaks to the emotions of the person and pushes for a reaction. This is usually based on his own ideas with little or no truth according to the Bible. Sometimes it is just that person's own ideas, just to get something from you such as money or control of your life just for the leaders benefit.

Sometimes, it is an individual that lives in a world of fantasy that goes into an emotional experience and says they have had a supernatural experience. I'm not in any way saying that the experience did not happen. But most of these experiences are deceptive and dangerous to the individual and those around them. Why you may ask? Simply put, this is because our emotions can change from minute to minute. There is no stability in trusting in your emotional experiences. Don't get me wrong, feelings are important when they are based on the truth. Then, from the truth, one must have a balanced understanding of the Major Doctrinal teachings in the Holy Bible. The reason for this is that the Doctrinal teachings in the Holy Bible are the immutable truths of God. By this I mean it is God's truth that never changes. So, based on good emotions or not, good feelings or not, God's Doctrinal teachings never change. Therefore, it is our God-given right and responsibility to correctly learn and understand the proper Doctrinal truths from God. Without these Doctrinal truths, we run into a dangerous risk. By this I mean that if one believes that they possess everlasting life on emotional feelings only, they are self-deceived and are in extreme risk of not having eternal life at all. Why is this? How can this be? The answer is very simple! Salvation and eternal life is only based on the Word of God (the Holy Bible).

You may be asking, "What is Doctrinal teaching or Doctrinal truth, for that matter?" The word doctrine is to be understood as a precept, belief, dogma or teaching. But you may even say if the word doctrine is similar to the word teaching, what is the big deal? Well, if one looks at the word doctrine, just by simply analyzing it, it resembles and looks close to the words doctor and document. A doctor is required to have a good deal of education and also the approval and monitoring of other doctors. If a doctor breaks the Hippocratic Oath, the doctor is in grave danger of losing his license to practice medicine. The word document has a great meaning. It is an account of a transaction, agreement or account that can be traced to a specific action or time. The word teaching is different than doctrine, in that teaching is not as specific as facts can change with time. The responsibility of the teacher is not as important, because of the fact that teachers many times can include their own opinon and distort the facts. On the other hand, the word doctrine, or as some say doctrinal teaching, especially in the biblical sense, has much greater impact and permanent importance. The word doctrine means that the teaching must be taught as it was taught from the beginning. This means that doctrine is not to be changed in any way. It is not to be added to or subtracted from. The Holy Bible is God's special Word to us and it must be taught His way. The creature has no right to change what the Creator has established.

The next kind of faith on the hierarchy is faith based on human authority. By this I mean ministers, priests, pastors, chaplains, evangelists, missionaries, teachers or professors, etc. I am in no way saying that we shouldn't listen to these types of clergymen. All of us are to listen to God's true ministerial clergy. The major problem today is that there are many in the clergy who are not living up to their responsibility (2 Timothy 4:1-8). Many are not preaching or teaching the True Gospel which is the true Good News centered around all the work that the Son of God has done for us (1 Timothy 4:1-2; 2 Timothy 3:10-17). Many are more concerned with the politics of their denomination or their standing in the group. Some will get you feeling good about yourself by psychologizing you. Others speak and teach about the history of the church building, etc. Even others will preach about being good, peace loving people and doing good things for mankind. This is all well and good, but it is devoid of God's Word speaking to us. There are also those that have huge ministries and yet they are not being responsible to God by not preaching the Good News to you. Some ministers are very topical in their preaching, but it is very unfortunate that these topics are not Gospel-driven. Sometimes the topics that are spoken about are very minor in topic in comparison to the doctrine from the Word of God pointing to the Gospel of Good News. For example: the gift of tongues as in comparison to the gifts of prophesy, teaching, or encouraging, service for the Lord, etc. There is no way a person can be brought to the truth of God's Word if they are only thinking of the exercise of the spiritual gift of tongues and putting the Good News of the Gospel to the side. It is not enough just to understand the Major Doctrinal Truths of the Bible. One must understand who the true God is and who we are and what God has done for us. This is the key in understanding the Good News, not some superficial experiential sign or feeling without the facts.

The next abuse of authority is that the Bible is taught like a history or a philosophy textbook. There are times that some even teach the Bible like it is a trivia game book to find out who knows the most trivia about it. Some examples are, "How many chapters are in the book of Genesis?" Fifty is the answer. Or, "How many books are in the Bible?" Sixty-six books are in the Bible. "How many commandments did Moses bring down from Mount Sinai?" Ten is the answer to this. So okay, you have the questions and the factual answers, but where is the spiritual truth or application to glorify the One True God? How does knowing these answers help your life? So if there are 10 Commandments, do you know them and how you can apply them to glorify God and benefit your life? As you can see, the understanding of the Word of God and applying it is what is needed for a person to live a godly life; not knowing wasteful crumbs of unimportant facts. Some may say, "but doesn't it stimulate the mind for learning?" Yes, but so does a comic book!

The Bible is the only book for salvation and that is an eternal salvation. This is the major understanding message of the Bible. Preaching, reading or only understanding it for trivia is eternally worthless so far as dooming one to Hell. There must be understanding and application of its truths. There are some ministers who play nice but are out to get your money. They will say this is God's money and that they need a new church building. They may try to push a guilt trip on you to tithe. In the Kingdom of God, this is wrong and I'll tell you why. It is wrong because the receiving of salvation is free and based on faith not money. God doesn't need money. Today it is very unfortunate that some churches do not ask the congregation if they disagree about monetary expenditures. It is even more unfortunate that if one person disagrees with the church, without the church asking why, the congregations will ostracize that person or that family. This is very wrong. It must be considered that if a person (or even a small number of people) disagree with a building project or a Sunday school addition, etc., that they consider that this one person or small group of persons may very well be enlightened about the will of God in this one particular situation. This may be due to a spiritual gift that God has provided to this believer or small group of believers and if God has provided it, to ignore the understanding of this person or small group could be dangerous as to the will of God. They may be for a new church building, but they may be enlightened about some problem that may be deep in their intuition or the eyes of their inner, spiritual, mindful heart. If one is to go forward without God in it, it will cause a major failure in the process according to God's will. This failure is not due to God but it is due to the pride of man. So what am I trying to show you? That the Word of God goes as far as giving us warnings. Yet many of them are ignored today! These warnings are not just for the wisdom in smaller decisions in our life, but the huge decisions like the direction of a country, etc. I'm sure you can see that all things need to be tested against the ultimate authority, which is the facts of God's Word the Bible based upon His Doctrine. I'm assuring you that there is the highest logic in all of this! This logic is not based on feelings that can change, and it is not based on human authority that can be wrong. It is based on the will of God that is given to us by His Word the Bible.

The third type of faith is evidential faith and it is the best, strongest and the most solid type of faith to have. Why? Because it is God's special revelation, which is His Word to humanity. God also reveals Himself through His general revelation, which is in nature, such as planets, animals, babies being born, and so on.

The Bible in the general sense has stood the test of time. Here are six broad, general aspects of the test of time that the Bible has withstood.

1) The Bible has been the best seller of all time.
2) The Bible has comforted millions of people throughout the generations.
3) Ignorant and evil governments have tried to destroy the Bible throughout history and they have never succeeded.
4) The Bible claims many blessings including the truthful claim of eternal life.
5) The Bible is still spiritually accurate as it was from the oldest writings of the prophets as well as all the books in the New Testament, including the last book, which is the book of Revelation written by the last living Apostle, John.
6) The Bible claims it is from God, and Jesus Christ the God-Man quoted the Old Testament Scriptures. He also claimed to be God's Son and that He would be crucified and rise on the third day, and He did. No other claim has surpassed this one in all of history, nor has it ever happened and been witnessed as the claiming of the resurrection. The resurrection of Jesus Christ goes beyond every area of life in history. No other faith or religion can not make a true claim such as this, nor can any area of science.

The Scripture is the recorded Word of God that is God breathed, or another way of saying this is the Bible is the only God inspired book. All 66 books in the Bible are equally inspired by God through its human writers. The writers of the Scripture were born along by God as He revealed His Word through them. Yet as God moved through the Prophets and Apostles in writing, giving His special message to humanity, one must understand that God didn't alter the personality of the writers in any way. God didn't, in any way, work through the writers as if they were robot-like or in some mystical trance. God inspired their minds to write as He revealed it to them. All of the prophecy, commandments and instructions, etc., down to the dotting of the i's and the crossing of the t's are inspired in the writings of the original form. That means the writings in the original Aramaic, Hebrew and the Greek language. These were the languages that the Old and New Testaments were written in (Matthew 5:18). We will get into the discussion of inspiration as we go further along and into more detail. This is important because these are all factual parts of the true evidence of the Bible as being God's Word to humanity.

This leads to an evidence of faith and that true faith is neither blind, emotional faith, nor is it based on human authority. The reason for this is because all types of faith or believing based on emotional feeling and human authority can lead to a faith that most of the time has great error. To go one step further, evidential factual faith is based on logic: God's Logic. Let me explain. All of God's Word is based on logic and reason, if we look at the Bible as God's logical and reasonable plan for life here on earth and salvation for everlasting life. This means we all need to study the Bible from the major basics and fully understand these basics, and we must continue to build and grow from there to gain more of a true understanding of God and His plan for us all.

Some of these basics are: Who is God? What does it mean that Jesus Christ is fully God and fully Man? Is there really a Devil and is he the real enemy? Is there really a Hell? What is sin, or is it just a word to control someone with? The list goes on! The Bible is based on God's logic, not our human logic. In fact, in the Gospel of John chapter one in verse one (John 1:1), one of the names for Jesus Christ is "the Word". First of all, to write a word correctly in any language the letters in that language need to be placed in a logical order for it to give meaning to communicate properly. If there is a different letter in a word then it will give a totally different meaning, such as the word saw as compared to the word sew. These words have two different meanings and those meanings are not even close to each other as words. This is also in the same way for the word "no" and "know", but these words even sound alike yet they communicate a totally different meaning. Being that one of the names for Jesus Christ is "Word" (John 1:1) it is this name for Jesus Christ, who is the God-Man, that was written about in its original form in the Greek language. The reason for this is that the Greek language, at the time, was the international language as well as the most precise language of that time. In fact, the whole New Testament was written in the Greek language. Now let's take a look at the English word for this name of Jesus Christ, also called the "Word". In the Greek language it is the word Logos and it means logic, reasoning, cause and work, and other words related to the logical order of God's Logic and God's Wisdom.

As one can see, the Bible claims that a true faith in God is based on His Logic by believing in His evidence, giving us an immovable faith based on the true facts given by God, not from the authority of men or our emotions. The evidential or factual way of having this type of faith is the most solid type. To have this type of faith prepares a person for any situation in life. It is also the safest because it is based on what God says. To understand the scripture properly, it needs to be understood within the context of its book within the Bible. The final test to keep it in context is to test it in the context of the whole Bible. This is very important in order for the truth of God's love to be understood.

Evidential faith tells you that if you know the truth, and it is telling you that you are forgiven for a sin of any sort because you have acknowledged and confessed it to the Lord Jesus Christ, God's Word says that you are forgiven. Now this forgiveness is absolute and that also means even if the person who has confessed the sin doesn't feel forgiven, that person is still forgiven. This goes even further even if another person would say that sin is not forgiven, according to God's evidential truth from His Word, that sin is forgiven.

No person on the face of the earth has authority over the Word of God, ever. But if one is a true child of God, they have authority because of their faith in the Word of God. But what does it mean to be a true child of God? You are a true child of God if you have accepted that Jesus Christ died on the cross and shed His blood for your sins (John 3:16; 1 John 1:9-10). If one puts their faith and trust in Christ, it is God who says you are forgiven and your feelings don't matter. It is His Word that matters, period. But remember, you are a child of God only if you have asked Christ to be your Lord and Savior. This doesn't mean that the person who has asked Christ to be their Lord and Savior now has a license to freely and carelessly go on sinning. The reason being is that this is not the way a child of God should act. It is not how to glorify the One who saved you from your sins. One must also realize that it is their responsibility to God that they grow in their spiritual walk with God. That means they must learn and understand the major basic Doctrinal Truths (Major Teachings) of the Word of God in the Bible. One needs to understand that this is not the responsibility of the ministers only, but it is each individual's responsibility. As I mentioned before, some ministers have been and are very irresponsible in this way throughout history. Even to this day!

God makes it our responsibility to learn and grow for a strong spiritual life. But some children of God are still infants. In the book of 1 Corinthians chapter 3 verses 1-3 as (1 Corinthians 3:1-3), the Apostle Paul is talking to a very rich and material-wealthy church, and yet we can see in reading this book many of those in that church are acting like infants that are not willing to grow in their faith. The Apostle Paul tells this group they still need to be fed milk because they couldn't eat meat yet. Meat in this sense represents one of having a mature understanding of their faith in God!

This maturity doesn't come from age but by studying and understanding the Major Doctrines (Major Teachings). These Major Doctrines were first taught in the early church from God's "Word", that is, His Logic. It is by these Major Teachings that the Apostles taught them in their time and they are to be taught and understood by each Christian today. It is then that the God of the Bible can give us the greatest understanding of who He truly is in His proper light. In this book you will get to learn these Major Doctrinal teachings in order to start on the right and correct path of who God really is and who we really are. Because if there is an improper foundation of knowledge set in place or a part is missing, the true blessing of God's salvation may be greatly misunderstood; this happens all because of a lack of this type of knowledge. Or the hope of a blessing could very well be missed in one's life here on earth and in heaven.

Here is the Gospel Good News Message that is found in God's Word, the Bible.

One must accept Jesus as Lord.

1) Believe that God loves you!
The first thing a person needs to believe is that God loves them. This is the reason He sent His Son Jesus Christ.

For God so loved the world, that He gave His only begotten Son, that whoever believes in Him shall not perish, but have eternal life. John 3:16

Some other verses in the Bible that you may look up and read about God's love are: John 4:8-14; 1 John 4:19.

2) Sin is in the way
The second thing is that you must acknowledge that you are rebellious and have a sin nature. You need to turn away

from sin. Because of this we all need to have a Savior, One who can save us from our sins.

...even the righteousness of God through faith in Jesus Christ for all those who believe; for there is no distinction; for all have sinned and fall short of the glory of God Romans 3:22-23

Some other verses you may like to look up and read are: Romans 5:8; 2 Corinthians 5:21.

3) God demands a perfect blood sacrifice for sin

You must believe that Jesus Christ the Son of God was crucified on the cross for your sins and He paid the price for you by His sacrifice, which is the shedding of His blood.

...and through Him to reconcile all things to Himself, having made peace through the blood of the cross; through Him, I say, whether things on earth or things in heaven. Colossians 1:20

Some other verses you may look up and read are: Romans 3:25, 5:6; 2 Corinthians 13:4; Galatians 3:13.

4) The Resurrection of Jesus Christ

Then, you must believe that Jesus Christ arose from the dead on the third day for the forgiveness of your sins.

He who was delivered over because of our transgressions, and was raised because of our justification. Romans 4:25

Other verses you can look up and read are: John 11:25; Romans 6:4; 1 Peter 1:21 and John 2:19, where Jesus talks about the temple of His body.

If you truly believe that Jesus died on the cross and was the perfect blood sacrifice for your sins and that He arose from the dead to give you everlasting life, say the Salvation Prayer below to accept Jesus Christ into your heart so He will become your Lord and Savior.

...for "WHOEVER WILL CALL ON THE NAME OF THE LORD WILL BE SAVED." Romans 10:13

The Salvation Prayer

I come to you, dear Father God, in faith knowing that it is your Son, Jesus, who came to earth and died on the cross for the forgiveness of my sins and that He arose from the dead and completed all the work for my salvation. Therefore, I now accept and ask you, Jesus Christ, to come into my heart as my Lord and Savior. Thank you Lord Jesus for saving me and giving me everlasting life. In Jesus name. Amen.

You made Jesus very happy! Just read what He said about you, in the next verse.

I tell you that in the same way,
there will be more joy in heaven
over one sinner who repents than
over ninety-nine righteous persons
who need no repentance. Luke 15:7

Just for your own personal record, sign your name and date it so you can have a record of when you received Jesus as your Lord and Savior and received everlasting life.

_____ __/ __/ ____
Sign Date

Realize that God has chosen you to be His child before the beginning of time.

If you have truly accepted Jesus Christ as your Lord and Savior consider this:

Jesus Christ's love for His chosen Child!

1) Jesus came for the world!
2) Jesus came at the right time!
3) Jesus came personally for you!
4) Jesus came for me personally, too!
5) Jesus would not have come if He couldn't get you, to give you everlasting life!
6) Jesus would not have come if He couldn't give me everlasting life, too!
7) Jesus Christ is the perfect and only God-man and came at the perfect time for all His chosen children too.

Anthony Galante

And we know that God causes all things to work together for good to those who love God, to those who are called according to His purpose.
For those whom He foreknew, He also predestined to become conformed to the image of His Son, so that He would be the firstborn among many brethren; and these whom He predestined, He also called; and these whom He called, He also justified; and these whom He justified, He also glorified. Romans 8:28-30

4

WHICH BIBLE TRANSLATION DO I GET

—◆—

It has been my experience that there are so many different kinds of Bibles of a novelty type. There are Bibles for hunters, servicemen, women, children and family Bibles. Then there are many types of study Bibles with the notes of a particular teacher or a group of teachers. Others are devotional and archeological or historical. All of these are good types of Bibles. The concern I have is that many people are not getting the proper understanding of the Major Doctrinal teachings the way the prophets, apostles and the Lord Jesus Christ taught. There is a lot to learn, that are the major teachings that God intended each person to know and be responsible for and to know in the Bible.

It has also been my experience that people who are looking for a Bible for the first time get quite confused about which type of Bible to purchase. There is a lot of bewilderment over not knowing which Bible to choose. The reason for this is most likely due to the knowledge explosion in this country. Sometimes they get a Bible that a friend may have suggested. Then when they open it, a very high majority will say to me "it's too hard to read", or the flow of it is just not there for them. There are many translations of the Bible that I believe are good from the original writers, that were written in Hebrew, Aramaic and Greek. I believe it is very important that we stay with the Basic English translations, which are more than adequate for the understanding of the Major Doctrinal truths from this Holy Book the Word of God.

There are five basic translations that I recommend to anyone who is starting to read God's Word. All five of these translations are accurate in spiritual meaning. They are the King James Version (KJV), New International Version (NIV), New American Standard (NASB), New King James Version (NKJV) and the Amplified Bible (AMP). Here is a little of what each translation is like. There are some differences among them, but there are no differences in their spiritual understanding and content. They are all the same concerning their spiritual meaning.

1) King James Version (KJV)–This is the oldest of all the translations. It is written in the old English language from the 17th century. If you feel comfortable with the older, traditional language, then this is the translation that may be for you. It has been widely used in America up to the 1950's and 1960's. There are still a good number of churches that use this translation even to this day. So if you like the older traditional styles, as well as its poetic style, this just may be your translation.

2) New International Version (NIV)–This is a translation that is very easy to read. The words and thoughts are easy to understand. Many of the churches today are using this translation throughout the country. It flows easily to read and is a favorite among teens, yet it is a very good translation for adults as well.

3) New American Standard Bible (NASB) is a true word-for-word translation. Its vocabulary is written in a mature form. It is moderately easy to read. Its words are of more intensity, similar to what is found in the Hebrew, Aramaic and Greek. This is a very good translation and is loved by many serious Bible students.

4) New King James Version (NKJV)–This is very similar to the older King James Version, but is easier to read because it is written in up-to-date English. This is for the person

who loves the style of the older King James Version but struggles with the older English style language.

5) The Amplified Bible (AMP) is written in easy moderate form and can be enjoyed by most. This is a Bible that gives many shades of meaning and applications by amplifying the original meaning word-for-word and verse-for-verse. This translation gives a much deeper understanding of God's Word.

5

ALWAYS READ THE BIBLE IN CONTEXT

—————

What does it mean to read the Bible in context, being that it is God's Word to all mankind? Why is it so important to read and understand the Word of God in context? First, one must understand that the Bible is made up of 66 books. Each one of these 66 books is from God to all of mankind. This means all races, nationalities, groups, etc. There are no exceptions. To go one step further, it is written to each individual on the face of the earth in a personal way. This is because Jesus died for all, not sparing one person. Each one of the 66 books in total brings about a context of the Major or Doctrinal teachings, and shows us God's true nature and character. Each one of the 66 books must be studied in its individual context to understand God's Gospel message to us that is in the Bible. There are two testaments: the Old Testament pointing to the coming Savior who is the Messiah (this is in the first 39 books in the Holy Bible). The second is the New Testament, which has 27 books. These books point to the arrival, work, death, burial and resurrection of Christ Jesus the Messiah. The New Testament also tells us The Lord Jesus will return for His Church and how He will set up His Kingdom here on earth. It is also imperative to realize that both the Old and New Testaments are equal in importance and that there are no contradictions in the Scripture from testament to testament or from book to book, for that matter. One can only understand this if the Bible is read in proper context. This is why reading the bible in context is so important! There are no contradictions from one book in the Bible to any other part of the Bible, if read in context. That means from chapter to chapter in the same book there are no contradictions and from paragraph to paragraph, as well as verse by verse. Many times a person can take a verse from a book and cross reference it properly, and experience the depth of God's character, wisdom, promise, prophecy, love, instruction, command and message as long as it is cross referenced properly. The only way to know this is to understand the Major Doctrinal teachings correctly. In this book, I will bring out the Major Doctrines (teachings) because these are the major foundations of the true Christianity as the way they were taught from the Prophets, Apostles and Christ Himself, the Son of God.

The title of the Son of God means that He, Jesus Christ, is fully God as well as fully Man. This means that He is the God-Man in Himself. This is why reading, studying and understanding the Bible in context is so important. God wants you to know what He means when He says He loves you! When one reads something in context they look to all of the circumstances around the situation to get the exact or best possible meaning from the text. Another way of understanding the Bible in context can go like this. If you read a verse in the Bible, see what the other verses in that paragraph say to shed light on that one verse. Then, see what the chapter does to shed light on the verse. To go further, what does that book in the Bible say about that verse? To go to the next step, if the book you are reading or studying is in the Old Testament, how does the verse compare throughout the whole Old Testament. From here on, you can compare the verse in the Old Testament to the New Testament to get the deepest understanding in the total context of the Bible. If you are reading and studying a verse in the New Testament then the process is the same, but, of course, starting from the New Testament you may end up in the Old Testament, or even any other book in the New Testament for the final comparison. The chart below is for basic clarification to this process of reading the Bible in context.

Very Basic Steps for Reading
The Bible in Context
O.T. = Old Testament and N.T. = New Testament

1) O.T. verse 1	1) N.T. verse 1
2) Look at the verses around that O.T. verse 1	2) Look at the verses around that N.T. verse 1
3) Look at O.T. verse 1 in full paragraph for meaning	3) Look at N.T. verse 1 in full paragraph for meaning
4) Look at O.T. verse 1 meaning from within the chapter	4) Look at N.T. verse 1 meaning from within the chapter
5) Look at O.T. verse 1 meaning from within the O.T. book it is in	5) Look at N.T. verse 1 meaning from within the N.T. book it is in
6) O.T. verse 1 meaning within the enter O.T.	6) N.T. verse 1 meaning within the enter N.T.
7) O.T. verse 1 meaning compared to the whole N.T. Good News	7) N.T. verse 1 meaning compared to the whole O.T. waiting for the Messiah and Christ

6

THE LOVE OF GOD CHANGES OUR THINKING

⌐∾∿∾⌐

Have you ever been in a state of misfortune, distress, grief, sorrow, tribulation, trouble, suffering, disaster or anguish? Remember a person is to have faith in Christ first. Because it is only after one's simple acceptance of Him we can understand that God can change our thinking with His promises.

Man's thinking!	God's has a promise in His Word!
I can't do it	You can do all things (Philippians 4:13)
I can't manage	I will supply all your needs (Philippians 4:19)
I can't go on	My grace is sufficient (2 Corinthians 12:9)
I can't figure things out	I will direct your steps (Proverbs 20:24)
Nobody really loves me	I love you (John 3:16)
It's impossible	All things are possible (Luke 18:27)
I'm too tired	I will give you rest (Matthew 11:28-30)
I'm not able	I am able (2 Corinthians 9:8)

It's not worth it	It will be worth it (Romans 8:28)
I can't forgive myself	I forgive you (1 John 1:9; Romans 8:1)
I'm not smart enough	I'll give you wisdom (1 Corinthians 1:30)
I feel alone	I will never leave you (Hebrews 13:5)
I'm frightened	I have given you power, love and sanity (2 Timothy 1:7)
I don't have enough faith	A measure of faith is given (Romans 10:17; Hebrews 11:1)
I'm always worried	Cast your care upon Me (1 Peter 5:7)
I don't know where to start	Seek God's way first (Matthew 6:33)
I feel so confused and pressured	My truth makes you free (John 8:31-32)
I feel like an outcast	Greater is He that is in me (1 John 4:4)
I have weaknesses	My perfect power works through your weakness (2 Corinthians 12:9-10)
I accepted Christ, but doubt my salvation	I have truly given you eternal life (1 John 5:11-13)

The Major Doctrines or Master Teachings as it was taught from Christ, the Son of God, and the Apostles and Prophets from within the Bible!

The word "revelation" is a very important word. In its purest form, revelation means the act of God revealing Himself to mankind. It also can mean to unveil or to make something previously not known revealed. In other words, God is unfolding His truths and realities to us that we could never

55

discover by ourselves. God does this in two ways. The first way is in a very general, usual, common, and regular way, like in nature. The second way is a special, unusual, individual, particular and extraordinary way. This appears to be similar in the way we communicate to each other as humans. In a general or common way by what clothing we wear, such as style of hair, and the way we move and act in our body language. Then we can also communicate in a more specific, special, individual and more particular way. This can be how we individually express ourselves, such as in our writing or the accent we use with our speech. Then there are our particular likes and dislikes in areas of our lives. This is how we reveal ourselves as humans.

So, you can see revelation is how God shows us who He is and this is how He communicates and speaks to us today. One must understand that each individual needs both types of revelation by God: the General Revelation in nature and Special Revelation from His written Word. This is the only way a person can understand who the true God is and how He is always present to help us in life. To put this in simpler terms, we all need to understand that just because a person is dressed like a doctor, fireman or policeman, doesn't mean they are one. In fact, a person can be dressed like this for the fun of going to a costume party, or they could be a dangerous imposter. So how can one really tell if one is real or an imposter? One can tell by their particular special or extraordinary way. That is how one can identify real from unreal. Understand, if one is a real professional doctor, fireman or policeman, they will have the right credentials and they will also communicate to you in the proper professional form. They will be as specific as possible in guiding you to a healthy and safer life. This is why God reveals Himself in two ways and both are very important, in understanding His nature in a general way, and who He is specifically.

7

THE MASTER TEACHING OR DOCTRINE OF GENERAL OR REGULAR REVELATION

—*ᴔᴔᴔ*—

General Revelation is the way God reveals Himself to all of humanity by nature and through nature. This also happens within history in the past, as well as living in the present and the future. It is by this type of common revelation that God provides and gives us proof, testimony, facts, and overwhelming evidences for His (God's) existence and His creative power. Let me explain what I mean about God's power. In the first book of the Bible and in the first verse we read:

> In the beginning God created the heavens and the earth.
> Genesis 1:1

The meaning for this word "created" is not used the same way as humans use the word create or creative, such as meaning clever, imaginative or to make something from something else. Similar to an artist with paint and canvas making or producing a painting. This also applies to an inventor who takes different types of materials and produces an order with them do something, etc. But the meaning of this word "created" as being stated in the Bible means that God created all things on the earth and all things that are seen as well as unseen in this universe, out of nothing! All the things that God created in the material world He creatively made from the unseen world of His power! But this is not all that God did; He created all things from the non-material "nothing" by His all-powerful spiritual Word. He also sustains and fosters life in a forward progressiveness according to His perfect and permissive plan, which is His overall plan. By perfect, I mean the way God wants humanity to live and make choices according to the way God has always intended. A good example of this is God never lies or could never lie because He is truthful. In turn, God hates lying, which leads us to His permissive will.

As humans, we all have lied at one time or another and God demands a blood sacrifice for all sin. Because of His love for mankind, God has provided a way of forgiveness through the shed blood of His Son Jesus Christ. This perfect blood sacrifice is for all the sins of humanity but is only in effect for those who accept Jesus Christ as their Lord and Savior. This is the way God reveals Himself to all. The reason for this is that God is the Creator and provider to all. The Bible says that God reaches out to all people without partiality (Matthew 5:45; Acts 14:17).

God reveals Himself in a common and general way throughout all of nature here on earth entirely. This can be seen in Psalms (19:1-2; 104:5-25). God also shows His power in a universal and prevailing manner by such things as light and heat from the sun. To take this matter further, God also keeps the earth on its course and on its turning rotation, as well as circulating around the sun (Psalm 19:4-6). Did you know that the Bible also claims that the earth was round 500 to 600 years before Christ? This is about 500-600 B.C.! You can see this in the book of Isaiah (40:22). There you will see it states that God "sits above the circle of the earth." So there you have it! As to the old, wrong claim 550 years ago that some believed that the earth was flat! One just needed to take a close look in studying the Bible and they would have gotten the right answer to the myth of the earth being flat.

God is revealed to man in a general or common way within themselves, primarily through the conscience. Some are more sensitive than others and some have made their conscience very insensitive. But it is the conscience that God has given to each and every person. This gives evidence that there is a God who created them by His invisible power and nature (Romans 1:19-20). This conscience that God has given to each person is an instinctive standard of God's law within the heart of each person. It is to let us know what is right and wrong (Romans 2:14-15). This conscience is not, as some say, something that developed through the generations of men. It is also not given to us by philosophy, religion, science or art. It is given to us by God. If I may go one step further, it is given to us *only* by God (Acts 17:23-24; 29). Therefore, if the truths of general or common revelation of the existence of God are rejected or not believed by any person, the Bible says "they are without excuse" (Romans 1:20). In Psalm 14:1, it says that "The fool has said in his heart, 'There is no God'." This disbelief brings about a just, blameful condemnation upon themselves. Because when one is like this, it is God who renounces and rejects them for their withholding denial of reality of the truth within their own conscience.

8

THE MASTER TEACHING OR DOCTRINE OF SPECIAL OR PARTICULAR REVELATION

———❧❧❧———

The Special or Particular Revelation of God has a much greater importance, as well as is a more specific way in which God speaks to us today. Everything an individual needs to know about who God is, is in His Special written Word the Bible. His plan is for all mankind and tells us what we need to know and believe so our spiritual needs can be met and fulfilled.

There are 66 books in the Holy Bible and this is how God speaks to us in all completeness, even for our time today. God has used other methods in the past before the 66 books were completed, and these methods are shown to us and written about in the Holy Bible. All of these methods are considered special and particular revelation for their time. But again, because the Bible is completed, this is the greatest and safest method of how God talks to us today. He has also given us His Holy Spirit, who indwells each and every believer to guide and teach each believer, as a promise from God that He will never leave the believer. So there is no reason for God to use the methods of the past in speaking to the believer. It must be said again, that if the person is a true believer, by having faith in God's work that He sent His Son and putting their faith in Him as their Lord and Savior, the Holy Spirit will indwell that person permanently and will never leave them. This is God's promise! Here are the methods God used to reveal Himself to the Old Testament and New Testament saints before the Bible was completed.

God's Methods of Particular or Special Revelation are:

1) **God spoke to men through the casting of lots.** This was a way of making a choice or getting a resolution for an issue and understanding for God's will in a matter (Proverbs 16:33; Acts 1:21-26).

2) **God spoke to the Old Testament High Priest through the Urim and the Thummin (these words mean light and perfections).** These were possibly two types of stones, one white and the other black in color. They were held within the breastplate over the heart of the High Priest, symbolizing and knowing that the decision had to come from God. They were to be held above the priest's heart and it was God who gave the illuminating choice to the High Priest for the matter of concern (Deuteronomy 33:8; Exodus 28:30; Leviticus 8:8; Numbers 27:21; 1 Samuel 28:6; Ezra 2:63).

3) **God spoke to men through dreams.** Found in (Genesis 20:3,6, 31:11, 24; 40-41; 1 Kings 3:5; Matthew 2:12 about the Magi, Matthew 2:19-22).

4) **God spoke to men through visions.** These visions were of a spiritual sight presented to the mind by God for showing a prompt concern to a near situation. The other kind of vision God used to speak to man was of the kind that was to reveal concerns of the distant future (Isaiah 1:1, 6:1; Ezekiel 1:3-28; Daniel 7:6-8:27; Acts 10:10-16).

5) **God spoke to men through theophanies.** A theophany is a true visible appearance of God. Most of the time, this is in a human form. This was a way God would

show Himself and talk to men of that time. As you look up these verses, one needs to understand that the Angel of the Lord is Jesus Christ pre-incarnate. Meaning that Jesus Christ appeared to those in the Old Testament even though He was only Spirit at that time as His Father in heaven (Genesis 3:8; 16:7-14; Exodus 3:2; 2 Samuel 24:16; Zechariah 1:12).

6) **God spoke to men through angels.** Angels are created heavenly beings that are spirits even though they have revealed who they were as angels in the form of a physical body, to men (Daniel 9:20-21; Luke 2:10-19; Revelation 1:1).

7) **God spoke to men through the Old Testament Prophets.** A prophet was God's spokesman who actually uttered the words that God spoke. Prophets had two responsibilities. They did forth telling and foretelling (2 Samuel 23:2; Zechariah 1:1). Then there were New Testament Apostles. Apostles are those men who are chosen by Christ and were sent out with all authority as representatives of Christ; thus the original Twelve Disciples. The New Testament also mentions other apostles in a non-official type. The twelve Disciples are messengers sent out by the Christian church of that time (Romans 1:1; 2 Peter 1:1; 2 Corinthians 1:1). Now as for the New Testament prophets, they were similar to the Old Testament prophets (Ephesians 3:5). But as for prophecy, there are those given this gift today, but only in the sense of forth telling the Word of God. There is no more foretelling because the Holy Bible is completed and God now speaks through His Word the Bible (Romans 12:6).

8) **God spoke to men through events, acts and judgments.** Found in these verses: Micah 6:3-5; Ezekiel 25:7, and there are many more! But everything is focused on

the event of the Son of God coming to us and taking on human flesh and a bodily form (John 1:14). Another event is that of the Wise men, also known as the Magi, following the Star of Bethlehem to find the child Jesus (Matthew 2:1-2; 9-10).

9) **God spoke to men through His Son Jesus Christ who is fully God and fully man.** He is also the second person of the Godhead (John 1:14, 3:2, 7:46, 14:9-10; 1 John 1:1-3). Christ the Son of God died for sinners (Romans 5:6-11). In the book of Hebrews, we see that God the Father worked closely with and through His Son, Jesus the Christ (Messiah) from the beginning of Creation and even still in these last days.

...in these last days has spoken to us in His Son, whom He appointed heir of all things, through whom also He made the world. Hebrews 1:2

Then there are also the acts and miracles of Jesus Christ (John 2:7-11) and by His words as well (Matthew 16:17).

Important!

Some believe that there is continuous unique revelation today. But this is truly a serious and grave error of belief because the Bible is complete, with the last book being a final prophetic book called the Book of the Revelation. Jesus commanded that nothing is to be added to the Bible and that no one is to take away from the words of the Bible, because there will be very severe consequences if one does such a thing (Revelation 22:18-19). One may ask why God is severe about this. The reason being is that to add to God's Word, or to take away from it, is one of the greatest dishonors to God after He has given humanity the Good News of His Son. This is the essence of the Gospel. Not only does it insult the one and true God, it also would cause great damage for the salvation of mankind. The process of the completion of the Bible is what is called the cannon of scripture. It is the complete official list of all 66 books in one book, the Holy Bible. It is this Holy Bible that is the only authority of one's Christian faith today. More of this will be discussed in greater depth later.

9

THE MASTER TEACHING OR DOCTRINE OF GOD'S INSPIRATION OF HIS WORD THE HOLY BIBLE

———⟨ఠ⟩———

Inspiration: Today's meaning of the word "inspired" can mean many things to us as humans. It can mean things such as a great idea (as in inventing something), or it can mean one has a great artistic ability (such as an artist or a composer). It can also mean that a person's speech compels one to wisdom, or to give them courage to press on in their goal or endeavor. But biblical inspiration from God means that God has inspired or breathed life in the situation, such as when God inspired or breathed life into the man He created called Adam. This can be seen in Genesis (2:7, 20-23). In these verses, you can see in verse 7 that God breathed life into the man and how the woman Eve came from the life that God gave Adam. The whole entire human race has come from this one man that was made of the dust of the earth that God breathed or inspired life into; this "first of all men". So inspiration from God means breathing life into man.

The Bible is also inspired by God. He breathed His life into the writing of the Bible Scripture where it is the Word of God to man. But how did this happen? What does this all mean that man with their physical hand inscribed or wrote the words? And is what they wrote exactly? How did God work through these Apostles and Prophets who wrote the Bible? Were they commanded to write like a robot acts after getting a command? Was the writer's personality altered in any way? The answer to all of these questions is no! There was no mechanical alteration of the writer's personality. The way God inspired His words to be written through the Prophets and the Apostles is that He influenced and carried them along to write the Scripture in a supernatural way. This means that these men were born along in the actual recording of God's message in the original languages and manuscripts. If we look at 2 Timothy 3:16 it says "All scripture is inspired by God...." and then the Bible also says:

But know this first of all, that no prophecy of Scripture is a matter of one's own interpretation, for no prophecy was ever made by an act of human will, but men moved by the Holy Spirit spoke from God. 2 Peter 1:20-21

Then we also read in the Bible:

...which things we also speak, not in words taught by human wisdom, but in those taught by the Spirit, combining spiritual thoughts with spiritual words.

But a natural man does not accept the things of the Spirit of God, for they are foolishness to him; and he cannot understand them, because they are spiritually appraised. 1 Corinthians 2:13-14

A deeper and fuller understanding of God's Inspiration of the Scripture is that all the words are inspired (2 Peter 1:20-21; Matthew 5:18; 2 Timothy 3:16-17). To go a step further, Scripture is also inerrant. This means that the Word of God, the Holy Bible, does not digress from any point of truth in it at all. But there is a stronger word still, and that is the Word is infallible. This means the Scripture, in no possible way, is able nor does it have the capacity to deviate from the truth in all matters, such as: historical facts, prophecy, genealogies, the account of creation, choice of words and also the use of grammar (1 Corinthians 2:13; Matthew 4:4; Galatians 3:16).

Illumination: When we think of the word illumination, many people think of things like a light bulb being turned on to give light or sight. The other words that may come to mind are to interpret, have clarity or to explain. But God, by the power of the Holy Spirit, has this ministry that gives the believer guidance and also teaches the believer to understand the scripture, as well as bring scripture to memory at the time the believer is in need of knowledge and comfort. This is all done through the Word of God, the Holy Bible.

Now we have received, not the spirit of the world, but the Spirit who is from God, so that we may know the things freely given to us by God, which things we also speak, not in words taught by human wisdom, but in those taught by the Spirit, combining spiritual thoughts with spiritual words. 1 Corinthians 2:12-13

Illumination of God's Word only happens to the spiritual man, not the natural man (1 Corinthians 2:14-16; Colossians 1:9; 1 Peter 2:2; John 16:12-15). God spoke to the writers, prophets and apostles in the past through revelation, as we indicated earlier. Now that the Bible cannon is completed, God speaks to man primarily today through the illumination of His Word, the Bible, through the indwelling of the Holy Spirit to believers. Therefore, because the Bible cannon is completed, there is no more revelation today. There is everything that a believer needs in the completed cannon, the Bible (2 Timothy 3:15-17; John 17:17).

Canonicity: So what is canonicity or the cannon? The cannon is the collection of 66 books that had to pass certain tests. By passing these tests, these books were only then considered to be truly authoritative and from God. It is by these books only that one is to consider them the only true Holy Bible, the rule of life eternal.

The Test for All Thirty-Nine Old Testament Books and their Canonicity for placing them in the Holy Bible:

Jesus Christ, the God-Man, had total confidence in the Old Testament. He mentions and teaches from its historical incidents as truth and factual.

Some examples are:

1) Adam and Eve being created by God and are not just symbols of mankind (Mark 10:6-8; Matthew 19:3-5).
2) The Flood and the Ark in Noah's day were real and not a myth (Matthew 24:36-39; Luke 17: 26-27).
3) The destruction of Sodom and Gomorrah and the history about Lot and his wife (Matthew 10:15; Luke 17:28-29).
4) Jonah being in the great fish for three days and nights (Matthew 12:40).
5) Then there is the acknowledgment and history of:
    Isaiah in (Matthew 12:17)
    Elijah in (Matthew 17:11-12)
    Daniel in (Matthew 24:15)
    Abel in (Matthew 23:35)
    Zechariah in (Matthew 23:35)
    Abraham, Isaac and Jacob in (Matthew 8:11; John 8:39)
    Moses and his writings in (Matthew 8:4; John 5:46)

The Test for the Twenty-Seven Books that were placed in the New Testament part of the Holy Bible and their Canonicity:

1) The test of authority.
2) The test of uniqueness.
3) The test of acceptance by general consensus from the true Christian church.
4) Prophecy fulfilled by Jesus as Messiah, who is Christ.

Here are just a few fulfilled prophecies:

Prophecy	Old Testament	New Testament
A descendant of Jacob	Numbers 24:17	Matthew 1:2
Born of a virgin	Isaiah 7:14	Luke 1:26-27, 30-32
Crucified with criminals	Isaiah 53:12	Mark 15:26-28
Christ's Resurrection	Psalms 16:10	Mark 16:6-7

In conclusion, a true understanding of the Bible and its authority and God's inspiration of His Word to humanity is very important because:

1) It is truly God's work.
2) It is truly God's message to humanity.
3) All are responsible to God and His will.
4) It is God's Word and not some man-made writing of deception.
5) It has its history from God Himself.
6) It will bring spiritual safety if it is believed in.
7) It points the way to eternal life.
8) It shows us God's love for us and if believed, that person will have a relationship with God because of God's Word and through God's work.
9) It shows us that Jesus Christ is the only way to God. Because no one else in all of history could raise Himself from the dead.
10) It gives believers peace no one else or nothing else could give.

10

THE MASTER TEACHING OR DOCTRINE OF GOD AND COGNIZANCE OF HIM

―――≈≈≈―――

The desires of many, if not all, worldly religious groups have a focus and yearning that gives testimony to the knowledge of a Greater being. We also know that each individual in the human race from the beginning of time has always had the desire to worship. It is sad that many worship a false being, but we all worship. This is even if one says they worship no one, they still worship someone or something. The reason is because each person is born to worship.

God has made each person with this innate desire to worship Him. The Bible tells us that God in all of his wisdom is incomprehensible. Therefore, the human mind cannot fully grasp the knowledge of God (Job 1:7; Isaiah 40:18, 25-31). Some may say God is too great and beyond human comprehension, but the Bible shows us that God gives us the ability to know who He is so man can truly know and understand something about God. There is no excuse!

Let's just look at what Jesus Christ the Son of God says about this matter:

> If you had known Me, you would have known My Father also; from now on you know Him, and have seen Him. John 14:7

Then Jesus Christ says we can have a true knowledge of the true and only God:

This is eternal life, that they may know You, the only true God, and Jesus Christ whom You have sent. (John 17:3)

The Bible also says that because of Jesus Christ that it was He who came to give us a real knowledge and grasp for the true God.

And we know that the Son of God has come, and has given us understanding so that we may know Him who is true; and we are in Him who is true, in His Son Jesus Christ. This is the true God and eternal life. 1 John 5:20

Jesus Christ is the second person in the God-Head. God revealed Himself through sending His Son, Jesus, who took on a body of human flesh. This is called incarnation. Because of this, Christ was able to reveal God to us. Looking in the Bible, it says:

No one has seen God at any time; the only begotten God who is in the bosom of the Father, He has explained Him. John 1:18

If we also look up John 17:3, we will see Jesus Christ is basically saying we can know God by knowing who He is as the Son of God.

If you had known me, you would have known My Father also: from now on you know Him, and have seen Him. John 14:7

Then there is the coming of the Holy Spirit after Jesus Christ went up to heaven. This is called the ascension of the Christ. Only after Christ ascended into heaven did He send the Holy

Spirit. The Holy Spirit is the third person of the God-head and when He came to indwell the believers of the true church, He revealed God to humanity in a much greater way.

This is Jesus Christ speaking:

But when He, the Spirit of truth, comes, He will guide you into all the truth; for He will not speak on His own initiative, but whatever He hears, He will speak; and He will disclose to you what is to come. He will glorify Me, for He will take of Mine and will disclose it to you. All things that the Father has are Mine; therefore I said that He takes of Mine and will disclose it to you. John 16:13-15

The Holy Spirit was not sent for just the early church, but for any person of any nation from past, present or future, to anyone and everyone who has accepted Jesus Christ as their Lord and Savior. This new believer will receive the promise and gift of the Holy Spirit who indwells every believer and He will never leave them.

Let's see what Jesus Christ says about this:

…but you will receive power when the Holy Spirit has come upon you; and you shall be My witnesses both in Jerusalem, and in all Judea and Samaria, and even to the remotest part of the earth. Acts 1:8

11

THE MASTER TEACHING OR DOCTRINE OF THE PERFECT CHARACTERISTICS AND ATTRIBUTES OF GOD

———⟳⟳⟳———

When one goes through the pages of the Bible, one can quickly see that God is a Spirit. He is a superior Spirit that was never created, and superior to angels and man in every way. He is all eternal, all holy, all powerful and all infinite. He is all Godly, all impeccable, all righteous, all wise, all good, and all truthful. GOD is also all love.

> The one who does not love does not know God, for God is love. 1 John 4:8

No characteristic or attribute is apart from God. Nor are any of them independent of one another. All of the attributes of God are possessed equally by the three persons in the God-head. The Father, the Son and the Holy Spirit have all the attributes and characteristics equally. All of the attributes and characteristics truly describe each person and the true nature of the triune God. There are two types of attributes that God has. The first type of attributes are ones that only God possesses. These are called incommunicable attributes. The second type of attributes are called communicable. These are attributes that are possessed by God and are also found in the nature of man.

Some Examples of the Incommunicable Attributes or Characteristics that Only God Possesses

The Greatest and Most conclusive Attribute is that God is GOD!

There is only One God! There are no other gods. He is the only and that is it! He always existed! He is the most unique being in all ways because He is the One and only God who is totally self-sustainable and needs no other being to continue to exist. No one else was ever God, nor is there anyone who was God or ever can be God.

In the beginning God created the heavens and the earth. Genesis 1:1

God Possesses the Attribute of Eternality. God exists endlessly in all ways. He is not bound by time or distance. He is eternal, past, present and future. God exists endlessly in Genesis 21:33; Abraham made claim that God was Everlasting. Then in the book of the Psalm we read:

Before the mountains were born
Or You gave birth to the earth and the world,
Even from everlasting to everlasting,
You are God. Psalm 90:2

God also has no limits in time whether it is a thousand years or a day or night, it is the same to Him.

For a thousand years in your sight
Are like yesterday when it passes by,
Or as a watch in the night. Psalm 90:4

God Possesses Immutability. This means that God is unchangeable and He is also unchanging. This basically means that God is in control of all things and is aware of all

74

things. This means that God's thoughts do not shift even in the slightest. For we read:

> For I, the Lord, do not change; therefore you, O sons of Jacob, are not consumed. Malachi 3:6

Everything that God does is perfect — and to the tee! There is no changing things midstream, and He doesn't even make things appear in one way and it is different then what it was before. To put this in easier human terms, if you went to a paint store to buy paint and you picked out a certain color of blue off a paint chart, and you had it mixed and you went home with your new mixed color blue and painted the wall, this color would be the exact perfect match in every way. To the identical color on the paint chart, down to the perfection of the paint being mixed again and again, over and over with not even the slightest difference. This would be this way even if the paint were to be mixed thousands upon thousands of times. The paint would be the exact same perfect color on the paint chart. This next verse will give you an even better understanding of God's unchangeable ability:

> Every good thing given and every perfect gift is from above, coming down from the Father of lights, with whom there is no variation or shifting shadow. James 1:17

God is Infinite. This means that God has no bounds at all and has no limits whatsoever. He possesses the attribute of infinity. God says heaven is His throne and the earth is under Him. God also says that man can't even build a house for Him.

He doesn't even need a place to rest (Isaiah 66:1).

Then we read:

The God who made the world and all things in it, since He is Lord of heaven and earth, does not dwell in temples made with hands. Acts 17:24

God is Omnipotent. The word omni means "all" and the word potent means "powerful". So the word omnipotent means God is all-powerful. He has more power than anyone in all things. This goes far beyond the power of all things created all together. He is also the author of power. He is the Almighty One and in the first book in the Bible we read about God's omnipotence:

Thus the heavens and the earth were completed, and all their host. Genesis 2:1

Then we read that God Almighty brought forth all generations from the beginning of Adam and Eve to the very last future generation from Adam and Eve:

Who has preformed and accomplished it,
Calling forth the generations from the beginning?
"I, the LORD, am the first, and with the last. I am He."
Isaiah 41:4

The all-powerful God wants us to be His family members.

"And I will be a father to you,
And you shall be sons and daughters to Me,"
Says the Lord Almighty. 2 Corinthians 6:18

Then we read the words of Jesus, the second person in the God-head, who says that He as the Son of God is the beginning. He is the Alpha, which is the first letter in the Greek alphabet. Then He also says He is the end, which is the Omega, the last letter of the Greek alphabet. The reason for the use of the Greek letters is because the New Testament was written in the Greek language. This was because Greek was considered the international language of that time. Today the international language is considered to be English. Let's see what Jesus tells us about His Almighty power:

"I am the Alpha and the Omega," says the Lord God, "who is and was and who is to come, the Almighty." Revelation 1:8

God is Omnipresent. First of all, this means that God is everywhere present. But this doesn't mean that God is in everything. Just to give you an idea, God is not in rocks or trees and so on. But He is aware of all and sees every rock and tree.

In the Bible, we read about David and Goliath and when young David killed the massive giant Philistine soldier Goliath. David used a stone and a sling. God's Spirit was in David and God knew that it was this particular stone that David picked up that was the one that David would use to kill Goliath. We must realize that God was not in the stone. In a Psalm, David tells us and expresses to us about God's omnipresence, we read:

Where can I go from your Spirit?
Or where can I flee from Your presence?   verse 7.
If I ascend to heaven, You are there;
If I make my bed in Shoal, behold, You are there.   verse 8.
If I take the wings of the dawn,
If I dwell in the remotest part of the sea,   verse 9.
Even there Your hand will lead me,
And Your right hand will lay hold of me.   verse 10.
If I say, "Surely the darkness will overwhelm me,
And the light around me will be night,"   verse 11.
Even the darkness is not dark to You,
And the night is as bright as the day.
Darkness and light are alike to You.   verse 12.
Psalm 139:7-12

This one particular passage tells us a lot about the all-presence of God.

1) It tells us that wherever we go, He is there, and that we cannot hide from Him. We can see this in verse 7.

2) It tells us that if we go up to High Heaven and even if we go to the grave or Shoal, He is even present there. We can see this in verse 8.

3) It tells us that God is present even in the air and in the early morning. He is also present if we were to go to the deepest and most unknowable part of the seas. This can be seen in verse 9.

4) It tells us God is always present to guide us and to hold us and protect us. This is seen in verse 10.

5) It tells us that God is present even in our unknown and in our time of danger. This is in verse 11.

6) It tells us that God is everywhere, present, and His presence never leaves. He sees all things and through all things. This can be understood in verse 12.

Overall, God is present everywhere here on the earth. Indwelling each true Christian believer and every place even beyond our knowledge and understanding in this universe. Even beyond the heavens. The full God-head — that is the Father, Son and the Holy Spirit — are present at all these places at the same time. Here are some other Scripture passages that will also shed some extra light about the omnipresence of God. They are:

2 Chronicles 7:2; Galatians 2:20; 2 Thessalonians 1:9; Revelation 1:8.

God is Omniscient. This means God knows all things and everything about all things. He knows the past, present and future. He knows about all actual outcomes and all possible outcomes. We read:

SAYS THE LORD, WHO MAKES THESE THINGS KNOWN FROM LONG AGO. Acts 15:18

God knows all things from afar also, He says:

He counts the number of stars; He gives names to all of them. Psalm 147:4

Jesus said that God knows all things, even down to the hairs on our heads:

Indeed, the very hairs of your head are all numbered. Do not fear; you are more valuable than many sparrows. Luke 12:7

God knows all of the outcomes, even possible outcomes. In other words, even those that could have been! Let's see what Jesus says to give us an example of this:

Woe to you, Chorazin! Woe to you, Bethsaida! For if the miracles had occurred in Tyre and Sidon which occurred in you, they would have repented long ago in sackcloth and ashes. Matthew 11:21

God knows all about us and our life before we were conceived. He also knows how long we will live. He is the one who knows and has formed our bodies. He is the life maker and giver, not man.

Your eyes have seen my unformed substance;
And in Your book were all written
The days that were ordained for me,
When as yet there was not one of them.
Psalm 139:16

God has Simplicity. God is not a composite of many compounds; He is a Spirit. He is not material, but is immaterial. He is made up of spirit stuff and yet He is the ultimate of Spirit beings.

God is spirit, and those who worship Him must worship in spirit and truth. John 4:24

Love is the overall simple character of the Spirit of God. Let's see what the Bible says:

The one who does not love does not know God, for God is love. 1 John 4:8

God is Sovereign. God is in complete control of all things. He is not subject to any rule or law. He is superior in all ways and He is in perfect control. God, in His sovereignty, has given each believer an inheritance and God has purposed this way before humanity was ever created.

We can see this in this next verse:

...also we have obtained an inheritance, having been pre-destined according to His purpose who works all things after the counsel of His will. Ephesians 1:11

To every true believer in Christ, God gives us the indwelling Holy Spirit as a pledge of our everlasting life. In speaking about the Holy Spirit in the Bible, we read:

Who is given as a pledge of our inheritance, with a view to the redemption of God's own possession, to the praise of His glory. Ephesians 1:14

God is sovereign at all times and He is in control, even if it doesn't seem to be so to us. The Word of God says:

The LORD has made everything for its own purpose, Even the wicked for the day of evil. Proverbs 16:4

God is in control of all things simultaneously; He controls everywhere and everything in all ways at all times.

Whatever the LORD pleases, He does, In heaven and in earth, in the seas and in all deeps. Psalm 135:6

Because God is sovereign and in control, He gives every true believer a wonderful promise. Even if things don't seem to be going well for the true believer who is a child of God here on earth, by going through trials and tribulations, etc., because of this promise from God, the believer can still be at peace with God even in the greatest of tragedies. We can see that God is always up to something good by reading this next verse:

And we know that God causes all things to work together for good to those who love God, to those who are called according to His purpose. Romans 8:28

These are just some of the attributes that only God has; there are many others. These were given to you as some examples about the eternal greatness of God.

Here are some examples of communicable attributes and characteristics that God possesses in His perfection. Man possesses these attributes and characteristics also, but man does not possess them in perfection as God does.

They are as follows.

God Possesses Freedom

God is not bound by limits, space and time, and is totally free from any need of anything. He is also free of any dependency from anyone. In other words, God doesn't need man, or the animals, or the sun or water to be God. God is also freely independent of His creation. We can see this by just looking at each sunrise and sunset each day! Not one of them from the beginning of time has ever been the same. He is the eternally free artist. God is also independent of His creatures. If we take man and woman as an example, He makes them all different for His reason. Some have blue, green, gray, hazel-brown colored eyes. Some have lighter color in their eyes and some have a darker color of the same color in their eyes. God makes everybody's fingerprint different and there are many other thousands upon thousands of things that God does just because He is and has perfect freedom to do so!

Who has directed the Spirit of the LORD,
Or as His counselor has informed Him?
With whom did He consult and who gave

Him understanding?
And who taught Him in the path of justice
and taught Him knowledge
And informed Him of the way of understanding?
Isaiah 40:13-14

The answer is, no one taught Him anything because He needs no teaching of any sort. God is perfect in His freedom. He does it all His way!

God Possesses Holiness

The word holiness here means that God is pure and right in all things. This is also where we get the word righteous or righteousness. This also means that God is separate and withdrawn from all things that are evil. To go further, if there is no harmony or there is immorality, God is separate because He stays separate from all that is unclean and evil.

In the book of (Exodus 3:14) God, who is the great "I AM", says that He is Holy and that we should live a holy life because He is Holy. In Psalm 99:3, 5, 9, it basically tells us that God is Holy and we need to give Him praise and lift up His name in adoration. Then we read:

"To whom then will you liken Me
That I would be his equal?" Says the Holy One.
Isaiah 40:25

In this verse God Himself says "there is no one to compare Me to", and that there is no one near equal to Him. Then the verse goes on and basically tells us that there is no other God and that there is no one as holy as He is. So God is the only God and the only Holy God.

In the Old Testament book of Habakkuk (1:12) it mentions that God is eternal, that He is Lord and Holy over all. When we look in the New Testament, Jesus Christ the Son of God is praying to His Father for His disciples, and this is what He prays to His Father:

...Holy Father, keep them in Your name, the name which You have given Me, that they may be one even as We are. John 17:11

Here we see Jesus starting His prayer to His Father by calling Him Holy. Jesus says that He too is Holy because as the God-Man, He has authority from the Father. Christ tells the Father that when His work is finished on earth, and He goes back to the Father, that His disciples will be more than united. They will be united because they will be one, because Christ will send the Holy Spirit, the third member of the God-head, from heaven to indwell all His disciples to make them holy in God as one. Here is a reference to the holiness of God found in the Old and New Testaments. We see the same phrase.

...Holy, Holy, Holy, is the LORD... Isaiah 6:3 and Revelation 4:8

Both of these verses point to the holiness of God the Father, God the Son and God the Holy Spirit. All three persons in one Holy God-head. Then in (1 Peter 1:15-16), it says again that God is holy and that He commands Christian believers to be holy.

We can see the extent of the pure holy character of God as the Apostle John states:

... that God is Light, and in Him there is no darkness at all. 1 John 1:5

God Possesses Love

The author of love is God. As humans, we all have loved ones and some believe that love is taught to us. But the truth is that God gave us the ability to love. It can be triggered by others loving us or by a person seeing one showing love for another. God's love is a love that never fails, even though many will reject God's love. God offers all types of people His saving love, as we read:

> For God so loved the world, that He gave His only begotten Son. John 3:16

And all that we have to do to receive this love of God, which is a sure thing, is to accept His Son, Jesus Christ, as our Savior and Lord. It is when we accept Jesus Christ's suffering and sacrifice for our sins and believe that because God the Father loved His Son so much that He raised Him from the dead, that we who truly believe have eternal life. This shows us that God's love is not a feeling that comes and goes but it is sacrificial and unchangeable and everlasting forever. In 1 John 4:8, this verse tells us that "...for God is love."

God also loved us way before we could ever understand it. Even in our sinful, rebellious state, Paul the Apostle in the book to the Romans writes:

But God demonstrates His own love toward us, in that while we were yet sinners, Christ died for us. Romans 5:8

Even as enemies of God, He loved us so much that He provided a way for all who believe in the shed blood of His Son Jesus Christ to have everlasting life. God's love is not conditional. This means that if as a believer you sin, His love will not stop but continue as it always is. A good Old Testament verse showing us this is:

> "But with everlasting lovingkindness I will have compassion on you," Says the LORD your Redeemer. Isaiah 54:8

But does this love of God for the believers mean that we can just do what we like and live a sinful life? The simple answer to that is no! Think of it this way, if a parent truly loves a child, the parent will still love that child but tell them they are wrong and will discipline them in love. Let's see what the last book of the Bible has to say about this matter.

Those whom I love, I reprove and discipline; therefore be zealous and repent. Revelation 3:19

As you can see in this verse, God loves His children and He wants us to be enthusiastic about changing our wrong ways because of His love for us. The reason for this is not because God just wants to tell us what to do, but because God is seeking the highest good and glory for His creation. Therefore, as we truly look right at the love of God, it is a love that shows His very best for the believer as well as His affection, and finally, His caring correction.

God Possesses Righteousness

The word righteousness is another word for right-ness. The righteousness of God is the character and attribute of His very nature. But what does this mean? In very basic terms, it means God is always right. God is not like the human race where we may need to think about what is right or wrong or what the best choice is. God doesn't need to think about these possibilities. He just knows and does the perfect thing always because it is His nature. Looking in the Bible, we can see that God always holds true to His righteous nature.

For the LORD is righteous, He loves Righteousness:
The upright will behold His face. Psalm 11:7

We can see that all of God's ways of doing things never contradict each other. To go further, they never conflict in any way. We can see this in the next verse:

...The judgments of the LORD are true; they are righteous altogether. Psalm 19:9

So, as we can see, because of God's righteousness, He will never violate His Word. The reason for this is because He cannot. He is so righteous that He doesn't have the ability to, because within His whole being and all in Him this attribute of righteousness is only His, because He is one God and the only God.

Righteousness belongs to You, O Lord, but to us open shame, as it is this day — to the men of Judah, the inhabitants of Jerusalem and all Israel, those who are nearby and those who are far away in all the countries to which You have driven them, because of their unfaithful deeds which they have committed against You. Daniel 9:7

The prophet Daniel in the verse above is stating that God is the only true possessor of all righteousness. This is because all humanity, from the beginning of time, has sinned against the all righteous One, God Himself.

As I said earlier, the righteousness of God is a communicable attribute. This means that at a limited degree, some people are righteous. But how can this be when the book of Romans in the Bible says that the whole world is guilty of unrighteousness? In Romans 3:10 we read:

...as it is written,
"THERE IS NONE RIGHTEOUS, NOT EVEN ONE."
Romans 3:10

So, how can a person be considered righteous in the eyes of God? A person can be considered righteous only by having faith in the work that Christ Jesus did by His crucifixion, burial and His resurrection.

For in it the righteousness of God is revealed from faith to faith; as it is written, BUT THE RIGHTEOUS SHALL LIVE BY FAITH. Romans 1:17

Due to the fact that the whole world is unrighteous before God, the only way a person can obtain any type of righteousness in the sight of God is by placing ones faith and trust in God's Only Son Jesus Christ, and to accept Him as their Lord and Savior (Messiah) that has saved them from their sins. It is in this way that righteous God the Father sees and accepts us through His Son and it is only then that God will see the believer as righteous. What a great God, Halleluiah!

God Possesses Truth

In short, God is Truth. There is nothing about God that is false and there is nothing that He has ever said or did in any false way. God is always consistent with His character and Himself as He is the only real true and living God.

This is eternal life, that they may know You, the only true God, and Jesus Christ whom You have sent. John 17:3

God keeps His promises and never lies.

…in the hope of eternal life, which God, who cannot lie, promised long ages ago. Titus1:2

God is so true that He will never go back on His Word or character. For Him there is no option:
If we are faithless, He remains faithful, for He cannot deny Himself. 2 Timothy 2:13
Here are some other verses that point to the truthfulness of God; here is an explanation of what is meant. In Romans 3:4, we see that God is always true and that in comparison all men are liars. We also see in the New Testament book of Hebrews (6:17-18) for God to ever lie in any way is an impossibility.

God Possesses Unity

God is never divided in any way. Humanity is different and can be divided in thought. For instance, a husband and a wife in their marriage may want to buy a new car but they may not like each other's color choice. The husband would like a red car and the wife a green car. But in the end, they both could compromise on a tan colored car. Another example of how we humans think is that we may be divided within our own choices. For instance, a person may choose to go to a movie with a friend at the last minute even though they had planned to paint their bedroom weeks in advance. This person made an emotional choice to get out and go to a movie at the last minute rather than to stay at home and start painting the bedroom. This is a person whose choice was divided.

God is not like that because every thought and action of His is never divided in the least but is always a single choice every time, as He is One.

> Hear, O Israel! The LORD is our God, the LORD is one! Deuteronomy 6:4

God is all three persons in the Godhead. That is, God the Father has authority over eternal events as well as temporal events and things because all goes through Him.

As the Bible says:

> ...one God and Father of all who is over all and through all and in all. Ephesians 4:6

The Apostle Paul, in writing to the Corinthian church, tells them that everything that has ever existed, is in existence because God is united in His own character. This can be seen in 1 Corinthians 8:6.

> ...yet for us there is but one God, the Father, from whom are all things and we exist for Him; and one Lord, Jesus Christ, by whom are all things, and we exist through Him. 1 Corinthians 8:6

12

THE MASTER TEACHING OR DOCTRINE OF THE NAMES OF GOD AND HIS SUPREMACY

When we read the Old Testament in English, we will see that the names of God are not necessarily giving an accurate picture of God's name in the passage. This is because many Old Testament verses, in translating to the English language, have substituted the name of God, or LORD as in comparison, to the meaning of the name type of the character of God. These are just some examples and they will all give you a better understanding of who God truly is:

Old Testament Original Name	English Translation
Elohim: a plural form, the true GOD singular plural, the strong one, mighty leader, Supreme Deity (Isaiah 54:5; Jeremiah 32:27; Deuteronomy 10:17)	LORD written in all capital letters
El Elyon: (Genesis 14:19; Isaiah 14:14)	"God Most High"

El Shaddai: The almighty, God standing on the mountain (Genesis 17:1; Exodus 6:3; Psalm 91:1-2)	LORD all in capital letters
El Olam: the everlasting God (Genesis 21:33; Psalm 100:5; Isaiah 40:28)	LORD all in capital letters
El Roi: "God who sees" (Genesis 16:7, 9-13, 13)	LORD all in capital letters
Yahweh: "I AM" God's personal name (Genesis 22:14)	LORD all in capital letters
Yahweh Yireh: "The LORD will provide (Genesis 22:14)	LORD all in capital letters
Yahweh Nissi: "The LORD is my Banner" (Exodus 17:15)	LORD all in capital letters
Yahweh Shalom: "The LORD is peace" (Judges 6:24)	LORD all in capital letters
Yahweh Sabbaath: "LORD of Hosts" (1 Samuel 1:3)	LORD all in capital letters
Yahweh M'Kaddesh: "LORD who sanctifies" (Exodus 31:31)	LORD all in capital letters
Yahweh Roi: "The LORD is my shepherd" (Psalm 23:1)	LORD all in capital letters
Yahweh Tsidkenu: "The LORD our righteousness" (Jeremiah 23:6)	LORD all in capital letters

Yahweh Shammah: "The LORD is there" (Ezekiel 48:35)	LORD all in capital letters
Yahweh Elohim Israel: "The LORD, the GOD of Israel" (Judges 5:3)	LORD all in capital letters
Adonai: is singular as God meaning Lord, master, owner and plural for His upper case L and then lower case ord. "Lord"	Singular as God meaning Lord. Lord is not all capitals but majesty (Joshua 7:7; Isaiah 6:8)

These sixteen Old Testament names of God are to show you more about who God is and also to show you that God's names are to be respected to the utmost.

God's name is not to be Jehovah! Who in the world would think of calling God a different name just because they may think it is okay. How dare a person do such a foolish thing. Just to give you an example, no one likes to be called by a wrong name. If my name was Tim and someone called me Tom, I may or may not respond to them. But I would have every right not to respond at all. So why should God be called by a name that is not His own, like Jehovah, when it is not His real name. His name is YAHWEH. It is true that God looks upon the heart, but to call God by an incorrect name is also disrespectful to Him as well. His name is YAHWEH.

God and His Supreme Deity

It is true that God is the only God and there are no other gods. But the truth of God is that there are no others who should be claimed as God and this has happened throughout all of history, past, present, and will continue into the future. God is supreme. This means that He is far above all that the human race could ever understand or imagine. The only true

God and Son of the Father, Jesus Christ, while He had His ministry on this earth, basically tells us that God is the Father of all creation. Jesus also tells us that the Father loves us so that we should never put anyone in His place within our lives. No one is greater then God.

"Do not call anyone on the earth your father; for One is your Father, He who is in heaven. Matthew 23:9

Some may say that this one God is the God of the Jews only, and some may say He is the God of only some Gentiles. Here again, the Scripture tells us that He is the God of all. The Jews believe in circumcision as part of their claim to the true God and the Gentiles never consider circumcision as important to worship the true God, nor has God ever required circumcision of the Gentiles. Again, He is the only true God to all. Let us see what the Bible says about this:

...since indeed God who will justify the circumcised by faith and the uncircumcised through faith is one. Romans 3:30

We can even take this one step further. The Scripture tells us that even those spiritual beings called demons believe that there is one God. Here is the proof in the scripture.

You believe that God is one. You do well; the demons also believe, and shudder. James 2:19

Interesting to note in this verse. If demons believe in God as one and true and that they are doomed for the Lake of Fire, which is Hell, it is not enough for us humans to just believe that there is one God as a fact about God. We must believe in Him and have a relationship with Him as He intended. After all, He is our Creator! This relationship can only happen by accepting God's Son Jesus and His work that He has done for us on the cross and by faith in Him making Him the Lord and

Savior of one's life. It is this relationship that leads us to doing good works, in turn only to glorify the only true God.

Because God is supreme, let us see what the scripture says about Him being the only God.

Now to the King eternal, immortal, invisible, the only God, be honor and glory forever and ever. Amen. 1 Timothy 1:17

In this verse we see that there is only one God and that He is King over all. He will always be God and He cannot be seen with human eyes. It was Jesus Christ, the second person of the God-head in bodily form, that claimed to be God, as the only God, and who said it was God the Father who sent His Son Jesus the Christ into this world. This is how Jesus explained this to us:

This is eternal life, that they may know You, the only true God, and Jesus Christ whom You have sent. John 17:3

Jesus also says in Matthew 6:24 that we are never to put money or the things that money can buy before the only true God. The warning here is that nothing on earth is to be put in the place of GOD. It is this only God that is to get our devoted attention in all things. Because if anything else takes our attention away from Him, we are making that object an object of worship! Then it is this object that is considered to be an idol and a false god in that person's life.

The only true God is worthy of all our worship and attention! Not objects, fame or people. In the book of Revelation (15:4) we can see that all of the nations of the world from throughout the ages will in fact worship the One and Only Holy God at the end of this age. Some may call this the end of the world. But it is not the end of the world for the believer; it is only the beginning of the blissful blessing of everlasting life.

God is Supreme because He is the Lord of the Universe

In His Lordship, God is the planner, creator and sustainer. For evidence of this we can turn to the beginning of the first verse in the first book in the Bible.

In the beginning God created the heavens and the earth. Genesis 1:1

In this verse we see that before time existed God had a plan and brought it about. The word "created" in this verse means out of nothing! So this means that God brought all things about out of nothing! Here are some other verses that tell us that God is the only creator and sustainer of all things: Acts 17:24; Hebrews 3:4; Revelation 10:6.

God is the planner, creator and sustainer of those who choose and accept His Son Jesus Christ as their Savior and (or) Messiah. The Bible says if we accept God's plan for salvation because of what Jesus did on the cross, and also believing that He arose from the dead, that we as a believer become a child of God and possess life everlasting.

For God so loved the world, that He gave His only begotten Son, that whoever believes in Him shall not perish, but have eternal life. John 3:16

God in His supreme plan sent His Son to die on the cross, in the place for all the sin of the world, to save all those who accept the Christ. In turn, for any one who truly and whole-heartedly accepts and believes in Jesus Christ as Lord, God gives without cost, eternal life.

He who did not spare His own Son, but delivered Him over for us all, how will He not also with Him freely give us all things? Romans 8:32

As God-Supreme He is the Father

The Father gives His children grace, which means unmerited favor and peace.

Grace to you and peace from God our Father and the Lord Jesus Christ. Ephesians 1:2

The Apostle Paul also states this in 1 Thessalonians 1:1.

God the Father also gives good gifts to His children (James 1:17).

God the Father also gives commandments (2 John 4).

Believers call Him Father in prayer (Ephesians 2:18; 1 Thessalonians 3:11).

As God-Supreme He is the Son

Jesus Christ is God the Son, and He gives protection and salvation to believers that put their faith and trust in Him. He is the only God-Man. He is also the only way to the eternal God. Because He is the only one who came to earth from heaven and taken on a bodily fleshly form as a man, the Scripture tells us this:

No one has ascended into heaven, but He who descended from heaven: The Son of Man. John 3:13

God the Son was always a person in the God-head. He was never created but is the one who created all things. God the Son was always present before the beginning of time. In these next verses we see Jesus Christ, who is God the Son, also has the name as "the Word".

In the beginning was the Word, and the Word was with God, and the Word was God. He was in the beginning with God. John 1:1-2

Jesus Christ, God the Son, took on a body to shed His blood and die for the forgiveness of sinners. Therefore, the birth of Jesus Christ was a perfect birth. Why? Because He was not born with a sin nature, that's why!

The angel Gabriel appeared to the virgin Mary and said to her that she was to remain a virgin and yet conceive a child and that He would be God the Son.

The angel answered and said to her, "The Holy Spirit will come upon you, and the power of the Most High will over-shadow you; and for that reason the holy Child shall be called the Son of God." Luke 1:35

Why did the Holy Spirit need to overshadow Mary? The answer to this is because Mary had a sin nature just like all of us do and it had to be overshadowed because the Christ Child, Jesus, had to be perfectly holy and without sin of any possible type. Christ needed to be perfect because He is God and God is always sinless. The other major reason is that the Father would only accept a perfect blood sacrifice for the forgiveness of sin for all humanity. In fact, because Jesus Christ is God, one must understand that God does not have the ability to sin. What is meant by this is, because Jesus Christ is God, He didn't, nor doesn't, have a sin nature. He is therefore void of the ability to sin. An example of what is meant by this is like a person trying to teach, pressure, and force an animal like a horse or a cat to read a book. They just do not have the nature and ability to learn even the letters, let alone to read. God will never go against His nature. God can't sin, ever!

As God-Supreme He is the Holy Spirit

As God the Father and God the Son are equal in the God-head, so is God the Holy Spirit equal to God the Father and God the Son. As you can see, the Holy Spirit is the third person of the God-head and in no way is He to be referred to as "it", as so many people make this mistake. He is God! Not an "it"! Jesus speaks of the Holy Spirit as God. He tells us that He the Holy Spirit will be sent as a comforting Helper:

I will ask the Father, and He will give you another Helper, that He may be with you forever. John 14:16

Jesus is saying here to the believer that God the Father is the One who sends the Holy Spirit from Jesus Christ's request, and is the believer's Helper, and that the Holy Spirit will never leave the believer. Jesus goes even further in that He says that the Holy Spirit is truth and guides and teaches all believers about God's truth. Jesus also says that we cannot see the Holy Spirit but the true believer has the witness of the Holy Spirit that abides within them.

> ...that is the Spirit of truth, whom the world cannot receive, because it does not see Him or know Him, but you know Him because He abides with you and will be in you. John 14:17

Looking at this verse, Jesus is saying that the world system, meaning the non-Christian system or sin system, cannot comprehend the truth of God. This is because of their unbelief. Therefore, the Holy Spirit cannot give them understanding, guidance and teaching of God because He only abides and indwells in the believer whose Lord and Savior is Jesus Christ and only Jesus Christ.

God is Supreme because He is LORD

The term "Lord" means that God is the ruler and master over all. It is a name that points to God's authority and the supremacy of Jesus. That is why titles such as Rabbi or Sir are used to refer to Jesus. You can see this by reading a verse in Matthew 8:6.

We can also see this speaking of Jesus Christ as Deity (God). In Matthew 20:27-28 you can see one of His disciples calling Jesus Christ as his Lord. The disciple's name was Thomas and it was this disciple who didn't go by hearsay, but went only by (at that time) what he could experience. But when he saw Jesus Christ alive and arisen from a very brutal death, he believed that Christ was truly Lord of all and that He even had power over death. At that point, Thomas even stated that Jesus Christ is God.

Thomas answered and said to Him [Jesus], "My Lord and my God!" John 20:28

Christ is also spoken of as Lord to the nation of Israel as well as to the rest of the world. This can be seen in Acts 2:36. Christ is also called and is all sovereign:

...He who is the blessed and only Sovereign, the King of kings and Lord of lords. 1 Timothy 6:15

God is the Supreme Master of All

As Master, this means He is over all and has complete ownership over all His creation. Because God is Master over all, He has a right to do as He pleases. He is sovereign and in control of all things.

God is Master and He hates falsehood. Even in the time of the Old Testament, New Testament and even today there have been many false prophets and teachers. God doesn't allow for this spiritual destructiveness, by those who have and are deliberately going against His Truth. The Master Teachings or Doctrines of the Bible need to be professed and taught as God expects, not by the will of men, but by the Will of God. The Apostle Peter gives a very strong warning about this for his time and even for today. He says:

But false prophets also arose among the people, just as there will also be false teachers among you, who will secretly introduce destructive heresies, even denying the Master who bought them, bring swift destruction upon themselves. 2 Peter 2:1

The word heresy here in the verse above means to bring forth a teaching that contradicts the Bible. If a teaching contradicts the Word of God, then it is a teaching that is denying God as Master. Those who do such things do not go unnoticed by the All-Powerful God.

These so-called teachers may feel confident because they have snuck into the church to teach false non-biblical teaching. But in the Bible, in the book of Jude (Jude 4), it says that God who is the Master of all knows who these false teachers are from long ago and that their condemnation is waiting for them.

The Triunity of God or as many say the Trinity of God

The Bible teaches that there is one God. This can be seen in Deuteronomy 6:4; Zechariah 14:9; Mark 12:29. These Old Testament and New Testament verses all point to God as one, yet within this one God-head there are three persons within the unity of the true God.

The Old Testament points to and gives strong emphasis on the Unity of God. God says in the Old Testament that He is a single one God and that there are to be no others with the title of god before the only God (Exodus 20:3). God does not want any person to just know the fact that God is one. He wants each person to believe that He is one God within their whole being.

Know therefore today, and take it to your heart, that the LORD, He is God in heaven above and on the earth below; there is no other. Deuteronomy 4:39

Not only does God say this to the individual, He also addresses His chosen nation collectively through His prophet, Moses, within His nation.

Hear, O Israel! The LORD is our God, the LORD is one! Deuteronomy 6:4

God also blesses those who are believers in that He is the only God and they believe in no others. This can be seen in Isaiah 45:14. God also warns the believers to remember that He has stated that He is one and that He is unique in His oneness (Isaiah 46:9).

The Old Testament also gives emphasis on the Plurality within the God-head

The Old Testament gives definite evidence of the One God in a plural form. We can see this as early as the first book in the Bible, the book of Genesis. We can even see evidence of plurality three times in one verse!

Then God said, "Let Us make man in Our image, according to Our likeness." Genesis 1:26

In this verse we can see that God addresses Himself in a plural form three times: "Let Us", "Our image" and "Our likeness". You can also see the same plurality within the same one God in many other verses in the Old Testament, such as Genesis 3:22; 11:7; Isaiah 6:8.

13

THE MASTER TEACHING OR DOCTRINE OF THE ANGEL OF (THE LORD) YAHWEH

—⟨⟨⟨⟩⟩⟩—

The Old Testament shows us distinctions within the God-head. Before going further, one must understand that the Angel of Yahweh, or as we may read in the Bible the "Angel of the LORD", is the person of the Son of God. He is actually Jesus Christ in the appearance of a human body, yet was a spiritual body in the time of the Old Testament. It would be many centuries later that the Son of God, the second person in the God-head, would take on an incarnate body and be the Savior of the World. In the book of Genesis (16:7-11, 13) we see Hagar, Abram's female servant, having a conversation with the angel of the LORD:

(In verse 7) The angel of the LORD found her by a spring of water...

(In verse 9) Then the angel of the LORD said to her, "Return to your mistress..."

(In verse 10) ...the angel of the LORD said to her "I will greatly multiply your descendants..."

(In verse 11) The angel of the LORD said to her further, "Behold, you are with child..."

(In verse 13) Then she called the name of the LORD who spoke to her...for she said, "Have I even remained alive here after seeing Him?"

Hagar knows that she saw the angel of the LORD who is God. We can know this by looking at her response at the end of verse 13. Hagar was very joyful because of what the Son of God in the form of an angel said to her. When the Son of God in an angel's form left her, she realized that she saw God, but not in His totality. The scripture says that if one could look upon God in His totality, they would no longer live and lose their life. Again, Hagar did see God but not in His totality. It was by looking upon the angel of the LORD, who is the second person of the God-head, Christ Himself in a pre-incarnate form. This type of event is called a "Christophany". There are other events like this in the Old Testament. You can look them up in these verses: Genesis 18:1-21, 19:1-28, 31:11-13, 32:24-30; 1 Kings 19:5-7. The most important thing to understand is that the angel of the LORD in the Old Testament is the foreshadowing of Jesus Christ, who is also the Messiah.

Distinctions of the Persons of the God-head in the Old Testament

There are three distinctive individual persons mentioned within a single God-head. Before we go further, I would like to mention that God Himself tells us in the book of Genesis (1:26) that God made man in His image. But what does this mean being that God is Spirit? It was God's choice to make us as He has with a will, intellect and emotions. This is what it means to be made in the image of God. As God has these invisible or immaterial qualities, so He also gave them to each person. If it were possible for a person to lack even one of these qualities, they would not be a human. We also, as humans, have three other parts 1) a body, 2) a soul and 3) a spirit. But with God to be complete, He must have three persons again in one God-head to truly be God. Here is the Old Testament biblical evidence:

The GOD-HEAD

1) The Father (LORD)
   The LORD (Father) to the Lord Found in (Psalm 110:1) the cross reference to where Jesus Christ is quoting this is (Matthew 22:43-44).

2) The Son (Redeemer) from the LORD found in (Isaiah 59:20).

3) Holy Spirit (Spirit)
   The Spirit from the LORD, God Found in (Isaiah 48:16, 59:21, 63:10-11).

New Testament Evidences of Three Persons in One God

The Apostle Paul, in writing to the Corinthian church for the first time in 1 Corinthians 8:4-8, tells them that there is one God. Paul mentions that these are man's idols or false gods. Please notice the small "g" in gods as they are called here. For in that day, even as some today in false religions will sacrifice foods to these false gods and idols, Paul says there are many false gods and it doesn't matter where someone thinks they are from as there is only one true God.

Therefore concerning the eating of things sacrificed to idols, we know there is no such thing as an idol in the world, and that there is no God but one. 1 Corinthians 8:4

And then Paul says that the true believer is to only believe in one God in the same context:

...yet for us there is but one God. 1 Corinthians 8:6

103

In the New Testament book of Ephesians (4:3-6), the Apostle Paul explained that there was to be a true attachment of peace from one believer to another in the Spirit. This is because the believers are to be united under one single Lord, having the same faith, all in the same baptism. This is to be under one and only one God, the only true Father. This is collective evidence and proof that there is one God in the New Testament. Here is another verse that points to God as being one. It is found in the New Testament book of James as listed before. Let's see again what he says:

You believe that God is one. You do well; the demons also believe, and shudder. James 2:19

James is telling us in this verse that yes, there is only one God, but that it should be common knowledge as, in fact, even the fallen angels know this in their rebellious state. They also know that this all-powerful God is sending them into eternal doom. This is one of the strongest evidences, if not the strongest, that the True God is one spiritual being!

The Three Persons in One God of the New Testament

These three persons are in no way totally separate of each other, nor are they totally the same individual persons. Just to give you some examples of what is meant by this, God does reveal Himself through nature, found in Romans 1:20. When one considers the three primary lights of blue, green and red, they are all one thing, and that is light. On the other hand, they are different in color. Now if you take all three of these lights and shine them together, you will have white light. Let's consider the spiritual side of white light and that is there is no darkness in it at all. In the world of color, white is not even considered a color but a tint. Black, on the other hand, is considered a shade.

The next example of the three-in-one is found in the world of dimensions. If we consider all things that are in nature, they will all have three dimensions. All things have height, breadth and length in nature. All have dimensions and all three dimensions together make the object, which takes up some form of space. The best example of this three within one is that of monozygotic triplets. Mono means one and monozygotic triplets are three infants from one fertilized egg. All three infants are of the same fertilized zygote or egg and all three children are very close to identical. There are very small physical differences but the only real differences are in personality, tastes, etc. But over all, they are very close to being truly identical because they originate from the same sperm and egg. This gives them the same DNA.

The New Testament of the Bible tells us that there is one God and only one God, but that there are three persons in the one God-head. These three persons are the Father, the Son and the Holy Spirit. The Bible also says that all three persons are equal as God.

God in Three Persons in the New Testament

(Verses to be looked up in your Bible)
The New Testament tells us that:

1) The Father is God
He is all knowing or omniscient (Matthew 6:4).
He is all powerful or omnipotent (John 16:23).
He is all loving (John 3:16).
He gave Jesus Christ authority over all things (John 6:27).
He forgives all wrongdoing which is sin only through the Son (Luke 23:34).
He is one with the Son (John 10:30).

2) The Son (Jesus Christ) is God:
He is all knowing or omniscient (Matthew 9:4).
He is all-powerful or omnipotent (Matthew 28:18).
He is all present or omnipresent (Matthew 28:20).
He is able to forgive wrongdoing which is sin (Mark 2:1-12).

He can raise the dead (John 11:1-45).
He holds everything together (Colossians 1:17).
He is Creator (John 1:3).
He is the Judge of all (John 5:27).
He is, and always was, God even before the beginning of time and throughout all eternity (John 1:1-3; 20:28).

3) The Holy Spirit is God:
He is a person in the God-head and was sent by Jesus Christ (Acts 2:1-12).
He can be lied to (Acts 5:3-4).
He is all-knowing or omniscient (1 Corinthians 2:10-13).
He is all-powerful or omnipotent (Genesis 1:2; Revelation 2:7)
He is all-present or omnipresent (1 Corinthians 6:19).
He regenerates only believers in Christ (John 3:5-8).

Evidence of the Trinity (Triunity) in the New Testament

To start, many will say that there is no word "Trinity" in the Bible. This is true but because this is the only spiritual book from God that counts and is valid, this needs to be seen and understood in a spiritual sense. For instance, air is not seen, but we are all breathing it. God is not seen but we understand that He exists. This is because God reveals Himself through nature. In the same sense, we can see the Trinity in the New Testament Scripture. Let's see what Jesus Christ the God-Man says about the only true Trinity, the Trinity of God:

> "I will ask the Father, and He will give you another Helper, that He may be with you forever; that is the Spirit of Truth, whom the world cannot receive, because it does not see Him or know Him, but you know Him because He abides with you and will be in you. John 14:16-17

Just looking at these two verses, we can see all three persons in the God-head.

Each Person in the God-head and their Love for the Believer

The Father
The Father–gives His Son the authority to ask for the Holy Spirit to be given.

The Father–is the giver of the Helper the Holy Spirit.

The Father–the Holy Spirit will never leave the believer because of the Father's authority.

The Son
The Son–Jesus by His authority sends the Helper, who is the Holy Spirit.

The Son–Jesus wants the believer to be comforted in the security of God by this

Helper, the Holy Spirit

The Son- Jesus wants the believer to know the truth of God and their security in

God the Father, Son and Holy Spirit.

The Son- Jesus also says that only the believer will know of the presence of the

Holy Spirit in their life and that the Holy Spirit will be in their life forever.

Here are some examples of the Trinity in the New Testament. These are verses that the reader needs to look up in their Bible.
(Matthew 3:16-17)
Here is the explanation!

1) Jesus is being baptized
2) Holy Spirit is coming down on Jesus, gently like a dove, and shining on Him.
3) Then the Father's voice is speaking from heaven to earth and announcing to all that Jesus is His Son, whom He is very delighted with.

(Matthew 28:19)
Here is the explanation!

In this verse you see that Jesus Christ commands His disciples to go throughout the world and make more disciples and to baptize them within the Father, Son and the Holy Spirit. All in one flowing statement. There you have the true Trinity of God.

Some of the Blessed Actions and Works of the Trinity (Triunity)

The Father
The Father elects or chooses those to be His children. Speaking of children:

… are chosen according to the foreknowledge of God the Father. 1 Peter 1:1-2

The Father loves the people in the world and extends salvation to all (John 3:16).

The Father is the giver of good gifts (James 1:17).

The Son
The Son had to be rejected, suffer and die in our place for the forgiveness of sin.

And He began to teach them that the Son of Man must suffer many things and be rejected by the elders and the chief priests and the scribes, and be killed, and after three days rise again. Mark 8:31

The Son is the only one who can buy or redeem back man into God's kingdom. This is found in 1 Peter 1:18.

The Son upholds all things because of the power of the Word of God (Hebrews 1:3).

The Holy Spirit
The Holy Spirit gives all believers a new start. Everything is spiritually anew. He does this by rebuilding, reestablishing and giving us a new, regenerated start by the power of His deliverance.

...by the washing of regeneration and renewing by the Holy Spirit. (Titus 3:5)

The Holy Spirit gives the believer power, stamina and energy to bring the true message of God's Word throughout the earth even to the most unreachable parts of the world. This can be seen by reading Acts 1:8.

The Holy Spirit sets the believer apart from this world's sinful ways. This is called sanctification. This allows us to have the power to live a life truly pleasing and glorifying to God bringing forth spiritual fruit (Galatians 5:22-23).

In conclusion, a true Biblical knowledge and understanding of God is so important in so many ways.

1) Because a true believer is to have an understanding of the nature of His Creator. This is because it gives them a rock solid faith, preparing them for the most troubling times in their life.
2) A strong knowledge of the true God prevents deception from false teachings. The facts and truths need to come from God through His Word the Bible, not a puffed up, arrogant manmade philosophy of thinking.

3) All people are responsible to know their true Creator and that He is Holy, loving and demands it to be His way and not the so many thousands of unholy and unloving ways that man may feel is better. God's way is better, safer, sane and most loving to all of mankind.

4) It shows us of the power of the One and only true God and the weakness of man. It is God and His way that promises man everlasting life. Man has no such power, not even to save himself.

14

THE MASTER TEACHING OR DOCTRINE OF CHRIST (MESSIAH), HIS PERSON AND WORK

—◦◦◦—

If you ask a person off the street today, "who is Jesus Christ?", most will say that He was the starter of the Christian faith. Some will give a better answer and tell you that He is the Son of God. But a great many will not understand what the Son of God means at all. He truly is LORD and Savior of all believers and Lord over all people. He is also titled "The Prophet", who proclaims God's Truth. He is also the Great High Priest who provides a perfect sacrifice for the sins of the world, because He is the perfect blood sacrifice. He is also King of all and over all kings of the past, present and over all eternity. So, He is Lord over all prophets, priests and kings. To have these titles He had to pre-exist, and did in the second person of the God-head before creation. Therefore He, Jesus Christ, is God and always was God in all eternity past and will always be God in eternity future. He also took on a physical body, yet He had to be totally sinless, and was and still is in every conceivable way. It is because He was totally sinless that Jesus Christ could be the only perfect blood sacrifice. This sacrificial death had to take place on the cross. Then He was raised from the dead to overcome the power of death so He could ascend into heaven and be seated at the right hand of the Father. The right hand of

God the Father is the place of His authority. Therefore, Christ Jesus is in the place of Authority over all things.

Christ's Pre-Existence as the Son of God and the Second Person of the God-Head

Jesus Christ, the Son of God, always existed because He is God. He pre-existed before His human birth and was even prophesied to come into this world in the Old Testament book of Isaiah in chapter 53. The Apostle John writes about Jesus Christ's pre-existence before His birth in the Gospel of John.

No one has ascended into heaven, but He who descended from heaven: the Son of man. John 3:13

This verse means that not one person can ever get to heaven on their own merits, but only by the work of the pre-existent Son of God who came to earth to redeem those who believe in Him and His work. This verse also tells us that Jesus Christ came in a human body made of flesh and bones like all humans. In other words, He is fully God and fully Man. This is why He is called the Son of Man. Then it goes further and tells us that Jesus Christ is above every one and every thing created.

He who comes from above is above all, he who is of the earth is from the earth and speaks of the earth. He who comes from heaven is above all. John 3:31

In this verse John tells us that Jesus Christ is from God in heaven because He is God. Jesus Christ's wisdom and truth is from the heavenly realm of God. He doesn't speak of earth's things that are all worldly, motivated by a fleshly sin nature, because the truth and wisdom of God is perfect, not like the shifting ideas of the earth. The last part of the verse shows that Jesus Christ has all authority over all things. We can also see that God the Father loves His Son and has given Him this rightful authority. You can see this in John 3:34-36. The Apostle

Peter, the leader of the Apostles, also tells us that Christ had to shed His perfect, priceless blood for us as a spotless lamb to save sinners. It was this Jesus Christ who was the Son of God and was the Son of God before any created thing was created. Here is evidence of this:

...but with precious blood, as of a lamb unblemished and spotless, the blood of Christ.

For He was foreknown before the foundation of the world, but has appeared in these last times for the sake of you. 1 Peter 1:19-20

The Work of Christ in All of Creation

Because Jesus Christ is the second person in the God-head, there is not one thing great or small that has not come about in all of creation. Everything had to meet with His approval.

All things came into being through Him, and apart from Him nothing came into being that has come into being. John 1:3

Everything that Christ created are not just the things we see with the naked eye, but also the things beyond our senses and understanding in all invisible realms, such as in the heavens and the different classes of angels. Christ created and did this for His purpose and to glorify God.

For by Him all things were created, both in the heavens and on earth, visible and invisible, whether thrones or dominions or rulers or authorities — all things have been created through Him and for Him. Colossians 1:16

In the book of Hebrews (1:2), we can also see that Christ was placed inheritor by God the Father over everything because of all He (Christ) has created.

Christ and His Equality in the Nature of God

First and foremost, Jesus Christ said that He was equal to God the Father. He said this before He had the opportunity to raise from the dead on the third day from a most horrible death. Some have made the claim that they would come back to life even after a much less horrific death, but never did, nor ever will as compared to sinless Jesus Christ! Also, none have made the claim of being God and giving up their life in such a way as having a crown of long, sharp thorns placed on their head and cutting the nerve endings off from the brain, then being mercilessly flogged to the point of nearly not recognizing Him. This would have killed another strong, healthy man! Then a crucifixion and being stabbed by a Roman soldier's spear that hit the heart. Through all of this murderous abuse, to the point where most, if not all, of His blood was drained out of His body, He rises from the dead as He, the Lord of Life, Jesus said He would. This is the power of the true and only God! No one, but no one, comes even close by far!

One other thing to consider is the emotional and mental trauma that Jesus Christ went through and to no effect. For one to be able to rise from the dead after all this, there should be no doubt at all that He Must Be GOD!!! He claimed His equality to God the Father by saying:

I and the Father are one. John 10:30

Let's see the statement that Jesus Christ made about His glory with God the Father before His incarnation (meaning taking on a human body) on earth.

Now, Father, Glorify Me together with Yourself, with the glory which I had with You before the world was. John 17:5

This verse shows us that Christ was with the Father long before the world. It also shows in this verse that Jesus Christ is telling us that He was always God in the past, present and future. Jesus Christ is truly God the Son, and always was and will be God.

The Fullness of Christ as Deity (God)

Christ Jesus pre-existed before all created things such as time. He, the Son, was always with the God-Head. The title of Christ before all things is "Word", for the Scripture says this person called the Word has been God from before all things, because He is truly God.

In the beginning was the Word, and the Word was with God, and the Word was God. John 1:1

The next verse that is in the Gospel of John drives the statement that Jesus Christ is God and that there is no other correct, sane way of understanding it. The next verse that the Apostle John gives us says:

He was in the beginning with God. John 1:2

This verse means that because He is God, not a single solitary thing took place without Him. It is only God that brought everything into existence because of His Supremacy, because He is almighty.

The Son of God also called the Eternal Son Became Incarnate Meaning He took on a Human Body

The Scripture tells us that the person called the Word had to take on a body of physical flesh.

And the Word became flesh, and dwelt among us. John 1:14

The Old Testament Law had the power to condemn man of his shame and weakness because of their sin. In one way, the law is powerful in a negative way to condemn man. In a positive way, this is why we need a living Savior. That Savior was sent by God! The Savior of the true believer is Jesus Christ. He had to take on a body of flesh but He also had to be in a state of perfection, without sin as the Son of God, in order to bring forgiveness to man in this sinful, dying world. This is due to the fact of the condemning power of the Old Testament Law. Let us read this in the Scripture:

For what the Law could not do, weak as it was through the flesh, God did: sending His own Son in the likeness of sinful flesh and as an offering for sin, He condemned sin in the flesh, Romans 8:3

It is only through Jesus Christ that believers have victory over sin! In other words, a true believer must have faith and acknowledge his faith by believing and saying that Jesus Christ, who is the God-Man, died for them and there is no one else past, present or future that can save them from their sins.

By this you know the Spirit of God: every spirit that confesses that Jesus Christ has come in the flesh is of God. 1 John 4:2

If a person does not believe or teach that Jesus Christ is God the Son, the second person in the God-Head, according to the Bible they are of an "anti" spirit of the true and only God. They are not to be considered in any way to know the true God. These people may even go as far as to say that Jesus Christ is a separate god or God. This is a lie from a false spirit who is trying to deceive and deflect a person to a life leading to Hell, not Heaven. Heaven is where God wants all people to be. This is why God the Father sent His Only Son to save mankind who believes and wants everlasting life with Him. This statement may seem blunt and sharp and to the point. But let us see what God's Word, the Bible, says!

For many deceivers have gone out into the world, those who do not acknowledge Jesus Christ as coming in the flesh. This is the deceiver and the antichrist. 2 John 7

Let me also say that, as you can see, the latter verse was written by the Apostle John also known as the Apostle of Love. I know for some this may seem like strong language, but the possible discomfort of the strong, firm and to-the-point language doesn't make it untrue, but very true. One must believe that Jesus Christ is the second person of the one and only true God who loves humanity.

15

THE MASTER TEACHING OR DOCTRINE OF THE VIRGIN BIRTH OF JESUS CHRIST

The question is why did Christ have to be born of a virgin? But before we go to the direct answer we must see that the Old Testament has given us a prophecy that tells us that the Christ or Messiah had to be born of a virgin. We can see this in the book of Isaiah. We need to realize that the book of Isaiah was written about 500-600 years before Jesus Christ, the God-Man, was born on this earth. Here is the prophecy:

Therefore the Lord Himself will give you a sign: Behold, a virgin will be with child and bear a son, and she will call His name Immanuel. Isaiah 7:14

Now if you don't know what the name Immanuel means, it means "God with us". This is the prophecy of the coming Messiah in which the Old Testament Jewish people were looking forward to, as well as the Savior of the World. The book of Matthew (1:23) tells us of the fulfillment of this prophecy in the New Testament. It would be wise to look up this verse right now and read it for yourself!

In the Gospel of John (1:14) it shows us that the child born of a virgin is truly God the Son, because He was sent from the Father in all perfection of God's grace and all truth. In Galatians (4:4), it tells us that Christ was born under the Law of the Old Testament and because He is God, He was the only one to fulfill the Law. This means that because of His perfection, He could never sin against the Law. Why? Because Jesus Christ did not have a sin nature. In other words, He didn't have the ability to sin in any way, nor was He born into sin as was the rest of mankind. But some may state, "How could this be because if we go to the Gospel of Matthew (4:1), we can see that Christ looks like He is being tempted by the enemy Satan?" It must be understood that this means that Christ in His humanity was to be severely troubled, yet He could never sin, ever! Yet He was troubled with a lack of food and was told He could possess all the kingdoms of this world if only He would worship the Devil and also test God! But because Christ is truly God, He could not fall for this test. It is foolishness to think that God would test Himself!

The reason that temptation exists is because of the fall of Adam and Eve in the Garden of Eden. Humanity took on a sin nature from Adam until now, except for the Lord Jesus Christ. We all get our sin nature from and through our parents. Yes, that's right, from your biological father and mother. Jesus Christ did not get a sin nature from His earthly mother, Mary, because God through the Holy Spirit overshadowed her sin nature at the time of conception. This took place from God overshadowing Mary's sin nature and conceiving the perfect God-Man—Child Jesus—with no sin nature.

Mary said to the angel, "How can this be, since I am a virgin?"

The angel answered and said to her, "The Holy Spirit will come upon you, and the power of the Most High will over-shadow you; and for that reason the holy Child shall be called the Son of God. Luke 1:34-35

To take this just a bit further, Jesus Christ did not have a sin nature, nor did He in any way have a way to sin because He cannot sin at any time. Just to emphasize this to the fullest degree, Christ didn't have the ability to sin. This would be like trying to teach a plant to read and write. The plant doesn't have the nature to read let alone write! This is why Jesus Christ is the Lord and Savior, because of His perfect God-Man Nature!

These are the Following Reasons for Christ to Have an Incarnate Body

To Reveal the True God to Mankind

No one has seen God at any time;
the only begotten God who is in the
bosom of the Father, He has explained Him. John 1:18

If one turns to John 14:7-10 in their Bible, they can see Jesus basically tells us by His conversation with His disciple Philip that if He (or we) know Him (Jesus) we will know God the Father also.

To be our Example for Living

One of the goals God has for us is to live like Jesus Christ did. If one turns to their Holy Bible, they will see this according to 1 Peter 2:21. We will also see that He suffered for the believer and that this was an example to us in that we should be living the same way after Him. Let's see what the Scriptures tell us about how deeply He suffered for us:

WHO COMMITTED NO SIN, NOR WAS ANY DECEIT FOUND IN HIS MOUTH; and while being reviled, He did not revile in return; while suffering, He uttered no threats, but kept entrusting Himself to Him who judges righteously.. 1 Peter 2:22-23

These verses are as you can see very self-explanatory. The Apostle John, in His first letter, also exhorts the believer to learn about Jesus Christ and to live a proper life as He did. This can be seen by looking up 1 John 2:6.

To be a Perfect Sacrifice

This, in fact, is the most important reason for God the Son to come to earth and be born in a human body. The reason for this importance is that all of the other reasons are under the umbrella of Christ being a Perfect Blood Sacrifice. It is by the

Perfect Blood Sacrifice that humanity can be saved from their sin. It is the sin of rejecting this that leads to eternal death, which is separation from God here on earth and in the eternal age to come. In the New Testament book of Hebrews (10:1-10), we can see the great importance of Christ being a perfect sacrifice. Here is the explanation of this passage:

Verse 1–It tells us that the system of all the sacrifices before Christ were to show and give us a look forward to the great sacrifice to come that was the blood sacrifice of Christ. It was after His sacrifice that the system stopped.

Verse 2–The reason that Old Testament sacrificing stopped is because a true worshiping believer was and is in the sight of God clean in their conscience because of forgiveness for their sin.

Verse 3–The Old Testament system brings memory of one's sins throughout the years.

Verse 4–The reason for this is that animal sacrifices have no power to cleanse one of their sins.

Verse 5–Basically says that God didn't like animal sacrifices because they had no power to forgive sin because God requires a perfect blood sacrifice. This is why Christ, the second person of the God-head, had to be born in a sinless human body.

Verse 6–This verse tells us that God does not care for the ceremonialism of animal sacrifice because it does not fulfill His perfect demand of a perfect sacrifice.

Verse 7–This verse tells us that Jesus Christ came to earth to do God's will.

Verse 8–This is a review of verses 5-6 to emphasize the weakness of the Old Testament Law.

Verse 9–This verse is to show mankind that the better and perfect sacrifice has come and He, Jesus Christ, has established a new and greater way. The verse tells us:

then He said, "BEHOLD, I HAVE COME TO DO YOUR WILL." He takes away the first in order to establish the second. Hebrews 10:9

The first order is the Old Testament system for sin. The second order is the New Testament order, which is the only perfect system for the complete removal of sin.

Verse 10–There are two great promises from God to His believing children.

Let us take a look at the first:

By this will we have been sanctified through the offering of the body of Jesus Christ once for all. Hebrews 10:10

This verse tells us that because Jesus Christ is the second person in the God-Head, He was born in a sinless human body and gave Himself up as a perfect sacrifice for mankind. To any who believe in Him, He has approved as a child of God by God's standards with forgiveness of sin. This is the first promise, that Jesus Christ is able to cover all sins at all times, past, present, and future in and throughout all of history. This includes the individual believers past, present, and also future life even if one becomes a Christian today. This is the greatness of the true God! He truly is a God of eternal love! All for accepting His Son by faith.

To Fulfill the Davidic Covenant

All of the prophets in the beginning of the Old Testament point to the coming Messiah. Later on, it was written and said that the Messiah was to be born through the line of King David. All of those from the time of the Old Testament, who truly believed in the coming Messiah, would receive eternal life on credit looking forward to the Messiah's birth, because He is the true God-Man. Let us see this in the next verse:

He will be great and will be called the Son of the Most High; and the Lord God will give Him the throne of His father David. Luke 1:32

As you can see, the Messiah or Christ is the second member of the God-Head. The scripture says He would humanly descend through the line of King David. The next verse in the passage of Luke 1:33 tells us He (Jesus Christ) will rule through Jacob and His kingdom will never come to an end.

To Destroy the Devil's Works

The Scripture also teaches that one of the main reasons Jesus Christ the Messiah came was to destroy the works of the enemy. The Apostle John says that the person who has no concern for God and sins as a practice is doing the devil's will and work. The reason why is because sin started from the devil and this is why Christ came:

...The Son of God appeared for this purpose, to destroy the work of the devil. 1 John 3:8

To become a Sympathetic Priest

Up until the death, burial and resurrection of Christ, the high priest of the temple was responsible to God for the performance of the sacrifices for the people of Israel. But he could not be truly sympathetic to the people because he himself was also a sinner. In the book of Hebrews (4:14-16) we can see that believers have a High Priest that is a great One because He is from heaven. We can see this in verse 14. But who is this Great High Priest? He is the God-Man, the Father's Son. Because He is God Himself, believers are to hold firm and stand self-assured in His understanding us because of our human weakness. So what does this all mean? This means that Christ the Great High Priest knows all about you and me and He came to assure us of His love for us, because He has tender compassion for His believing children. We can see this in the next verse:

For we do not have a high priest who cannot sympathize with our weaknesses, but One who has been tempted in all things as we are, yet without sin. Hebrews 4:15

Verse 16 tells us that a believer has the privilege to call on Christ with assurance and trust as his King knowing that we deserve nothing, but that His love for us is unmerited, merciful and that in our time of need He is ready to help us.

To be a Qualified Judge over All Humanity

God the Father is the one who has given Jesus Christ, His Son, the authority to Judge all humanity. The best reason is that Jesus Christ is fully God and fully Man. He is 100% God and 100% Man at the same time. He is not half God and half Man, but 100% God and Man in one person. Therefore, He is the most unique of all beings that has ever been or ever will be. All of this gives us reason to understand that Jesus Christ is the qualified Judge. He is qualified because He is a righteous and Holy God, as well as one who can sympathize with His believing children.

For not even the Father judges anyone, but He has given all judgment to the Son. John 5:22

This is so that those who believe in the Father are to honor the Son as well. If a person rejects Christ as from the Father, they are also rejecting the Father. On the other hand, if the Son of God is rejected, that person does not have eternal life. This can be seen just by reading through John 5:23-27.

To Save His People from their Sins

The meaning of the phrase "His people" means that it matters not what race, color, nationality, Jew or non-Jew (gentile) you are. If one is a true believer in Jesus Christ as their Lord and Savior, they have eternal life from God. This is not by their work or by the work of any other sinful man, but it is the work of God that saves. It is not the work of what man does to get to God.

For the wages of sin is death, but the free gift of God is eternal life in Christ Jesus our Lord. Romans 6:23

In Romans 1:3, it tells us that Jesus Christ was born through the line of King David as was prophesied that the Messiah would be. Then Romans (1:4) tells us because Jesus Christ arose from the dead by the power of the Holy Spirit, this gives evidence that He is the Son of God and the Lord of all.

To Condemn Sin in the Flesh and to Fulfill the Law

Jesus Christ has come in an incarnate body to condemn sin, not people. But this is only for those that believe and claim Him as their Lord, no one else. For those who reject Jesus Christ, they are condemned because of their sin according to the Law.

Therefore there is now no condemnation for those who are in Christ Jesus. Romans 8:1

Only Jesus Christ could fulfill the demand of the Law to destroy its power to condemn a believer. The reason is because Jesus Christ was the sinless sacrifice who overcame death and its power and was raised to life to give believers eternal life through Him.

For the law of the Spirit of life in Christ Jesus has set you free from the law of sin and of death. Romans 8:2

Again, these are just a few reasons why Christ had to take on and be born into an incarnate body.

The Fullness of Christ Being God in His Body Incarnate

Some people, when they hear or read in the Bible that Jesus Christ is the Son of God or the Son of man, have trouble understanding or believing that He is fully God. These people are very limited in understanding the truth of the Scripture. This is because the Scripture clearly tells us that Jesus Christ is God. Here is what the Apostle Thomas said, and this statement is to and about Jesus Christ after He arose from the dead.

Thomas answered and said to Him, "My Lord and my God!" John 20:28

Next, the Apostle Paul, in writing to the believers at Colossi, says that Jesus Christ is in no way a part of God or next to God, but that Jesus Christ is truly, fully God in an incarnate body. Christ is fully God and fully Man in one body.

For in Him all the fullness of Deity dwells in bodily form. Colossians 2:9

In the next two parts of understanding Jesus Christ as God and His incarnation, we will be first investigating His attributes as God and then secondly, will be investigating His works as God. Jesus Christ possesses attributes that only God possesses, such as eternality. It was Jesus that stated that He was with the Father in His glory before the creation of the world. Here is how Jesus prayed and stated this:
Now Father, glorify Me together with Yourself, with the glory which I had with You before the world was.John 17:5)
Previous to this statement, in a prayer to the Father, He also stated that He existed before Abraham. He makes this claim by stating that He (Jesus) has the name of God which is

"I am". One can see this by looking up the verse John 8:58 for this evidence.

Jesus Christ as God Incarnate also Possesses Omnipresence

Omnipresence means that He is present in all ways, but this does not mean that He is in things like trees, rocks, etc. It means He sees all things and that He is aware of all things. This is how Christ states this:

> For where two or three have gathered together in My name, I am there in their midst. Matthew 18:20

Jesus Christ as God Incarnate also possesses Omniscience

This word omniscience is made up of two words: omni meaning "all" and the word science, which means a systematic understanding of knowledge. Therefore, Jesus Christ as He is God knows all things correctly without error. Because Jesus Christ is God the Son, He knows all things even down to the thoughts of men. The other thing is that He even knows the motivation of those thoughts. Let's see what the Scripture tells us about Jesus being all-knowing.

> But He knew their thoughts and said to them, "Any kingdom divided against itself is laid waste; and a house divided against itself falls. Luke 11:17

This verse tells us that Jesus knew the thoughts of those trying to trap Him and He alerted those who believed in Him to stay strong in faith in Him. Other verses show us of the infinite knowledge of Christ. In Luke 6:8-10, it shows us that the self-righteous were trying to trap Jesus Christ and accuse Him of breaking the Old Testament Law. But Jesus knew their thoughts. In the passage of John 4:15-29, Jesus basically explains to a woman at the well that He is the Messiah (Christ).

Then He proceeds to tell her all about her past husbands. He did this and yet this is only the first time they ever saw and met each other. In verse 29 of this passage, in the Gospel of John, this woman goes back into town and she tells others there that she met a man and He told her about all the situations in her life. Then from there she gives a strong indication that He was most likely the Christ. This shows us that Jesus Christ knows all things.

Jesus Christ as God Incarnate also Possesses Omnipotence

Omnipotence means He (Christ) has power over all things, not some things, but every single thing ever created or imagined. The first, most important thing that Jesus promises to do for those that truly believe and love Him is that they are always being watched over. No matter where we are or where we may go, He promises to always be with us. Here is how we can know for sure. Christ says to His disciples:

> ...teaching them to observe all that I commanded you; and lo, I am with you always, even to the end of the age. Matthew 28:20

Jesus Christ, being all-powerful, has the power to destroy 6000 demons — or as some call them, evil spirits — in one fell swoop! This can be seen in Mark 5:11-15. You can see that Jesus exorcised a whole legion of demons and they even begged Him not to destroy them. But Jesus, in His power, expelled all of them and sent them to Hell. In this passage one can even see the 6000 demons asking Jesus Christ if He could allow them to possess about 2000 pigs in the countryside. Jesus allowed them to possess the 2000 pigs, and then He sent them to their death. Jesus did all of this for the benefit of saving one man! It is in this passage that one can see a great demonstration of the power of the love of God. It also shows that in His power He knows the one who will ultimately believe in Him, as in the case of this man.

In John 11:38-44, Jesus Christ shows us that He has all power over death. If one looks up this passage, Jesus raises up His friend Lazarus from the dead, after he was dead and placed in a tomb for four days. This is a great miracle that illustrates to us about the promise that Jesus Christ said that He will never leave the believer no matter what the danger is, even death.

Jesus Christ as God also Possesses Immutability

What is immutability? This word means that Jesus Christ never changes. What He says He will do, He will do. He will not go against His nature as God. He is unchangeable. If a person reads the Bible, it tells us that He is the same today as when He walked on this earth over 2000 years ago. In the New Testament book to the Hebrews it says this:

Jesus Christ is the same yesterday and today and forever. Hebrews 13:8

Here are some other verses to look up about the immutability of Jesus Christ. They are Hebrews 1:12, 7:22-24 and Revelations 1:8.

Jesus Christ in His Incarnate Body as God demonstrating the works of God

His works are only the works of God. Jesus can and wants to forgive sin. But you may say, "There are so many people who can forgive my sin, so what is the big deal about forgiving?" One must truly and fully understand that it is only Jesus Christ who has all the power to forgive sin and to give the believer eternal life. In Mark 1:5-12 we can see a demonstration of the healing power of God's forgiveness through Jesus Christ. First, He tells a man who is paralyzed that He is forgiven:

And Jesus, seeing their faith said to the paralytic, "Son your sins are forgiven." Mark 2:5

But the religious leaders didn't like this because the leaders were so hard-hearted they were in disbelief that Jesus was their Messiah and possibly just trying to keep their positions as leaders. So Jesus showed them all His power as God. How did He do this? He commanded the paralyzed man to get up and walk home. Now one must realize that the man didn't need help up from his friends. Why? Because he had no struggle in getting up at all. He just got up and walked home as Jesus told him to do. So Jesus, by this miracle, basically proves His power of forgiveness against the power of sins condemnation. In 1 John 1:9, we can also see that the same forgiveness that Jesus Christ had then is still available for us today. Any person, again, any person who believes that they need eternal forgiveness from the one and only God will receive it through Jesus Christ. How? By having faith in Christ Jesus and realizing He did all the work to save you on the cross to give you forgiveness. His forgiveness has no resentments toward the one being forgiven. He lovingly and willfully forgives all who confess their sin(s) to Him and have faith in Him.

Jesus Christ Gives Eternal Spiritual Life

It is only through the Son of God, who is Jesus Christ, that one can receive eternal life. It is not enough to believe in God the Father, but you must also know that the Father sent the Son for the forgiveness of sin. So it is through the Son that one can receive life eternal. It is the Father who gave authority to the Son to judge all individuals with the Father. This is because the Father and the Son are God. They are always in agreement. Let us see this in the next verse:

"For just as the Father raises the dead and gives life, even so the Son also gives life to whom He wishes. John 5:21

One can get a better understanding of this inter-authority of God the Son and God the Father by reading the whole block of scripture in the Gospel of John 5:17-24.

Jesus Christ, Because He is God Has the Power to Raise the Dead

Jesus Christ will raise all the dead from the first man, Adam, to the very last person on this living earth. It will not matter how long a person has been dead, or even if a person's body was separated in pieces or if every single molecule (building block of physical life) of a person's body is separated. This is because our bodies are made of matter, and matter cannot be destroyed. In this process, Jesus Christ will first restore all the decayed and destroyed bodies and then place the proper soul and spirit into the person and then and only then raise that person from the dead. We can see that Jesus Christ has the power to raise the dead as mentioned earlier in the Bible, in the famous passage of raising and restoring Lazarus in the Gospel of John 11:1-45. In this passage, one can see that Jesus, only by the power of His word, raised Lazarus after he had been deceased and in a tomb for over three days. Here is the outcome of the power of Jesus Christ found in His Word.

The man who had died came forth, bound hand and foot with wrappings, and his face was wrapped around with a cloth. Jesus said to them, "Unbind him, and let him go." (John 11:44)

This is the power of the Lord Jesus Christ.

Jesus Christ because He is Fully God Will Judge All People

Some may think that only the Father in Heaven will be judge over all. But that is not true. The Scripture tells us that the Father has given the responsibility to His Son Jesus Christ.

For not even the Father judges anyone, but He has given judgment to the Son. John 5:22

Jesus Christ will judge all believers. Not for their sin, because their sin was judged on the cross with Jesus Christ, and it is from that point on that all believer's works will be judged for rewards from Christ. For the non-believer, there is no excuse for their sin. The non-believer will be judged for their sin by Jesus Christ. He, Jesus Christ, will also judge all the nations of the world. They will be judged for their ways of promoting the true God or not.

You may be thinking, "Why is it that God the Father gave all authority over to Jesus Christ the Son to be the Judge over all?" This is to glorify the Father and so that no man cannot be understood because of their humanity. This is one of the reasons why Jesus Christ had to take on a human body, so that we may truly know that God could empathize with us in our human weakness. That is why Jesus Christ also has the title of Son of Man. You can see this by looking in the Bible in John 5:27.

Jesus Christ Has Titles of Deity (GOD)

Son of God
1) Jesus Christ's responses to the Jewish critics (John 10:36).
2) The Jewish high priest stated it (Matthew 26:63).
3) Jesus agrees to the high priest's statement (Matthew 26:64).

Lord and God
1) Zacharias, a temple priest and the father of John the Baptist, claimed Jesus as Lord (Luke 1:67, 76).
2) The Apostle Paul points to Jesus Christ as Lord (Galatians 1:3).
3) Talking of Jesus Christ as Lord to save those that turn to Him as Lord (Joel 2:32).
4) The Apostle John claims Jesus Christ as God from before creation (John 1:1).
5) God the Father claims that Jesus Christ is His Son and is God (Hebrews 1:8).

6) In the book of Revelation the Apostle John wrote that he saw an inscription on Jesus Christ in Heaven that shows that He is above all kings and lords (Revelation 19:16).

His Claim as God

I and the Father are one. John 10:30

This verse shows that Jesus Christ is God and is equal with the Father and in no way is beneath or inferior to His Father who is God.

The Perfect Humanity of Christ Incarnate (in a Human Body)

Humanly, Jesus Christ was perfect because He was sinless. On the other hand, He grew up like any other child. He had a need for water and food and care just like any other child. He could feel pain, thirst and all the emotions. He was able to get sick, such as having a fever. He was able to feel tired and so on. The Bible says Jesus was always growing in a wise way and also correctly maturing physically in the sight of God and humanity. We can see this in Luke (2:40, 52). In the book written to the Hebrews (2:14), it tells us all children are made of flesh as well as blood and Jesus Christ was not any different than all of mankind in this way.

Therefore, since the children share in flesh and blood, He Himself likewise also partook of the same, that through death He might render powerless him who had the power of death, that is the devil. Hebrews 2:14

This verse claims that Jesus Christ was born in a human body just like all of us, made up of flesh and made up of blood.

Jesus Christ also had a Human Soul and Spirit

He had no shortcuts in His life here on earth. He experienced sorrow, grief, rejection, being misunderstood, being falsely accused, humiliated etc. Jesus Christ has gone through all that we humans go through and so much more. Just imagine the pain He went through because He is perfectly sinless and had to come into an imperfect world. Here is some insight as to how His soul felt before His crucifixion:

Then He said to them, "My soul is deeply grieved, to the point of death; remain here and keep watch with Me." Matthew 26:38

Let us go one step further about the humanity of Jesus Christ, as I mentioned earlier, Christ also had a human spirit. At the time of His crucifixion, just before He died, He gave His spirit to His heavenly Father. Let's look at the verse that shows us this:

And Jesus, crying out with a loud voice, said, "Father, INTO YOUR HANDS I COMMIT MY SPIRIT." Having said this, He breathed His last. Luke 23:46

Jesus Christ had a body, soul and spirit. It is these three elements or parts that make up a human being. Jesus Christ was and is fully God and fully human. Jesus Christ had all the characteristics of being a human. Here are some of them from the scripture.

He felt hunger (Matthew 4:2)
He felt thirst (John 19:28)
He felt weariness (John 4:6)
He would sleep (Luke 8:23-24)
He felt loving compassion and showed it (Matthew 9:36)
He bled (John 19:34)
He experienced suffering (1 Peter 4:1)
He experienced death (Matthew 27:50)
He wept is the shortest verse in the Bible; the exact words are: Jesus wept. John 11:35

But what did Jesus weep about? Not because of fear, because He was very bold in the purest sense of the word. Jesus wept because of the lack of faith others had in Him before His resurrection. Why did He have such deep sorrow? Because those close to Him, as well as those who believe in Him, had trouble grasping that He, Jesus Christ, was truly the only God in a human body as well as the only God of the resurrection. Not only did He raise His friend from the dead (John 11:17-44), but Jesus Christ also raised Himself from the dead (John 10:17-18).

Because Jesus Christ is the second person of the God-head and because of His incarnate human body, He set aside the full manifestation or advantage of His attributes as God. He did this only for His earthly ministry, yet He was and still is fully God. In laying aside some of His attributes as God, Jesus Christ totally listened to His heavenly Father for guidance. Some may say, "But how is this possible if Jesus Christ is fully God? How and why would He lay aside His attributes as God if he truly is God?" First of all, there are many times a person could lay aside attributes of their profession or a career; such as a medical doctor on vacation in another country, and also not being licensed in that country to practice medicine. An attorney can only practice law in the states that they are licensed in, and he or she is not to practice law in any other state(s). The other reason is that He (Jesus) set aside His attributes as God is in order to fulfill the demands of God the Father's Old Testament Law. This had to be done as a perfectly sinless sacrifice, with God the Father calling the shots or making the choices for Christ's life and in His life. This was so the heavy demands for sin could be met. This can be seen in the book of Philippians (2:5-11). The main two verses on this subject are verses 6-7:

...who, although He existed in the form of God, did not regard equality with God a thing to be grasped, but emptied Himself, taking the form of a bond-servant, and being made in the likeness of men. Philippians 2:6-7

By all these verses you can see the ministry of Jesus Christ being fully God and fully man. Therefore He is the God-Man.

16

THE MASTER TEACHING OR DOCTRINE OF THE SINLESSNESS OF CHRIST

—◊◊◊—

Every human being, from the first person who was Adam to the last person ever to be born to the human race, has been born into sin and will have a sin nature. Therefore, all humanity is born into sin. We have all gotten our sin nature from our parents and we all pass our sin nature on to our children. Jesus Christ is God the Son, the second person of the God-head, and when He took on a human body to be sacrificed for the sins of the world, the sacrifice had to be perfect, as the Old Testament lamb had to be perfect and without any physical blemish or the lamb could not be sacrificed.

Christ Was and Is Impeccable and Unchangeable because He has the Nature of Sinless God.

At the conception of Christ, the Bible teaches that the Holy Spirit, the third person of the God-head who is equal to the Father and the Son, was responsible for Christ's conception with the virgin named Mary. It was the Holy Spirit who overshadowed the sin nature of Mary. The Scripture is very self-explanatory on this subject in Luke 1:34-35. In verse 34 it explains that Mary was a virgin. Then in verse 35 it explains how Jesus Christ was conceived:

The Holy Spirit will come upon you, and the power of the Most High will overshadow you; and for that reason the holy Child shall be called the Son of God. Luke 1:35

The conclusion to this is that Jesus Christ was truly born of a virgin and did not have a sin nature. He is the only person on this earth who did not ever have a sin nature. Therefore, He was the perfect sacrifice, and a sacrifice that was totally sinless in every possible and even probable way. It was His sacrifice that met the total requirements of God's holy Law. It is through this sacrifice that salvation would be available to the human race from their sin, to those who believe in Christ as the Son of God.

Jesus Christ Always Pleased the Father

All believers can see that, based on the Father's statement found in Matthew 3:17, that Jesus Christ pleased His Father in heaven. But behind that statement is a very important question. How did He do it? The Scripture tells us that He always had a willing heart and a single mind and will to please His Father in Heaven. Jesus did nothing out of His own enthusiasm (John 8:28). But all things that Christ did were by what His heavenly Father told Him. Jesus Christ had and still has an ongoing and continuous loving relationship with His Father. Again, this ongoing relationship still exists today and this relationship is one that no other person on earth has ever had. It is a perfect sinless relationship. This is what Jesus said about His relationship with His Father:

And He who sent Me is with Me; He has not left Me alone, for I always do the things that are pleasing to Him. John 8:29

Jesus Christ Knew No Sin

This is a statement that tells us that He never experienced sin, not even in the slightest way. He never thought in a sinful, lustful or deceptive way, nor did He speak deceptively (1 Peter 2:22). Being totally absolutely sinless was, first of all, the true nature of Jesus because He is God. Secondly and thankfully, for the person who is a believer in Jesus Christ, because it was Jesus Christ the God-Man who took the place of the believer for the punishment of sin and that punishment was eternal death. It was only Jesus who could pay the price for sin so a believer could be declared righteous through Him.

He made Him who knew no sin to be sin on our behalf, so that we might become the righteousness of God in Him. 2 Corinthians 5:21

Not only did Christ have a perfect love for His Father in Heaven, He (Christ) also obeyed His Father in every perfect way along with perfect trust. Jesus always knew (and knows) even today of this perfect love, trust, and will that the Father eternally has for His Son Jesus Christ. But the Father also has an ongoing ministry for His Son throughout eternity, past, today and forever.

Jesus Christ was and is the Lamb without Blemish or Spot

In the Old Testament, a lamb had to be sacrificed to God (Exodus 34:20; Leviticus 14:10) because God's demand is that blood had to be shed for the covering forgiveness of sins. This lamb had to be perfect with no defects at all. May I also say that all Old Testament sacrifices were only designed to cover the sinner's conscience, and not the sinner's sin. For that time, sin was only forgiven through having faith in the coming Messiah and we can all see that this Messiah is called Christ Jesus. The Apostle Peter makes reference to this perfect blood sacrifice of Jesus in these verses:

...but with precious blood, as of a lamb unblemished and spotless, the blood of Christ. For He was foreknown before the foundation of the world, but has appeared in these last times for the sake of you. 1 Peter 1:19-20

137

There are no more Old Testament sacrifices because Christ fully met the demand of a perfect sinless blood sacrifice. This is why it only takes a true faith in Christ for anyone to receive everlasting salvation today.

Jesus Christ was perfectly and wholly Innocent and Never was in Need of a Sacrifice

In the Old Testament, all of the people, just as today, had sinned. Even the Old Testament priests! These priests had to first give a sacrifice for themselves and then they performed the sacrifice for the people. But Jesus Christ never needed to have or perform a sacrifice for Himself. It is His sacrifice on the cross that was done for humanity. This sacrifice was for the whole world, not just those that God elected before all creation. In this sacrifice and because of His sacrifice, Jesus Christ is given the title of the High Priest. The Apostle Paul under the inspiration of the Holy Spirit says it best when speaking of Jesus:

For it was fitting for us to have such a high priest, holy, innocent, undefiled, separated from sinners and exalted above the heavens; who does not need daily, like those high priests to offer up sacrifices, first for His own sins and then for the sins of the people, because this He did once for all when He offered up Himself. Hebrews 7:26-27

All people, whoever they may be, are elected to receive salvation in Christ Jesus today only by faith in Him because of His ultimate sacrifice on the cross. This promise is by His Word and that is the Word of GOD.

Jesus Christ was Tempted, which means He was Troubled, Just as we are Yet without Sin

We can see one example of this as we read the Gospel of Matthew (4:1) and in the following verses (2-11) we can see the severity of the devil tempting, meaning troubling Jesus Christ. In the book to the Hebrews (2:18), it tells us that Jesus

Christ suffered and was in reality troubled — or as some may say, tempted — so He can come to the aid and support of those that are being tempted and troubled today. We must realize that Christ was truly troubled to a much greater degree then all of us on the face of this earth.

For we do not have a high priest who cannot sympathize with our weaknesses, but One who has been tempted in all things as we are, yet without sin. Hebrews 4:15

Then the next verse gives the believer great encouragement and a great promise from God because of Jesus the God-Man.

Therefore let us draw near with confidence to the throne of grace, so that we may receive mercy and find grace to help in time of need. Hebrews 4:16

Realize that this verse is super positive and is uplifting. We see words like confidence. Grace is a very beautiful word here, and it means that it is a gift that we do not deserve. We also see the word mercy and this is a word that is a positive, loving act after one is offended. Jesus Christ truly is the most perfect High Priest. There is no one else like Him!

17

THE MASTER TEACHING OR DOCTRINE OF THE RESURRECTION OF JESUS CHRIST

———

C hrist's death, burial and resurrection is the Gospel message in three words. The whole Bible rests on these three very important words. Therefore, these three words are of first importance. If a person does not agree with the death, burial and resurrection as the most important part of the Good News message from God to man, and if they cannot truly believe this, then their claim to being a Christian is false in every way. Many people can act Christianized, but the death, burial and resurrection is in no way to be forfeited in Christianity. The Apostle Paul boldly put it this way.

For I delivered to you as of first importance what I also received, that Christ died for our sins according to the Scriptures, and that He was buried, and that He was raised on the third day according to the Scriptures,
and that He appeared to Cephas, then to the twelve.
After that He appeared to more than five hundred brethren at one time, most of whom remain until now, but some have fallen asleep;
then He appeared to James, then to all the apostles;
and last of all, as one untimely born, He appeared to me also. 1 Corinthians 15:3-8

Verse 3. This verse tells us that the most important thing that the Apostle Paul understood was that Christ died on the cross for our sins just as the Scriptures said He would. This was the first, important, master doctrinal teaching that Paul was passing on to others as the foundation for true Christianity.

Verse 4. Then Paul goes further and deeper into this most important topic. He says that then the Lord was buried and on the third day of His death, He (Christ) resurrected. Again, as the Scriptures said He would.

Verses 5-6. These verses say that the resurrected Jesus Christ appeared to the man originally called Cephas, who is the Disciple, who is also the Apostle, with the translated English name of Peter. Then He appeared to all twelve of the Disciples together. One must realize that an individual person may hallucinate, but for all twelve Apostles to hallucinate at once is truly an impossibility. An unbelieving person could say that all twelve apostles were conspiring to fool the public in saying that Jesus Christ arose from the dead. But Paul goes on even further to say that more than five hundred people witnessed Jesus Christ alive after the death and burial of His body. Then Paul goes on to say that most of those five hundred witnesses of Jesus Christ are still alive to this day. This means the day that Paul was writing this first letter to the Corinthian church in Greece, that most of those five hundred witnesses were still living.

Verse 7. After all of this, Jesus Christ appeared to His human brother who didn't believe in Christ's claims during His ministry. It was only after Christ's resurrection that James, His brother, powerfully believed that Jesus Christ was his Messiah. From there Jesus Christ also appeared to not only the original Twelve Disciples and Apostles, but also all of the secondary apostles. Some of the names of the secondary apostles are Barnabas (Acts 13:2, 7) and Silas (Acts 15:22, 32, 40).

Verse 8. The Apostle Paul says He appeared to him last and he even goes as far as to allude to the fact that he, Paul, was born in a wrong time meaning that before Jesus Christ got Paul's attention, it was Paul who persecuted the true Christian church, even to the point of putting some to death. This was because of His zeal and ignorance at the time. Then Christ got a hold of Paul and Paul believed. Christ also had other plans for the Apostle Paul. The Apostle Paul is the one apostle extraordinaire. He is responsible for writing most of the New Testament that we have today. Here is another verse that Paul wrote to the Roman Christians of that day, pointing to Christ's death on the cross for our sins and His resurrection to save us from our sins. What a great and glorious God!

He who was delivered over because of our transgressions, and was raised because of our justification. Romans 4:25

Jesus Christ Predicted His Resurrection would Happen

Because Jesus Christ is the God-Man, and because God the Father was in control of the events that His Son had to obey in order to fulfill the Law by never breaking the Old Testament Law, Christ had full knowledge of the events that would take place. Christ predicted that He, in total innocence from sin, would be delivered to those high officials of the temple and be sentenced to death. He also predicted that He (Christ) would be given over to the gentiles (Romans) and that they would cast insults at Him, beat Him and then nail Him to a cross to die a horrible death. Then He said after being dead He would rise on the third day. You can see this in Matthew 20:18-19. On the third day Jesus did resurrect from the dead. Three women went to the tomb where Jesus was buried and an angel of the Lord of God told them that He (Jesus Christ) was not there, but that He arose. You can see this again in the book of Matthew (28:1-20). But the key verses in this passage that show that Jesus Christ predicted His resurrection are the ones where the angel told the three women about Jesus. It was only after this event that Jesus appeared to them. Here is what the angel said to the three women:

He is not here, for He has risen, just as He said. Come, see the place where He was lying. Matthew 28:6

And again it was only then that the three women saw Jesus and touched Him and worshiped Him, because He is God:

And behold, Jesus met them and greeted them. And they came up and took hold of His feet and worshiped Him. Matthew 28:9

Jesus Christ Raised Himself from the Dead

First, it needs to be said that God the Father and God the Holy Spirit raised Jesus from the dead (1 Peter 1:21). Next, it is very important to know that the God-Man Jesus Christ did not allow anyone to take His life, but, that He gave it up by His own will. Also, because He is the God of the resurrection, He was able to bring His lifeless body back to life. This is for the believer and the unbeliever to know that Jesus Christ will raise the believer to life everlasting and to the unbeliever into everlasting punishment. The unbeliever into everlasting punishment because of their lack of faith and their lack of thankfulness for His (Christ's) work on the cross, that would save them from their sins if only they would have believed.

Let's see what Jesus predicted about being able to take up His life after His death on the cross.

No one has taken it away from Me, but I lay it down on My own initiative. I have authority to lay it down, and I have authority to take it up again. This commandment I received from My Father. John 10:18

Because of Jesus Christ's Resurrection there appeared a New Prototype Body

We can see this in Colossians 1:15-20. This prototype body is called a glorified body and because of Christ, all believers will receive a glorified body. This means no more sin nature and no disease. This new glorified body will be indestructible and the body will appear in the beauty as it was to be before sin entered into the world from Adam. No disease, underweight, overweight or deficiencies of any kind. The author believes that light may even emanate from our new glorified body. Christ is the first to receive this glorified body so believers of His church would receive a glorified body. Why is this?

He is also head of the body, the church; and He is the beginning, the firstborn from the dead, so that He Himself will come to have first place in everything. Colossians 1:18

When Jesus Christ Resurrected He was Well Recognized

It has been stated and known that because Christ was given a crown of thorns to wear as a mockery for being King; His body was severely beaten and bruised. He was then crucified on the cross. Because of all this trauma, He was unrecognizable at His death. After He (Jesus) arose from the dead, Scripture also tells us that He was very recognizable to His disciples. First He told them to be at peace (John 20:19), and then they saw that it was truly Him because He showed them His crucifixion scars.

And were He had said this, He showed them both His hands and His side. The disciples then rejoiced when they saw the Lord. John 20:20

The Wounds of Jesus Christ Will Always Visibly Remain

They where visible on earth after His resurrection (John 20:25-29) and they have and will continue to remain visible also in heaven eternally. We can see this in the last book of the Bible written by the Apostle John. Here is what it says as John was viewing future events in heaven. Keep in mind that Jesus Christ is the sacrificial Lamb (John 1:29) and that He was slain for the sins of the world.

144

Pointing to Jesus Christ as the Lion, from the tribe of Judah from the line of King David who overcame all, this is seen in (Revelation 5:5). Then pointing to Jesus Christ as the slain Lamb that is standing. Of course, this makes sense that this Lamb is a symbolic name of Jesus Christ the God-Man. Here is what it says in the next verse:

And I saw between the throne (with the four living creatures) and the elders a Lamb standing, as if slain... Revelation 5:6

But one may ask, why is it that the God-Man would want to continue throughout all eternity future with His crucifixion scars remaining on His Glorified Body? Well, there are at least two good reasons. First of all, I as a child who was born in the 1950's with a digestive problem, that was severe enough to the point that if I would have not had surgery at ten days old, I would have died within a few days from malnourishment. But at the age of three years old, I noticed that I had quite a large scar on my abdomen and I realized that other children in their bathing suits didn't have a mark or scar on their stomachs. Well, my father and mother told me that I needed an operation when I was ten days old and that if I didn't get the operation I would have died. Then my parents told me not to be ashamed of my scar but to be joyfully proud of it, because the scar was a way of showing me that God really wanted me to live. It was at that point that I as a little boy went around happily showing off my scar, by going up to people and asking them, "would you like to see my operator on my tummy?", and then picking up my shirt and showing them my scar that I knew was a way of reminding me and my parents of that life-saving event that God was with me.

In a similar way, Jesus Christ is glorified because of His life-giving crucifixion scars. He died on the cross to glorify His Father, God. He did it to save every true believer from their sins and gave them everlasting life. Secondly, Jesus Christ's crucifixion scars will remain as an eternal memorial and remembrance of the great anguish, suffering, humiliation and death He went through for His true children, who are His true believers, saving them by His work.

Jesus Christ was Able to Eat after His Resurrection

Now that Jesus Christ was in His true glorified body, He was able to eat food even though there was no physical need for Him to eat! I believe that Jesus ate fish with His disciples as a way of enjoying the fish without a physical need for nourishment from it. It is also very possible that He also wanted to enjoy a meal with His disciples. Realize that, because Jesus Christ was in His glorified body, that the fish He ate was totally consumed and that there was no waste. It is good to read this whole account in Luke (24:39-47). But the key verses for this topic are:

They gave Him a piece of a broiled fish; and He took it and ate it before them. Luke 24:42-43

All of Jesus Christ's Claims are True and His Greatest Claim also has the Greatest Proof, His Resurrection!

Because He is the God-Man and cannot lie, all His claims are true even without a visual showing of proof. The reason being is that because He is God, His claims will happen. But His greatest claim was that He would rise from the dead and He did. Just think of it, here is a person who claims to be God, is murdered in the most torturous way and three days later He raises from the dead in a better condition than before with a glorified body. He claimed He would rise from the dead and here is the answer as an angel said:

He is not here, for He has risen, just as He said. Come, see the place where He was lying. Matthew 28:6

Proof of the God-Man, Jesus Christ as Lord and also the Messiah

The verse of Romans 1:4 states that because of the resurrection, Jesus Christ is truly declared the Son of God by the Holy Spirit as Lord. Therefore, His predictions and claims are true. Jesus Christ also claimed to be the Messiah that Israel was waiting for, and He also proved that He was and is the Messiah of Israel because He was crucified, died and was resurrected from the dead on the third day. This also fulfills Hosea 6:2 as Hosea claimed He would resurrect on the third day to Israel.

18

THE MASTER TEACHING OR DOCTRINE OF THE ASCENSION OF JESUS CHRIST

The meaning of this statement points to Christ's departing bodily from this natural earthly world and His returning into the heavenly spiritual world. The timing of this ascension was forty days after His resurrection. The Bible is full of verses pointing to the ascension of Jesus Christ.

Old Testament Prophecy about the Ascension of Jesus Christ

Old Testament (Psalm 68:18) States that Christ ascended into Heaven

New Testament He led captives (Ephesians 4:8) He gifted men

Old Testament (Psalm 110:1) God the Father tells God the Son to sit at the right hand of His authority until God made His enemies to stay under His feet.

New Testament Pre Ascension (Luke 9:51) Jesus Christ knows of the day of His ascension and looked forward to it, but He made sure all things were done according to God the Father's plan, and done to perfection.

(John 7:32:33) Jesus Christ knew that when the Pharisees were seeking to stop Him and to put Him to death. Jesus knew His ascension was near.

(John 16:5, 10, 28) Verse 5, Jesus Christ tells His disciples that He will soon ascend to His Father, but it didn't seem important enough at the time so the disciples didn't question Him.

Verse 10 Jesus Christ got more specific and deeper, and told His disciples it was God's righteous will that He would ascend to God the Father and that they would not see Him anymore.

Verse 28 Jesus Christ says He came from heaven where His Father is, and that He came to this world. Then He tells His disciples He will leave this world again, meaning He was here to create the world and now He will be leaving the world a second time to be with the Father.

The Ascension Event of Jesus Christ

The event of the ascension of Jesus Christ is found in (Luke 24:51) and (Acts 1:6-11).

Again, one needs to understand that the ascension of Christ took place forty days after His Resurrection.

Here is the explanation from Acts 1:6-11: His disciples basically ask Jesus if it is time for the restoration of the kingdom, and Jesus says to them that this is only for God the Father to know the time for this event. Then Jesus Christ tells them that the Holy Spirit will come with power and they will get their power from the Holy Spirit to be His witnesses through every part of the earth. Now after He said this to them, He started ascending up until He (Jesus) was out of sight. As the disciples were still looking up skyward for the Lord Jesus, two angels in white appeared and asked them why they were still looking skyward. Then they said, "Jesus has ascended to heaven and will be coming back just the way He left." Again, it is much better to read this straight from the Scripture—as well as all Biblical Scripture. But the Gospel of Luke has the ascension of Christ in one simple verse. Here it is:

While He was blessing them, He parted from them and was carried up into heaven. Luke 24:51

The epistle of 1 Timothy 3:16 leads one to an overview of events that leads up to the mystery of the Lord Jesus Christ's Godly ascension:

...He who was revealed in the flesh,
Was vindicated in the Spirit,
Seen by angels,
Proclaimed among the nations,
Believed on in the world,
Taken up in glory.
1 Timothy 3:16

Jesus Christ's Present Ministry

Unfortunately, many people who believe Jesus Christ has ascended into heaven think He is up there and that is it! Many do not realize that He still is very active in glorifying His Father and He is very active in taking care of His children. This goes for each and every one of them at every second of the day! His ministries are ministries that are ongoing and eternal.

Jesus is the Head of the True Church

After God the Father raised His Son, Jesus Christ, from the dead He placed Him at His right hand in heaven. The right hand is symbolic of all power and all authority. Jesus Christ is the Greatest above all rulers and authorities and powers, as well as dominions in the heavens, as well everywhere in the universe and this world. He is in total absolute control from the beginning of all things and throughout all eternity. Again, God the Father gave the God-Man power over all things past, present and future. Jesus Christ is also the head over all things that have to do with all His beloved children. Therefore, Jesus Christ is the Head of the Universal Church. Being that the God-Man Jesus Christ is the head of His church, the Bible says that the church is called the Body of Christ. We can see this in Ephesians 1:20-23. In this passage we can see Christ's ministry to His church are as follows.

> And He put all things in subjection under His feet, and gave Him as head over all things to the church, which is His body, the fullness of Him who fills all in all. Ephesians 1:22-23

Jesus Christ sent the Holy Spirit Originally to Form and Bring about His Church

Jesus told His Apostles that God the Father had promised the sending of the Holy Spirit and that Jesus Christ would send the Holy Spirit to His church (Acts 1:4, 2:33). This is so each and every believer would be baptized into and with the Holy Spirit (Acts 1:5). He spiritually marks all believers that are in His body, the church, and indwells in them to guide them and teach them, also giving them power over sin. The Apostle Peter, in the book of Acts, also tells us that in the very early church the believers and others had actually seen and heard the coming and the manifestation of the power of the Holy Spirit on the day that Jesus Christ sent the Holy Spirit to the church (Acts 2:33). Today, anyone who has truly accepted Christ as their Lord and Savior also receives the gift of the Holy Spirit at that point of acceptance. He, God the Holy Spirit, comes into the life of the true believer. He marks the believer as God's child and gives them power over sin. The Holy Spirit also guides, teaches and illuminates the believer. The believer is also then baptized into the body of Christ, which is what is called the universal church. God is not prejudiced in any way and He accepts all races and all types such as black, white, oriental, American Indian, Jew or Gentile and from those that have a form of status and those that are less fortunate and have no status at all. Then there are those that are living in bad circumstances because of the way the world imposes it's will on one's life. Then there are those who, due to one's own rebellion against society, have had their freedoms of society taken from them. God hates sin, but He is never partial to anyone and always invites one to put their faith and trust in Jesus Christ as Lord and Savior, in turn freely receiving everlasting life. All believers are given the Holy Spirit to fill their spiritual needs. It is the promise of God. We can see this in the next verse:

> For by one Spirit we were all baptized into one body, whether Jews or Greeks, whether slaves or free, and we were all made to drink of one Spirit. 1 Corinthians 12:13

Jesus Christ Sanctifies His Body which is the Church

The Bible says that Jesus Christ the God-Man is the head and the church is His body (Ephesians 5:23). The meaning of this is that Jesus Christ is the sanctifier and that He cleanses the church and sanctifies it and declares it holy. This is only through Him because He is God.

> Husbands love your wives, just as Christ also loved the church and gave Himself up for her, so that He might sanctify her, having cleansed her by the washing of water with the word. Ephesians 5:25-26

Jesus Christ Gives Gifts to the Body which is the Church

Again, His body is made up of members and each member is given a spiritual gift for the sake of building up the church. You can see this in Ephesians 4:7-13. But the key verse in this passage for this topic of doctrine is:

But to each one of us grace was given according to the measure of Christ's gift. Ephesians 4:7

Christ also gives each member different ministries. We can see this in the following verse:

And there are varieties of ministries, and the same Lord. 1 Corinthians 12:5

Jesus Christ also Empowers His Body of Believers

He does this by giving each member encouragement to keep them growing and this also keeps them strong in their faith. Jesus Christ also disciplines His true children which are part of His body, to keep them from sin and also to make them stronger and stronger for spiritual warfare. This can, again, be for sin that is in one's life, or to give one a proper understanding to overcome a lack of faith.

Another name that Jesus Christ has is the Vine and this Vine has many branches, which are the believers attached to Christ because of their faith in Him. Jesus tells us this in John 15:1-10. It is by encouragement and discipline that Jesus Christ shows us His love for us and it is by this method that we can bear much fruit because if He didn't do this for us we would not be His children. This is Jesus speaking:

I am the vine, you are the branches; he who abides in Me and I in him, he bears much fruit, for apart from Me you can do nothing. John 15:5

Jesus Christ is the Faithful Great High Priest

It was the High Priest in the Old Testament that was appointed by the people to bring gifts, as well as sacrifices, to God as He commanded for the sins of the people. But it was and still is only Jesus Christ whose sacrifice, which is His death on the cross, burial and His resurrection, that can forgive sins. There is no one else that can forgive sin! He is the only

One who has ascended into Heaven. This is because He is the God-Man (Hebrews 4:14). It is because of this reason that He can understand all of our situations and circumstances. Because He is God, He knows where we came from. Some of us came from a poor family. Maybe we had a sick parent or child. Maybe we had an evil parent. Maybe we have a physical problem or an emotional problem. He knows if we are in a hard marriage and so on and so on. Whatever it is, the Great High Priest understands all His believers. This is because Jesus Christ was tempted, meaning troubled, in every possible way, just like us. This is the reason He can understand all of His believers and why He is called the Great High Priest (Hebrews 4:15).

So what does God want us to do from here on? He wants us to get closer to Him with the faith He has given us and trust Him by approaching His Great heavenly throne undeservedly (Hebrews 4:16). This is so that Jesus will assist, support and help us right in the midst of the most troubling and devastating situations of our lives. This goes for spiritually, physically, and even mentally, in all and in every type of trial that happens to and with the believer.

For since He Himself was tempted in that which He has suffered, He is able to come to the aid of those who are tempted. Hebrews 2:18

Jesus Christ the Great High Priest Intercedes for His Own

When one puts their faith and trust in Jesus Christ, that believing person becomes a child of God. If one is a true child of God, their sins are all forgiven. If a child of God has a sin problem and he goes on sinning, God will not reject him but He may discipline him and may even take him home to heaven sooner then his time should be here on earth. But one must understand that a true child of God is never rejected by God or sent to Hell. Why? Because He loves His children! One must also understand that if a child of God sins, he or she needs to

154

confess that sin to stay in fellowship with Christ, so that they can move on with a clean slate and not go into deeper sin. It is Jesus Christ who is an intercessor and advocate, who defends His children before God the Father. Because the Father sent His Son Jesus Christ and shed His blood for forgiveness of our sins, the Father looks at a believer, even if they are the most pathetic of sinners, and He (the Father) looks through the shed blood of the Great High Priest who is Christ Himself, and sees them as forgiven because of their faith in God's Son. The reason for this is because Christ is innocent of any sin, and as believers we are declared forgiven (Hebrews 7:25). It is Jesus Christ who is the God-Man who takes up the gap for us. He is the bridge to the Father's throne. He is also our go-between.

Here is a verse packed with great blessing:

Therefore there is now no condemnation for those who are in Christ Jesus. Romans 8:1

WHY IS THIS?

...who is the one who condemns? Christ Jesus is He who died, yes, rather who was raised who is at the right hand of God, who also intercedes for us. Romans 8:34

That is Why! There is no greater interceder and defender than Jesus Christ the God-Man.

Jesus Christ is preparing a Place for His Believing Children in Heaven

Jesus Christ the God-Man tells His believing children to not allow the world and all its troubles, problems and tragedies affect your faith in Him. Yes, it is true God may have allowed all these things to take place in this sinful world, yet one is to look to the One who is greater and bigger than all the struggles in the world. Jesus also comforts believers by saying that God the Father was the One who has sent Him. This can be seen in

John 14:1. Next there is a great promise of comfort. The Father is in heaven and He has many rooms for His children to live in and stay in. This is a comforting truth about the living God. Then Jesus tells His disciples that He will be going to arrange everything in preparation for their arrival. This is just one of the things Jesus Christ is doing right now for all His believers right now (John 14:2). The next verse in this passage puts it all together and points to His coming again for all His saints who are His believers.

> If I go and prepare a place for you,
> I will come again and receive you to
> Myself, that where I am, there you may be also. John 14:3

Jesus Christ's Future Ministry

It is Jesus Christ that Will Raise All Those Who Are Dead

First, Jesus Christ will raise the dead by the power of His voice (John 5:28).

Second, Jesus Christ will, at two different times, first raise the believers and then He will raise the unbelieving shameful from the dead. You can see this in the New Testament but also in the Old Testament and it can be found in Daniel 12:2.

Third, the New Testament shows us the event called the rapture. This word means that Jesus Christ will come to snatch away all His believers. This includes all believers in the past and up to the time just before the great and terrible event called the Great Tribulation. Jesus will come to get His own before the antichrist will appear and it will be that God will pour out His wrath in judgment against unrepentant practicing sinners.

Now this rapture or snatching away is found in verses 1 Thessalonians 4:13-18.

Here is an explanation of these verses:

156

Verse 13. Paul tells us that there is absolute hope for believers who have died to be raptured.

Verse 14. Paul tells us, if we are believers, that Jesus was put to death and He arose from the dead to life. God will raise to life those that have died believing in Jesus.

Verse 15. Paul says that those true Christians who are living at the time of Christ's coming, which is also called the rapture, will be snatched away. But not until all those who have died in Christ first are raptured, and only then, will those believers who are alive be raptured up after those that died in the faith.

Verse 16. Quote is very clear to understand here it is:

For the Lord Himself will descend from heaven with a shout, with the voice of the archangel and with the trumpet of God, and the dead in Christ will rise first. 1 Thessalonians 4:16

Verse 17. Then Paul tells us that the living believers will be snatched up with those that were previously snatched up. This will all happen by the sounding voice from the archangel using God's trumpet. So the dead believers in Christ will be raised first.

Verse 18. The Apostle Paul says that we as believers should always remind and encourage other believers by this promise God has for those who believe.

Fourth, as mentioned earlier, there will be a seven-year tribulation where the antichrist will deceive all the non-Christians remaining on the earth after the rapture (snatching away) of all the believers. But during this very evil time on the earth called the tribulation there will still be some people who will turn to the true Lord and Savior Jesus Christ and these believers will suffer death even to the point of being decapitated for their faith in Christ.

After the tribulation, the Lord Jesus Christ will raise those dead, decapitated believers from their death to everlasting life (Revelation 20:4-6).

Jesus Christ Will Reward All of His Saints According to Their Work

Unfortunately, there are some people who may say, "If Jesus Christ saves me from my sins then I can do as I please, after all my sins are forgiven and I am saved!" WRONG!

First of all, if Jesus Christ is truly your Lord and Savior, the believing saint (for a saint is nothing more then a true believing child of God) would not want to sin against God and just do what they want. The reason being is that Jesus Christ will be rewarding His children for their works. Be aware that these rewards are eternal rewards. Also realize that these works are to be based on the Word of God (2 Corinthians 5:10). I believe if a Christian who has been a Christian for twenty years and a person who is a Christian for twenty days are both called home to be with the Lord, there is a very good possibility that they could receive the same reward. The reason being is that time is not necessarily a factor with God in this case. One can see this in Matthew 20:1-16. The most important thing is that the good work was done within the truths of the Word of God, and with a proper heart striving to love and to glorify God. We can see this from reading 1 Corinthians 3:11-15.

Verse 11. Paul basically tells us that Jesus Christ is to be our foundation. How do we know Jesus Christ? Only by His Word, the Holy Bible, that so few truly read today.

Verse 12. We as believers are to understand and live the Word of God by learning its truths and live a holy life for God. One must understand that nothing else is needed or proper in comparison. No horoscopes, no fortune telling, no philosophy that contradicts the faith of Christianity or is anti-God, is to be practiced at all!

Verse 13. On the day that the believer is before the Judgment seat of Christ for his or her works (not their sins because all their sins are forgiven), they (the works) will be tested by fire. Here is what the Bible says about this process:

…each man's work will become evident;
for the day will show it because it
is to be revealed with fire, and the
fire itself will test the quality
of each man's work. 1 Corinthians 3:13

Verse 14. Paul then tells us that after the work of the believer goes through fire, if it is built on the foundation of God's Word and it survives the test, that person will get a reward from Christ Himself.

Verse 15. If the person's work will be consumed by fire, it will be loss, but the person will be saved with nothing else, meaning no rewards.

We are not to judge the works of another man if it is done with pure motives or not. Christ will be the Judge and give praise if He needs to. A believer is to only judge if their works and the works of others are truly based on the Word of God. If it is not, we are not to start or continue in that work. Again, this is because it is not based on God's truth.

Some examples are: a minister claims Jesus Christ was not born of a virgin. This is not biblical because Jesus Christ was born of a virgin. Her name was Mary and it is in the Bible in Luke 1:26-35. So one must not stay under this false teacher. They need to stay away and find another church or Christian group. If one claims it is okay not to pay their taxes, and they even claim to be a Christian, this also is not biblical. The Bible claims we must pay our taxes (Matthew 22:17-21). In plain

English, anything that is not based on the foundation of the Bible is dead works.

Jesus Christ Will Also Judge the Unbelievers

This is an act of the righteousness of God. Yes it is true, God is love, Jesus Christ is love but He is also Holy, righteous and longsuffering with His patience. Unbelievers may have done some great things for mankind; some may have been great doctors, leaders, CEO's, etc. Each and every person had an opportunity to accept the God-Man, Jesus Christ, for the forgiveness of their sins to become a true child of God. But whether it was their pride, power or persuasion of other people, they didn't accept that God the Father sent His Son, who is also God the Son, for the purpose of giving them everlasting life. So because of their rejection of God, they are not and will not be placed into the family of God.

Jesus Christ, after His one-thousand year reign, will then cast the devil and the beast and also the false prophet into Hell because of the wicked, evil and deception they have caused to so many billions throughout the centuries (Revelation 20:10). Then Jesus will be sitting on His Great White Throne and prepare to judge the sinful unbelievers. This is found in Revelation 20:11. The Lord and King Jesus Christ will raise all the unbelieving dead.

And I saw the dead, the great and the small, standing before the throne, and books were opened; and another book was opened, which is the book of life; and the dead were judged from the things which were written in the books, according to their deeds.

And the sea gave up the dead which were in it, and death and Hades gave up the dead which were in them; and they were judged, every one of them according to their deeds. Revelation 20:12-13

According to the two verses above, because this group of unbelievers did not believe that God the Father sent His Son for their sinful unrighteousness, and yet they had all the opportunity to accept the Son of God as their Savior but did not, it is because of this rejection of the Son of God that they sealed all their fate. All because of their actions and temporal achievements. This is what is meant by the word "deeds" as it is written in the last word of these two verses.

The next verse tells us that Jesus will dispose of the holding tank where all the unsaved are and this is because Christ will show the unsaved His righteous power as God, as He told them in the past but was rejected. Therefore, the unbelievers will suffer a second death away from God for all eternity (Revelation 20:14).

The last verse that is in this chapter, verse 15, tells us if anybody's name is not listed in this great book, the book of life, the outcome is simple; the lake of fire or as some may call it, Hell, awaits them (Revelation 20:15). Jesus Christ is just putting these rebellious people where they belong safely away from His believing children.

Jesus Christ Will Judge All of the Nations of the World

This pertains to the time before the one thousand year reign. Jesus will judge all nations and destroy all of those nations that rejected the true cause that God had for all of mankind, from the first man and woman, Adam and Eve, to those that tried to destroy the Jewish race and Israel, and also those that from the time of Christ tried to destroy His work and His believers. These are the nations that Jesus Christ will drop His wrathful judgment upon.

> From His mouth comes a sharp sword, so that with it He may strike down the nations, and He will rule them with a rod of iron; and He treads the wine press of the fierce wrath of God, the Almighty. Revelation 19:15

> For the unbelievers, God's condemnation, judgment and wrath awaits them. For the believers, God's love, mercy and just reward awaits them.

19

THE MASTER TEACHING OR DOCTRINE OF THE HOLY SPIRIT

First there are some false conceptions about the Holy Spirit. The Holy Spirit is not a force. The Holy Spirit is not a dove. The Holy Spirit is not to be referred to as "it". He is not a separate Spirit of God. The Holy Spirit is a person. He is the third person in the God-Head.

Just because He is the third person does not put Him in third place in the God-Head. The Holy Spirit is equal to the Father and the Son. He is God the Holy Spirit. As you will read, He has a ministry to all people, the unbelievers and the believers from the time of creation and through eternity. But if He is rejected by any unbelieving person in this life, there is no hope for that person of ever obtaining eternal life from the Lord and Savior Jesus Christ. The Holy Spirit's ministry to the unbeliever is to effectually bring a sinner to salvation. This is done based upon the work of the Lord Jesus Christ that is also based upon His Word, the Holy Bible.

Scripture also refers to the Holy Spirit as the Spirit with a capital "S".
The Holy Spirit is referred to as a Person in the Scriptures.
The Holy Spirit is Intelligent.

He, the Holy Spirit of God, is referred to as the third person of the God-Head. Therefore, He knows all things and He also has the ability that investigates and searches everything and all things.

... for the Spirit searches all things, even the depths of God.

For who among men knows the thoughts of a man except the spirit of the man which is in him? Even so the thoughts of God no one knows except the Spirit of God. 1 Corinthians 2:10-11

The Holy Spirit Has a Mind

The true test of any person is that he has a mind. There are three parts of the mind such as a will, intellect and emotions. The Holy Spirit has all three of these non-material capabilities. The Holy Spirit with His mind will search the believer's heart and understands what is best because He, the Spirit, knows God's will. From there, He mediates for the saintly believer to stay in tune to the will of God.

...and He who searches the hearts knows what the mind of the Spirit is, because He intercedes for the saints according to the will of God. Romans 8:27

The Holy Spirit Teaches the Believers

Jesus Christ promised the believers that God the Father would, after His (Christ's) ascension in His name, send a Helper to His saved children (John 14:16). This Helper is the Holy Spirit who indwells all believers and would be their teacher and bring to memory all the truths in the Scriptures which is our Holy Bible today (John 14:26). He can do this because the Holy Spirit can take the Word of God and do this only by God's wisdom. Again, this only will happen by Godly wisdom (James 3:17-18).

This is not possible by human wisdom. I believe it is very unfortunate today that the church has been allowing human wisdom to enter into the church. To a very large degree, this is one of the primary reasons why there is so much weakness in the church today. It is not because God is not with the church, but it is that the church has allowed the wisdom of the world into the church. That is why some of the readers of this book may even say this book is all head knowledge. This is because they are used to a steady diet of emotionalism from their worldly-type church. God wants us to live by His Word, not by weak, non-eternal, worldly ways. We are all here from the acts of God and His sovereign (supreme overall) plan. Not my plan or your plan, their plan and so on. No wonder the world is in its weak, sinful state. So again, the Holy Spirit takes the Word of God, which is the will of God, and brings together thoughts that are spiritual with words that are spiritual. This is how we are taught by the Holy Spirit.

...which things we also speak, not in words taught by human wisdom, but in those taught by the Spirit, combining spiritual thoughts with spiritual words. 1 Corinthians 2:13

The Holy Spirit Has and Shows Emotional Feeling

The Holy Spirit can be grieved. The emotion of grief is an emotion that covers a lot of different feelings, like unhappiness, sadness, concern, sorrow, love, anger, betrayal and so on. The Apostle Paul tells us in the epistle to the Ephesians that a disobedient believer can actually bring unhappiness and sorrow to the Holy Spirit for their unrepentant sin.

Do not grieve the Holy Spirit of God, by whom you were sealed for the day of redemption. Ephesians 4:30

The Apostle Paul says in the verse above that the Holy Spirit can be sorrowful and grieved from a believer's sin, even though the Holy Spirit has marked that person with a seal promoting him or her to heaven. Then the epistle from James

164

tells us that the Scripture has a proper and righteous purpose for each believer and if a believer is not living properly (James 4:5) for God, The Holy Spirit who indwells the believer feels the emotion of jealousy. Jealousy is a feeling which senses betrayal, sorrow, and the pain of someone's unfaithfulness, love for their return and so on. As you see, the Third person of the God-Head truly has emotions and feelings.

The Holy Spirit Has a Will

As with the Father and the Son and human beings, the person of the Holy Spirit also has a will. He has the power to make conscience decisions and choices all within the will of God.

By His Will the Holy Spirit Directs Believers Activities

A very good example of this is how the Holy Spirit acted in directing the Apostle Paul on his missionary journey. This is found in the book of Acts (16:6-12). Just a side note about the book of Acts, some people have taught that this book is about the acts of the Apostles. This is dangerously incorrect. It is true that the Apostles were great men of God, but that is how far they should be praised, no further. The other thing is that the book of Acts doesn't cover all the Acts of these Apostles mentioned in it. This book is a book that shows us the ministry of the Holy Spirit and points to the Acts of the Holy Spirit. This is the truly the wisest conclusion one can come to in knowing that the Holy Spirit is fully God.

In the passage in (Acts 16:6-12), if one reads it, they will see how the Holy Spirit has a loving way of showing how He guided the Apostle Paul and even as how He can guide believers today. I, in my own life, on different occasions have been guided by the Holy Spirit in ways that have saved my own life and other family members by His prompting, and I must say that there was an enormous amount of pressure from others around me to go in a different way or to do things differently. But by holding strong to the prompting of the Holy Spirit, I know that He was the one who had the greatest concern for my life and those closest to me at the time.

The Apostle Paul had an experience where the Holy Spirit actually forbade him from preaching in a region that is in the modern country of Turkey (called Asia then).

They passed through the Phrygian and Galatian region, having been forbidden by the Holy Spirit to speak the word in Asia; and after they came to Mysia, they were trying to go to into Bithynia, and the Spirit of Jesus did not permit them; and passing by Mysia, they came down to Troas. A vision appeared to Paul in the night: a man of Macedonia was standing and appealing to him, and saying, "Come over to Macedonia and help us."

When he had seen the vision, immediately we sought to go into Macedonia, concluding that God had called us to preach the gospel to them. Acts 16:6-10

As one reads this passage, one can see the Holy Spirit continued to guide the Apostle Paul by not allowing the Apostle to enter the city of Bithynia in Acts 16:7.

If one reads Acts 16:8-12, they can see that the goal of the Holy Spirit was to guide Paul to preach the Gospel in the northern Greek city of Macedonia for a good number of days.

The Holy Spirit Distributes Spiritual Gifts to Believers by His Will

Each and every true believer has at the very least one spiritual gift, if not more than one gift. There are a total of nineteen spiritual gifts. The purpose of a true believer in having spiritual gifts is for the strengthening and building up of the true overall Christian church, which is also called the universal church. The gifts are not for one to be prideful about, because the exercise of the gifts are all to glorify the Lord Jesus Christ and to build and encourage His church in love.

There are seven motivational spiritual gifts listed in the book of Romans (12:1-13). Every true believer has at least one of these gifts:

1. Prophecy
2. Service
3. Teaching
4. Exhortation
5. Giving
6. Leading
7. Mercy

Each believer is responsible to find out what their gift or gifts are and to use them to glorify God to the fullest (1 Peter 4:10). What each believer must understand is that there are different gifts from the Holy Spirit, who is the third member of the God-Head. All of these gifts can be used for different ministries to glorify the same Lord God (1 Corinthians 12:4-5). It is also true that each and every true believer receives their gift or gifts according to the Holy Spirit's will.

Here is how the Scripture says it:

But one and the same Spirit works all these things, distributing to each one individually just as He wills. 1 Corinthians 12:11

The Holy Spirit Has Actions of God because He is God

The acts of God toward man have always been to encourage faith and to protect each believer. These are the actions of the Holy Spirit from the first man, Adam, to the end of this age and forever.

The Holy Spirit Acts by Guiding

In this Church age, the Holy Spirit indwells each and every real believer, never leaving them, and it is from this position that He guides all believers to do the will of God. He guides the believer to discern what is of God and what isn't. He also guides a believer to glorify Jesus Christ and it is Jesus Christ who speaks through the Holy Spirit to the believer. The Holy Spirit teaches us the Word of God. He also points to prophecy in the Scripture to protect us and make us aware of things and events that will take place. One of the names for the Holy Spirit is the Spirit of (biblical) prophecy. For prophecy to be 100% accurate, it must be biblical and true prophecy is only biblical. No other source is valid.

But when He, the Spirit of truth, comes, He will guide you into all the truth; for He will not speak on His own initiative, but whatever He hears, He will speak; and He will disclose to you what is to come. John 16:13

The Holy Spirit Acts by Convicting

The Holy Spirit convicts of sin. He convicts the world, and even within the world, He convicts individuals. For believers He convicts of sin because through Christ and because of His work, they have the power to overcome the power of sin. To the unbeliever they are convicted of sin because of their pride and fear in not wanting to turn to the Lord Jesus and allow Him to be their Savior. Rather than turn to the Lord Jesus to save them, they prefer to stay under God's judgment and do not truly believe that the ruler of this world is Satan and that because of this they will die in their sins. Some may not truly realize that Satan has already been judged. This can be seen in John 16:8-11. But the key verse for this topic is verse 8, speaking of the Holy Spirit:

And He, when He comes, will convict the world concerning sin and righteousness and judgment. John 16:8

The Holy Spirit Who is God Acts in Performing Miracles

The book of Acts is again the book of the acts of the Holy Spirit (Acts 1:1-8) and one can see by reading the book of Acts that all the apostles in the book of Acts were the vessels that the Holy Spirit worked through performing miracles. This was another way for the Holy Spirit to reveal who He was to this world. In chapter 8:26-40 in the book of Acts, we see a situation of Philip being guided to a eunuch from the official court of the queen of Ethiopia. The Holy Spirit told Philip to go to this man and explain the Good News of the Gospel of Jesus Christ to Him. After He did this, the eunuch wanted to be baptized and Philip did as he requested. But immediately coming out of the baptismal water, Philip was suddenly taken up by the Holy Spirit, and Philip found himself about thirty miles away from where he was. He found himself in the city of Azotus. The main verse in this passage that shows this miracle from the Holy Spirit is:

When they came up out of the water, the Spirit of the Lord snatched Philip away; and the eunuch no longer saw him, but went on his way rejoicing. Acts 8:39

The Holy Spirit Acts by Interceding for Believers

Because a believer is still in his or her weakened human state with a sin nature and sin still is present in this world, a believer may not know how to pray to avoid sin because of the pressure of temptation. It is the Holy Spirit who is always powerfully involved and helps the believer to overcome falling into sin. The Holy Spirit also benefits and helps the believer in times of minor trouble as well as times of great tragedy. There is a normal, good human analogy for this that He is like a big brother who protects His youngest brother or sister. He is like the paramedic who pulls you out of a raging flood. He is also like the doctor pulling you out of a heart attack in the emergency room. With all these instances, the person is in trouble, but he doesn't know how to ask for help! Be aware that the Holy Spirit is always on the scene to help and benefit the believer and He does this with moans similar to a powerful man in the process of fighting to lift a very heavy weight. In other words, the Holy Spirit moves with great effort in helping the true believer within the will of God. Here is how the Scripture says it:

In the same way the Spirit also helps our weakness; for we do not know how to pray as we should, but the Spirit Himself intercedes for us with groanings too deep for words. Romans 8:26.

The Holy Spirit is treated as A Person in Scripture

Because He is the third person in the God-Head, He needs to be totally respected as God.

The Holy Spirit needs to be obeyed

Within the book of Acts (10:19-23), the Holy Spirit spoke to the Apostle Peter as He was thinking through about a revelation from God. The Holy Spirit then told Peter that there were three men who were searching for him (Acts 10:19). Then the Holy Spirit commanded Peter to go down to the first floor and the Holy Spirit instructed Peter to be kind to them despite their cultural differences. Then the Holy Spirit told Peter that it was because He (the Holy Spirit) guided them to Peter (Acts 10:20). So what did Peter do?

Peter went down to the men and said, "Behold, I am the one you are looking for; what is the reason for which you have come?" Acts 10:21

And then we can see in Acts 10:23 Peter continued to obey the Holy Spirit by letting them in and giving them a place to stay because the three men told Peter that they were divinely lead to him, as we can see by looking previously in Acts 10:22. So we can see that the Holy Spirit must be and should be obeyed willingly. But one may ask, "How does the Holy Spirit speak to believers today?" The answer is by the completed Word of God, the Holy Bible.

Scripture Tells us that the Holy Spirit Can be Lied To

In the Bible, in the book of Acts, we see that the Holy Spirit can be lied to. There are many people still today saying that they are doing some type of work for God but they really are working for themselves. This is lying to the Holy Spirit but there is no severe consequence for this because God will judge their work. In the passage in Acts 5:1-11, we see a husband and a wife selling some land and then making an agreement to keep some of the money back for themselves. But this couple presented the amount of money to the Apostles as if it were the full amount. In other words, they were being deceptive to the church and lying to the Holy Spirit so the Holy Spirit took both husband and wife out of the situation by taking their lives. Let me make you aware that the amount that they gave to the church was all right, and it was ok that they kept some of the money for themselves. But it was the lying to God the Holy Spirit that was the problem. Many people lie to the Holy Spirit today in another way and that way is by their pride in believing in themselves and not a true God of Salvation.

But Peter said, "Ananias, why has Satan filled your heart to lie to the Holy Spirit and to keep back some of the price of the Land?

And as he heard those words, Ananias fell down and breathed His last; and great fear came over all who heard of it. Acts 5:3, 5

Scripture Tells Us That the Holy Spirit Can Be Resisted

First we must realize that the Holy Spirit always moves in a loving and effectual way, not in a deceitful or manipulative way. He works toward each person, in bringing each individual to the point of allowing that person to open their eyes, in understanding that they need a Savior because of their sins. From this point they will either choose to accept Christ or reject Him. By rejecting Jesus Christ as the Messiah, it is this sinful action that is resisting the Holy Spirit. This is a very dangerous situation to be in because it may be that person's last time to accept the Lord and His work on the Cross for them. But God in His mercy continues until that person accepts Christ through the power of the Holy Spirit if he or she is truly one of God's chosen children. This is also called God's election.

In the book of Acts (7:1-60) we read about how the Holy Spirit spoke through this bold servant of the early church. His name was Stephen and he preached one of the greatest prophetic sermons of all time to the Jewish religious leaders of that time. In his sermon, he even said that they were resisting the Holy Spirit. By this they were also resisting the true work of God. Stephen said that they were proud and foolish to the degree that they didn't want to bend their head forward to understand properly. Then he tells them that their hearts are far from God despite their positions as religious leaders. Then Stephen goes further and tells them that they are covering their ears in resistance to God, Himself the Holy Spirit. Then Stephen gives the final bold warning and tells them to break loose of the prophet-killing ways of their fathers. It is the Holy Spirit that can give a person this kind of loving and warning boldness as He gave the prophets, and this boldness is still available to us today. But this boldness is not an act of one's will, but only by the leading of the Holy Spirit, Himself.

You men who are stiff-necked and uncircumcised in heart and ears are always resisting the Holy Spirit; you are doing just as your fathers did. Acts 7:51

Scripture Tells Us That the Holy Spirit Can Be Blasphemed

Blasphemy against the Holy Spirit is the only unpardonable sin; it cannot and will not be forgiven by God. But what is this sin, one may ask? This is an act of one's will to reject the activity and finished work of Christ for one's salvation and not claiming that Jesus Christ is God, but that He is not God. Some go as far as to say that He, Jesus Christ, is of the enemy of righteousness, who truly is Satan. This is blasphemy against the Holy Spirit. Another very simple way is when one rejects Christ and will not accept Him as Lord and Savior. This is blasphemy against the Holy Spirit. One can see this in Matthew 12:31-32, Mark 3:28-29 and Luke 12:10. If one turns to Matthew 10:24-25, one will see an example of how some of the Jewish religious leaders committed blasphemy against the Holy Spirit. We see Jesus Christ referring to a time when these Jewish religious leaders said that Christ's miracles were not of God, but from the devil.

This is a very grave sin as Jesus Christ the God-Man says in the next verses, that blasphemy against the Holy Spirit is unpardonable. This is Jesus speaking:

> Therefore I say to you, any sin and blasphemy shall be forgiven people, but blasphemy against the Spirit shall not be forgiven. Whoever speaks a word against the Son of Man, it shall be forgiven him; but whoever speaks against the Holy Spirit, it shall not be forgiven him, either in this age or in the age to come. Matthew 12:31-32

Scripture Tells Us that the Holy Spirit Can Be Insulted

How can the Holy Spirit be insulted? First of all, this happens when a person who calls themselves a believer and claims that Jesus Christ is their Lord and Savior, because of some event, now believes that the work of Christ (which is the death, burial, and resurrection) is not sufficient for them to receive salvation. Instead, they believe that someone else's work or someone else's work with Christ's work is then sufficient. Or to go further, they stop believing in Christ altogether and lose their sight of God. The Bible tells us that this is like stepping on Christ, Himself, and on the precious blood that He shed to give one who has true faith in Him everlasting life. It is the person who at one time said he was a believer and then fell away and abandoned the faith as mentioned in Hebrews 3:12. It is this person that insults the Holy Spirit.

How much severer punishment do you think he will deserve who has trampled under foot the Son of God, and has regarded as unclean the blood of the covenant by which he was sanctified, and has insulted the Spirit of grace? (Hebrews 10:29)

These are just some of the examples in Scripture that show us that the Holy Spirit is a true person. He is intelligent, shows feelings, and He has a will and He has actions.

The Holy Spirit is God

The Scripture is always the ultimate authority in knowing who the true God is. The Scripture tells us that the Holy Spirit is equal to God because He is the third person in the God-head.

The Scripture shows us the Holy Spirit's Equality in the God-head

In the Old and New Testaments, the Holy Spirit is shown with diverse titles connecting Him to the God-head as God. Here are a few examples of this. As the Apostle Paul was on his missionary journey written in the book of Acts, he says that the Holy Spirit would not allow them within the will of God to enter Asia (Acts 16:6). Be aware that the Asia in that time was a Roman province, and was Southwest of Asia Minor, which is today modern Turkey. After that experience, the Apostle Paul refers to the Holy Spirit in Acts 16:7 by a different name, "the Spirit of Jesus". Here is the whole verse:

> ...and after they came to Mysia, they were trying to go into Bithynia, and the Spirit of Jesus did not permit them. Acts 16:7

This took place after Paul and the others with him in Mysia were hoping to go to Bithynia. I believe that Paul made reference to the Holy Spirit with the name Jesus because Paul had connected with the love and warning of Jesus Christ through the power of the Holy Spirit. The next connective name of the Holy Spirit will again show us that He is God because He is equal to Jesus Christ as well as the Father. The Apostle

Paul, in writing His first letter to the Corinthian Church in chapter 6, strongly discouraged lawsuits among church members and was reminding them that these things should not be happening. Then he reminded the Corinthians that as believers they were cleaned by Christ, and in the process of maturing in Christ, because of God's forgiveness and acceptance as His children through the work of Jesus Christ and through the power of the Holy Spirit of God. This is how Paul wrote it:

> ...but you were washed, but you were sanctified, but you were justified in the name of the Lord Jesus Christ and in the Spirit of our God. Corinthians 6:11

The Holy Spirit is spoken of as (YAHWEH) the Lord

The Apostle Paul makes reference to this in Acts 28:25-27, by telling us that it was the Holy Spirit that spoke to and through the prophet Isaiah in the Old Testament. This is found in Isaiah 6:1-13. But the key verse for this subject in this text, that shows us that the Holy Spirit is spoken of as the Lord (YAHWEH), is in verse 3. May I also say that this verse also shows us the equality of the Father, Son and the Holy Spirit by pointing to each of the three persons in the God-Head as equal within the name of the LORD.

> And one called out to another and said,
> "Holy, Holy, Holy, is the LORD of hosts,
> The whole earth is full of His glory." Isaiah 6:3

The Holy Spirit, who is the Third Person in the God-Head, is God

By this it is shown by God's Word that the Holy Spirit is not an individual attribute of the Father or of the Son. In other words, there is a third person and as a person the Holy Spirit is a separate person of the God-Head. Now it must also be said that the three persons of the God-Head cannot be divided, for all three are God. With that said, Jesus Christ the Son shows us this in Matthew 12:31-32, telling us that the Holy Spirit, if rejected, will not forgive a person this blasphemous sin. There are no exceptions at all! One must accept Jesus Christ as their Lord and Savior in order to avoid this eternally damning sin. This is the authority and power of God the Holy Spirit.

> Therefore I say to you, any sin and blasphemy shall be forgiven people, but blasphemy against the Spirit shall not be forgiven. Matthew 12:31

Another example of the Holy Spirit as God showing His authority and power is shown to us by the example of the Apostle Peter in Acts 5:3-5. Looking at verse 3 of this passage, we see that Peter discerned that a person by the name of Ananias fell into sin by trying to be deceptive to the church and lying to the Holy Spirit about a false amount of a contribution. Then in verse 4, Peter rebukes Ananias with this statement, speaking about the Holy Spirit as God:

> ...You have not lied to men but to God. Acts 5:4

And the end result was that Ananias and also his wife, who was of the same mind and heart as her husband, had cost themselves their lives on earth because the Holy Spirit in His power and authority took them out of the picture because He was lied to. He has this power only because He is God.

The Holy Spirit and His Equality with God

Jesus Christ, in His commandment to His disciples in what is called the Great Commission, announced that as disciples we are to go to every nation and make other disciples. We need to baptize them as a testimony to others present and in the specific designation of all three persons in the God-Head. Here is this powerful verse that shows equality of all the three persons in the God-Head.

Go therefore and make disciples of all nations, baptizing them in the name of the Father and of the Son, and of the Holy Spirit. Matthew 28:19

The Holy Spirit Has the Attributes of God and is All Knowing and is Omniscient

To be all-knowing is only an attribute of God. Because the physical material world has come from the spiritual world and the Holy Spirit is God, He knows all things. There is not one thing He doesn't know. The Holy Spirit knows everything, such as how many cells it takes to make the entire world. We can even go much further than this. Consider this: He knows how many molecules there are in all the entire universe in total.

He knows fully the past, present and future of all things beyond mans capabilities of thinking, knowing and understanding. The Apostle Paul brings this out in 1 Corinthians 2:6-16 about the believer relying on the Holy Spirit for guidance. This is the key verse in the passage:

Now we have received, not a spirit of the world, but the Spirit who is from God, so that we may know the things freely given to us by God. 1 Corinthians 2:12

In (Isaiah 40:13), it tells and shows us that the Holy Spirit is Sovereign over all, and knowing and does as He pleases for He is God. He never goes against His character in any way and because He is God, He never needs advice of anyone, ever.

The Holy Spirit is All Present and is Omnipresent

The first man in space was a Russian by the name of Yuri Gagarin, and when he got into space he mentioned that he could not see God in space so he came up with the conclusion that God must not exist. This is truly a false and foolish statement! Let me say that nature attests to many things that we can't see, but that doesn't mean that they are not present. For instance, we do not see air but we breathe air. We can't really feel air if it is still. Sometimes we smell a certain fragrance or odor but we don't know where it is coming from or what it is! Just because we don't see God with our eyes that doesn't mean He doesn't exist!

The Bible tells us that God is all-present and no one can escape His presence. Think of it this way: if an infant child is placed in a playpen and the parent is in the same room with the child, but the child's back is turned away from the parent, the child will not see the parent being in the same room, but the parent is still present with the child.

Another thing is that the Holy Spirit is present wherever a person can go. Even if it is possible for a man to truly go to mars, the Holy Spirit is still present. Another point to understand is that the Holy Spirit is present everywhere but He is not in things. Some examples are: He is not in trees, stones, etc. But He does indwell believers. King David the psalmist tells us about the all-presence or omnipresence of the Holy Spirit in Psalms (139:7-12). It matters not where one goes; the Holy Spirit is always present. The main verse in this passage that shows us the omnipresence of the Holy Spirit is:

> Where can I go from Your Spirit?
> Or where can I flee from Your presence?
> If I ascend to heaven, You are there;
> If I make my bed in Sheol, behold, You are there.
> Psalm 139:7-8

Note: the word Sheol in these verses is referred to in the Old Testament as a place for departed souls.

The Holy Spirit is All Powerful and Omnipotent

Being all powerful to the end degree, even using the greatest power of logic and imagination collectively as a human race, cannot in any way come close to the power of God the Holy Spirit. In the Old Testament book of Job (33:4-6), Elihu states that it is the Holy Spirit of God who had the power to assemble, shape, construct and form us so we became a living human being, just as all men have by the all-powerful God. In all reality, this cannot be refuted because the truth about reality starts with knowing the all-powerful and omnipotent God. Because God is all-powerful, the third person of God, the Holy Spirit, is all-powerful which means He is omnipotent. As the psalmist in all of Psalm 104 said, the Holy Spirit as He is God cares for all of God's works. When God told the Holy Spirit to go forward the Holy Spirit in His omnipotence created and He was part of creating all things spiritual and material. This means from the angels to the most minute dust particle. He also is responsible for the day-to-day changes of the growth of all living things such as the growth of children, animals and plants. He is also responsible for the sun rising and setting in the evening. The verse that says it all in Psalm 104 is:

You send forth Your Spirit, they are created;
And You renew the face of the ground. Psalm 104:30

The Holy Spirit Has the Actions of God

The Holy Spirit was and is the cause of a One of a Kind Miracle and that is the Virgin Birth of the God-Man, Jesus Christ. Now one must understand that the whole human race is a sinful and rebellious human race. Because of this, even Mary the mother of Jesus Christ was also a sinner, and even she had a sin nature, and even she needed a Savior from her sins, as well as everyone else in the human race with no exceptions.

Mary was esteemed by God to be the woman to bring forth the Messiah and Christ to save those who believe in this God-Man Jesus Christ from their sins. Mary was a virgin which means she had never been with a man. She was told by the angel Gabriel that she was going to bring forth the birth of the Messiah and she was perplexed about how this could happen. The best passage for this is found in Luke 1:26-38. But the two key verses in this passage about the Holy Spirit's involvement in this situation are in these two verses:

Mary said to the angel, "How can this be, since I am a virgin?"

The angel answered and said to her, The Holy Spirit will come upon you, and the power of the Most High will over-shadow you; and for this reason the holy Child shall be called the Son of God. Luke 1:34-35

There are four key points to understand in the two verses above, they are:

1. In verse 34, Mary herself claimed to be a virgin.
2. In verse 35, the angel Gabriel said that the Holy Spirit (God) would be the other person to bring about this special conception.
3. In verse 35, the Holy Spirit (God) would be responsible for not allowing Mary's sin nature to be brought into this conception by overshadowing or blocking her sin nature so the Child would truly be Holy.
4. In verse 35, because this child was conceived without a sin nature and this was the work of God the Holy Spirit this child, was and is the only person who is the Son of God, who is the Savior of the world, because He is the only one who was able to meet the demand of God the Father in being a perfect blood sacrifice for the sins of the world.

The Holy Spirit was the Agent in Giving the Inspired Scriptures

This means that the whole Bible has come about because of the Holy Spirit working through chosen men such as the Old Testament Prophets and the New Testament Apostles. From the book of Genesis to the last book of the Bible (Revelation), the Scripture is inspired which means it is God-Breathed. The writers didn't write based on what their intelligence and creative mind told them, but they were born along by the Holy Spirit unfolding and writing the will of God. Therefore, no man can make up his own interpretation of who God is or what the will of God is. Whether a man or group of people use all the logic or love they can muster up, if it does not go along with the will of God in the Bible, these self-proclaimed spiritual leaders are out of God's will and living a lie!

Let us see what the Word of God says about this matter. The Apostle Peter in 2 Peter 1:16-21 explains this perfectly. He tells us that under any circumstance the Scripture, which is the prophetic Word of God, is the most sure thing to go by, and nothing in human history or human experience will ever come close. We see this in this verse:

So we have this prophetic word made more sure, to which you do well to pay attention as to a lamp shining in a dark place, until the day dawns and the morning star arises in your hearts. 2 Peter 1:19

Peter then gives us a powerful conclusion in this matter and is stating this under the inspiration of the Holy Spirit.

But know this first of all, that no prophecy of Scripture is a matter of one's own interpretation, for no prophecy was ever made by an act of human will, but men moved by the Holy Spirit spoke from God. 2 Peter 1:20-21

The Holy Spirit was Involved in the Creation of this Entire World and Universe

We can see the act of God in His creation in the first two chapters of the first book of the Bible, which is the book of Genesis. One doesn't have to go too far in the first chapter of Genesis in seeing that the Holy Spirit is mentioned in the second verse of the first chapter. It says:

The earth was formless and void, and darkness was over the surface of the deep, and the Spirit of God was moving over the surface of the waters. Genesis 1:2

The first verse of Genesis tells us that God created the heavens as well the earth. The Holy Spirit is also included in this creation because He is the third person in the God-head.

The Holy Spirit was also involved in all of the seven days of creation.

Here in very brief are all of the seven days of creation that God the Holy Spirit was involved in.

Day 1, Light (Genesis 1:3).

Day 1, Day and Night (Genesis 1:4-5).

Day 2, The Atmosphere–Sky and land (Genesis 1:6-9).

Day 3, Plant growth (Genesis 1:10-13).

Day 4, The visibility of the Sun, Moon and Stars (Genesis 1:14-19).

Day 5, The fish, birds, insects, very large sea animals (Genesis 1:20-23).

Day 6, The cattle, ground animals like snakes and wild animals and finally Man (Genesis 1:24-31).

Day 7, God's creating was completed (Genesis 2:1-3).

As you can see, the Holy Spirit is truly a person and not a thing or an it!
HE TRULY IS GOD!

The Ministry of God the Holy Spirit

As the Father and Jesus Christ have their ministries, the Holy Spirit also has His ministry. His ministry is for the unbelieving sinner to repent and to turn always from a sinful life. He strengthens the Christian who truly believes in heart, mind and body. The believer is to be centered on the Word of God, which means that the Word of God is the only true guide for their spiritual life, nothing more nothing less. They are to know this and stand by this. They are not to be secure by the label or title of being a Christian, but by their faith and stand on the Word of God.

The Holy Spirit's Ministry to the Sinner

He convicts man of sin. The Holy Spirit does this in an affectionate and concerning, loving way. He helps the sinner in a patient manner and He doesn't quit on the person because the Holy Spirit has the view of eternity for that individual. He also glorifies Jesus Christ because of His work of convicting sinners and guiding them to accept Jesus Christ, based on His righteousness, as their Lord and Savior. It is at that point that one becomes a true child of God and is declared righteous in the sight of God. One must understand that no one can achieve salvation based on one's false thought of their own righteousness, but only on the true righteousness of Jesus Christ.

To the sinner who will not accept the saving work of Jesus Christ, judgment awaits him for his sins. Let me assure you, the Bible states this for everyone, no matter who they are or what status they have or how loving they were to mankind, it matters not at all. Why? Because if they do not accept Jesus Christ as Savior before their death, the judgment of Hell awaits them. The Bible says that the devil is the one who rules this world and he is judged already. It is the Holy Spirit that lovingly desires salvation for an individual but God the Father lovingly has sent His Son, Jesus Christ, to supply salvation for all. If the sinner doesn't want to believe, trust and listen to God in telling him that the sacrifice of His Son was offered in a perfect and only way that is pleasing to God, in the sight of God, the Bible says that this person is calling God a liar. The reason is because the person is not of God but is under the dominion of the devil who has, as said earlier, been judged already by God. This can be found in the passage of John 16:7-15. The major verse for this topic is verse 8. This is Jesus speaking about the Holy Spirit:

And He, when He comes, will convict the world concerning sin and righteousness and judgment. John 16:8

The Holy Spirit's Ministry to the Believer

The Holy Spirit is involved in many forms of ministry to the believer.

The Holy Spirit Regenerates the Sinner Only
After the Acceptance of Jesus Christ, It is then
that that person becomes a Born Again Believer.

He, the Holy Spirit, at the time of a spiritual birth of a person is responsible for washing the believer clean, coming into a believer's life by indwelling them and brings about a new born again spiritual state and gives the believer a true new and living spiritual life.

He saved us, not on the basis of deeds which we have done in righteousness, but according to His mercy by the washing of regeneration and renewing by the Holy Spirit. Titus 3:5

The Apostle Peter tells us we are not born again in a natural way but in an eternal, ongoing way by the power of the Word of God (1 Peter 1:23).

The Holy Spirit Baptizes Each Believer into the Body of Christ

This Holy Spirit baptism is not water baptism. Water baptism is commanded by Christ as a symbol of ones acceptance of Jesus Christ as Lord and Savior. One thing is to be clear: that water baptism could take some time after the accepting of Christ depending on the time and availability of the baptizer, but it is commanded by Christ and it needs to be obeyed to honor and glorify the Lord Jesus. On the other hand, the baptism of the Holy Spirit happens simultaneously or at the same time one puts their faith and trust in Jesus Christ as Lord and Savior of their life. It is at that point they are baptized into the one body of Christ and they are saved from their sins and belong to Jesus Christ. We can see this in the next verse:

> For by the Spirit we were all baptized into one body, whether Jews or Greeks, whether slaves or free, and we were all made to drink of one Spirit. 1 Corinthians 12:13

In this verse we see that race, nationality or social rank makes no difference. All belong to God and all believers get spiritually nourished by the same Holy Spirit. In 1 Corinthians 12:27, the Apostle Paul tells us that we are all individuals in one body, and that body is the body of Christ.

There is a beautiful example of how each believer is baptized into the body of Christ and it is found in the book of Romans.

Or do you not know that all of us who have been baptized into Christ Jesus have been baptized into His death?

Therefore we have been buried with Him through baptism into death, so that as Christ was raised from the dead through the glory of the Father, so we too might walk in the newness of life. Romans 6:3-4

The Holy Spirit Gives the Believer Power

This power is to give witness of Jesus Christ without fear of one's death and the power of love for all people to hear about Jesus Christ, and the power to know that regardless of the circumstances or a different culture, climate, language, rejection or acceptance, one knows of the power of their faith to bring others to the God-Man, Jesus Christ. This is the working power of the Holy Spirit.

> ...but you will receive power when the Holy Spirit has come upon you; and you shall be My witnesses both in Jerusalem, and in all Judea and Samaria, and even to the remotest part of the earth. Acts 1:8

The Holy Spirit Sanctifies Each Believer

Sanctification, in short, is where the Holy Spirit helps the believer to grow more and more like Christ. It is a conforming to the image of Christ (Romans 8:29). As a person yields their life to God, the Holy Spirit is in the process of sanctifying that person and just as a fruit tree grows fruit so does a believer grow spiritual fruit. This fruit is because the Holy Spirit is working in the believer's life.

But the fruit of the Spirit is love, joy, peace, patience, kindness, goodness, faithfulness, gentleness, self-control; against such things there is no law. Galatians 5:22-23

The Holy Spirit Who is the Third Person of the God-Head Indwells All True Believers

Every true believer is not to live under the power of the fleshly sin nature. Therefore, the Holy Spirit lives within them because of their faith in Christ Jesus. It is also the Holy Spirit, that raised Jesus Christ from the dead, that also indwells each believer and because of this each believer needs not to fear death, because it is the Holy Spirit who will raise the believer from the dead as He raised Jesus Christ (Romans 8:9-14). The main verse in this passage for the Holy Spirit indwelling the believer is:

But if the Spirit of Him who raised Jesus from the dead dwells in you, He who raised Christ Jesus from the dead will also give life to your mortal bodies through His Spirit who dwells in you. Romans 8:11

The Holy Spirit also Convicts the Believer of Sin

As mentioned earlier, the Holy Spirit convicts the unbelieving sinner of sin. But He also convicts the believer of sin that is in his life and to live a more Christ-like life. This can be seen in John 16:8, as Jesus Christ tells us that the Holy Spirit will convict all humanity of sin. This is how Jesus said it:

"And He, when He comes, will convict the world concerning sin... John 16:8

The Holy Spirit also Guides All Believers to the Truth about God and His Word

It is very unfortunate that we live in a world today that says that there are no absolutes. Many people have learned so-called facts in the past and these facts have failed to be facts. Many people have been brainwashed into believing that because of this, there are no absolutes.

The Word of God is a true absolute and accepting Jesus Christ never fails, because He is God and He never could fail nor will He ever fail. The Holy Spirit was sent by Jesus Christ and He even said that the Holy Spirit would lead the believer into the real truth:

But when He, the Spirit of truth, comes, He will guide you into all the truth; for He will not speak on His own initiative, but whatever He hears, He will speak; and He will disclose to you what is to come. John 16:13

I believe that the person reading this book is being lead in a loving way by the Holy Spirit into understanding this truth. And that truth is the Word of God, the Holy Bible.

The Holy Spirit Seals the Believer

Each believer is marked or sealed by the Holy Spirit because of their faith in the work of Jesus Christ which is the Good News of the Gospel. This seal is a seal of ownership and a security in God and for the believer. Because the believer is a child of God, he or she needs to act properly as a child of God and not give the Holy Spirit grief and sorrow by falling into sin. They need to act in a loving way as Jesus Christ the Lord (Ephesians 1:13; 4:30-32, 2 Corinthians 1:21-22). Here is the main verse for the topic that the Holy Spirit seals believers:

In Him, you also after listening to the message of truth, the gospel of your salvation — having also believed, you were sealed in Him with the Holy Spirit of promise. Ephesians 1:13

All because of Jesus Christ, the believer is sealed with God the Holy Spirit within their heart.

The Holy Spirit Fills the Believer

The Holy Spirit empowers believers to do the extraordinary by filling them and allowing them to exercise their spiritual gift(s). In other words, the Holy Spirit gives each believer a supernatural capability to overcome sin. Why? Because the Holy Spirit indwells the believer and fills the believer to overcome the evil ways of the world (1 John 4:4). In the time of the beginning of this church age, in Acts chapter two, on the day of Pentecost, the Holy Spirit gave the Apostles the supernatural capability to speak the Good News of the Gospel to many others in earthly languages they never learned. This is an example of — and what — the sign "gift of tongues" is all about. Just think of it! Not to know a totally foreign language and to start speaking it and communicate to many others is a supernatural capability.

And they were filled with the Holy Spirit and began to speak with other tongues, as the Spirit was giving them utterance. Acts 2:4

The Holy Spirit and His Ministry to the Body of Christ the Church

God the Holy Spirit is responsible for starting the church age that we are currently in. The starting date was fifty days after the ascension of Jesus Christ. This is found in the book of Acts (2:1-47).

The Holy Spirit Formed the Universal Church

But what is the true Universal Church? The Universal church is every true Christian that has faith in the finished work of Jesus Christ and accepted Him as Lord and Savior because of His death, burial, resurrection and ascension. It matters not if the person is from the U.S.A., China, Russia or any country in Africa or the Middle East, or even to the remotest part of the world. The person that is in the Universal Church is a person that has true faith in Christ Jesus and only the kind of faith that is based on His Word (the Bible). A person's status in this life means nothing. You can be the richest person in the world or the poorest, the smartest or the least smart, you can be the most powerful, such as a president of a great nation or the most handicapped person with the ability to understand and reason. Also you can be the most religious, such as the top leader of any size church or group of churches of any type, sort or denomination on the face of the earth. If their faith is not based on the whole Word of God (the Bible), then there is something very wrong. A true Christian spiritual leader is to preach and teach God's Word without interference from politics, in or out of the church. He is not to be swayed by tradition or the size and history and beauty of the church or church buildings. To God these are nothing! To God, He is only concerned with the church truly growing and living according to His Word! True faith is putting absolute trust in the facts of God's Word and then, in that true faith, that person belongs to the Universal Church of the true one and only God. Another way of saying this is a universal group of believers in Christ Jesus, that are true believers belong to the family of God and are patriots of Heaven (Ephesians 2:19-22). Here is the primary verse for this topic of the Universal Church:

So then you are no longer strangers and aliens, but you are fellow citizens with the saints, and are of God's household. Ephesians 2:19

The Holy Spirit Aides in the Worship of the Local Church

True worship is an attitude of praise, thankfulness, service and acknowledgement of the true and only God. The Holy Spirit is within the presence of believers to bring forth these things in worship. True worship is a joyous occasion. It takes place when one is filled with the power of the Holy Spirit. There is harmony in songs of praise to God from the heart. It is also to uplift each believer and glorify Jesus Christ as well, as to honor God the Father. All of this is the work of the Holy Spirit.

And do not get drunk with wine, for that is dissipation, but be filled with the Spirit, speaking to one another in psalms and hymns and spiritual songs, singing and making melody with your heart to the Lord. Ephesians 5:18-19

The Holy Spirit Directs in Missionary Work

Because the Holy Spirit indwells the believer, He can guide and direct an individual in missionary work in many ways, such as:

1. He spoke to Philip and said: "Go up and join this chariot" (Acts 8:29).
2. The Holy Spirit forbade or prohibited the Apostle Paul to go to Asia (Acts 16:6).
3. The Holy Spirit resisted or prevented the Apostle Paul to go to Bithynia (Acts 16:7).
4. He guided the Apostle Paul with a vision (Acts 16:9-10).

The Holy Spirit directs the believer today. He directs the believer by speaking to one's heart, by prompting, saying no, saying yes or giving us a visual desire in our heart. But mostly, and again I say mostly, through the Word of God which is the Bible.

The Holy Spirit Warns Church Members

The Holy Spirit in the First Letter to Timothy warns us that in the end times we are currently in, there will be those that will say that they don't believe the Bible anymore, because they are liars and deceivers and also teachers from the Devil and his demons. One such teaching is that Jesus Christ is not God. This is a lie and false teaching from the pit of Hell! Another is that there are many ways to get to Heaven; this is another lie from the pit of Hell! Jesus said that He was the only way, the only truth and the only way to eternal life. This is because He is the Great "I AM" and there is no other way to God the Father but through Jesus Christ (John 14:6). Let's see what the Holy Spirit says in warning the church about false devilish teaching:

But the Spirit explicitly says that in later times some will fall away from the faith, paying attention to deceitful spirits and doctrines of demons, 1 Timothy 4:1

The Holy Spirit is the One Who Appoints the Pastor to the Church

The Holy Spirit is the one who guides the pastor as well as the church together to make the pastor the overseer of all spiritual matters in the church. The Holy Spirit is to be the one in this process and the potential pastor and the potential church needs to make sure that God is truly in this matter, or else the outcome can be disastrous. God is to be first, not man's political pull. All people involved need to be totally honest as well, because it is God's church and the potential pastor is God's servant. Otherwise, there will be problems and things that will most likely bring about disaster for the church or the pastor or both. The Holy Spirit needs to be in control!

Be on guard for yourselves and for all the flock, among which the Holy Spirit has made you overseers, to shepherd the church of God which He purchased with His own blood. Acts 20:28

The Holy Spirit Gives Spiritual Gifts to the Church

Every believer is gifted!
Every Believer Possesses at Least One Spiritual Gift

The Apostle Paul tells us that he wished each believer was like him with the superior gift of being an apostle because the apostle is gifted with all the gifts. But still, it is well that each believer has at least one spiritual gift (1 Corinthians 7:7). The Apostle Peter also states that each believer has a spiritual gift and the purpose is to glorify God with it. Here is the verse as Peter stated it:

As each one has received a special gift, employ it in serving one another as good stewards of the manifold grace of God. 1 Peter 4:10

No Believer Today Has All the Gifts

As stated earlier, the gift of apostleship is the gift that has all the other gifts within it. There are no apostles today because the Bible is complete and there are no additions to be made to the complete Word of God. The Apostle Paul in 1 Corinthians 12:29-30 shows us that no believer today has all the gifts, by bringing a question to mind and tells us, is everyone a prophet or a teacher? But he says that the greater type gifts need to be aspired for:

But earnestly desire the greater gifts. And I show you a still more excellent way. 1 Corinthians 12:31

So what is this greater way? It is the way of love (1 Corinthians 13:1-13) and it is the greatest way. This love is for all believers to apply in their lives.

The Purpose of Receiving a Spiritual Gift from the Holy Spirit is to Glorify God the Father

It was God the Father who planned all things and then created everything for His glory and honor. So when a believer uses their spiritual gift or gifts that God gave them, the believer is to utilize his or her giftedness to the glory of God.

> Worthy are You, our Lord and our God, to receive glory and honor and power; for You created all things, and because of Your will they existed, and were created. Revelation 4:11

The Holy Spirit also gives Believers Spiritual Gifts to Edify the Church

The word edify is similar to having the proper tools that give the potential for a good outcome. But to go further, it also includes the process of bringing that potential into volition or to a positive outcome. For example, a doctor who has great skills to do heart surgery because he or she needs to know and understand the correct procedure for the surgery to be a success, but within this, it is vital to have the right tools to perform the surgery correctly. The Apostle Paul tells us that spiritual gifts are to edify the church. Here are his words inspired by the Holy Spirit:

> ...for the equipping of the saints for the work of service, to the building up of the body of Christ. Ephesians 4:12

Sometimes a Person Does Not Use Their Spiritual Gift and It Must Be Stirred Up

The Apostle Paul used all of his spiritual gifts including exhortation or encouragement, as in the case with one of his most precious disciples that he knew at a very young age. His name was Timothy and now he was a young pastor and evangelist on a mission, but because of pressure and persecution, Timothy got a little discouraged and timid. Paul, in 2 Timothy 1:7, told him not to be fearful because he had a spirit of power, love and a soundness of mind that God the Holy Spirit gave him. This is part of the encouragement. But in the previous verse Paul tells Timothy how to get out of the rut of not moving forward. He tells Timothy that he was called of God for this work, and that he needed to get newly stirred up and put the gift in gear. This is good advice for all believers today. Here are Paul's words:

For this reason I remind you to kindle afresh the gift of God which is in you through the laying on of my hands. 2 Timothy 1:6

It is Very Important for All Believers to Exercise their Spiritual Gift(s) in Love

Love is to precede a person's spiritual gift, or the work that a person is doing is nothing, as Paul the Apostle says. Now let me say that this means that love is to be the motivation for the use of the gift. This doesn't mean that every person around the individual that is applying their gift by love will understand it to be from love. That is between God and that person. Paul tells us about this and gives us an example in 1 Corinthians 13:1-13 of what love is. Here is the first verse of the passage:

If I speak with the tongues of men and of angels, but do not have love, I have become a noisy gong or a clanging cymbal. 1 Corinthians 13:1

Love is very important!!!

There are about Nineteen Listed Spiritual Gifts in Scripture by the Holy Spirit

Of the nineteen gifts, there are some gifts that were temporary and there are those that are permanent gifts. The temporary sign gifts were just that, they were sign gifts. This was God telling the believers that the age of God's Grace was started and in effect. For instance, the temporary sign gift of Apostleship is no longer a gift that is needed by the church because the Bible from the book of Genesis to the book of Revelation is complete. There is no longer a need for more

Scripture regardless of how many millions of other books have been printed. The inspired, breathed Word of God is the ultimate authority over all humanity and forever will be.

The Apostle Paul, in writing to His Christian Hebrew brothers, brought this out by explaining to them that they need to realize that their Messiah has come and they are not to be pulled in the direction of being under the Law, but under Grace, and that God has given proof of this, including spiritual gifts:

God also testifying with them, both by signs and wonders and by various miracles and by gifts of the Holy Spirit according to His own will. Hebrews 2:4

One must also understand that the Holy Spirit gives the gifts He wants to give each believer, not the other way around. There are many who wish they had a certain gift but it is the Holy Spirit who is the giver.

The Temporary Sign Gifts

There are seven temporary sign gifts. These are apostleship, prophecy (in the sense of foretelling the future will of God with 100% accuracy), miracles, healings, tongues, interpretation of tongues and knowledge. These are seen in 1 Corinthians 12:8-10 and 2 Corinthians 12:12. When a person looks at these verses, they will see all of the temporary sign gifts listed with some of the permanent gifts listed, such as wisdom and discernment of spirits. This is because these were the gifts that were active at that time. As one reads the New Testament through from the beginning to the end of the New Testament, one can see no exercise of the temporary spiritual gifts. Just to be clear, does this mean that God doesn't perform miracles or healings today? The answer to this is no, God can perform miracles and healing even today. It is just that these were temporary sign spiritual gifts to show us and assure us that the Age of Grace has started. No one truly has these temporary sign gifts today that were given at the start of the Church Age of Grace. And again, they are no longer active today. The reason for this is that God wants believers to truly live and believe in His Word by faith and live through His Word for Salvation, not for signs of spectacularism, such as healing or miracles. Besides, if God chooses to perform a miracle or healing on someone of any disease, He can surely do it without a person having a gift of miracles or healing.

What the Temporary Spiritual Gifts Are

Apostle: The true apostle had a personal calling from Christ (Mark 3:14) and had been with Jesus from the beginning (Acts 1:21-22). They witnessed the Resurrection (Acts 1:22) and laid the doctrine (John 16:13) and structural foundations (Ephesians 2:20) for the church. God gave them power to perform miracles (Acts 5:12) of all sorts. Their names will be placed in the New Jerusalem (Revelation 21:14).

Prophecy: In the time of the New Testament in the Bible a prophet could foretell the future will of God with 100% accuracy, such as found in Acts 11:27-29. This is also the same as with all of the Old Testament prophets. They warned, rebuked, protested hypocrisy, exhorted, instructed only in the will of God. They were and are driven by truth and moral duty and have a great love for the Scripture.

Miracles: There are three types and (or) parts to miracles (1 Corinthians 12:10, 28). They are of supernatural power like power over death (Acts 9:39-41). Then there are wonders like walking on water as Jesus did (Matthew 14:24-29). Finally, there are signs from God's servant to authenticate the power of God in the Church Age such as Paul asserting blindness to the sorcerer in Acts 13:8-12.

Healing: This gift was able to heal many illnesses but not all of them. Paul could not heal Epaphroditus who was very sick for a long time (Philippians 2:25-27). The healing was not dependent on the amount of faith one has, like in the case of the man born blind in John 9:1-12. Another thing that is important to know is that all healing is not from God. This can be seen in Acts 8:9-11. But it was Peter's shadow that went onto a lame man named Aeneas and through that shadow the Holy Spirit healed him. Then a woman by the name of Tabitha was also raised from the dead by the power of the Holy Spirit's gift of restored healing working through Peter. This is found in Acts 9:32-41.

Tongues: Is the gift of speaking a language or languages that a believer never knew before their salvation in Christ (Acts 2:1-15; 1 Corinthians 12:10, 28-31). It is a known language, not some mystical babbling. This is not exercised by the Holy Spirit today, even though some may claim they have this gift today.

Interpretation of Tongues: This gift was the understanding of a language spoken to them that the receiving person never knew before their acceptance of Jesus Christ as Lord and Savior of their life. In other words, after conversing with the person who had the gift, they immediately understood the foreign language spoken yet they were never taught the language. Again, this was a sign gift and it is not active today (1 Corinthians 12:10, 30-31; 13:1).

Knowledge: This gift is more like the utterance of knowledge. This means knowledge of a biblical matter that was given to a believer to share with their church or another believer that was not previously known. This was knowledge that the Holy Spirit gave to that unknowing person. This is not an exercised gift today, but was exercised before the Bible was completed from Genesis to Revelation. This is why Paul first mentions the gift of wisdom and then the gift of knowledge in 1 Corinthians 12:8. The understanding in this is that the gift of wisdom is still active today but the gift of knowledge is not exercised today because having wisdom is the correct application of knowledge. But to have knowledge doesn't mean one has the understanding to apply knowledge, which is wisdom. A good example is a very young child may know the ABC's, but will not have the wisdom to coordinate their ABC's to write words from them so that they can write a note or letter. This is knowledge without wisdom.

What Are the Permanent Spiritual Gifts of the Holy Spirit

These are the spiritual gifts that are still active today. They are prophecy; only in the sense of foretelling the Word of God. There is no foretelling of future events in the exercise of this gift for today. The reason being is there is no need for this because the Bible is complete. Then there is giving, exhortation, service, mercy, ruling, teaching, wisdom, discerning of spirits, faith, evangelism and pastor-teacher. All of these gifts were and are present throughout the Church Age since the day of Pentecost. This can be found in Acts 2:1-47. You can find these gifts listed in Romans (12:3-8), James (3:13-18), Philippians (1:9), Ephesians (4:11) and 1 Corinthians (13:2).

Here is a listing and explanation of the permanent spiritual gifts of the Holy Spirit.

Prophecy: The gift of prophecy for today is as stated before; there is no foretelling the future or making predictions from the person with this gift. The person with this gift of prophecy is a person that loves the truths of the Scripture. Because of this, they exercise this gift by foretelling the truths of the Word of God (the Scriptures) in a fearless manner in the same way that the Old Testament prophets did. The person with this gift points to the will and conscience of the person they are speaking to. Not holding back the mention of sin if needed. They have a supernatural capability that can detect what is biblically true and false with the responsibility of the balance of the truth. Those with this gift are the truth hounds. The person with this gift can, most of the time, preach but not all will preach. Many times it is just their life that makes others, Christians and non-Christians, uncomfortable about their own life. Because they love to speak God's truth to many, this is the thing that brightly drives responsibility in the face of the one who is irresponsible. The person with this gift is the announcer of God's will. The person with the prophecy gift is very Bible driven, truth driven, encouragement driven and comfort driven. It has been said that he or she comforts the uncomfortable and discomforts the comfortable. The reason is that they point to the lack of responsibility and one's sinning (1 Corinthians 14:1-3). Prophecy is the highest ranking of the gifts for the church today (1 Corinthians 12:28; Ephesians 4:11). This gift is listed in the book of Romans (12:6) along with the other most fundamental and basic gifts for the church today (Romans 12:6-8). But some may say prophecy is not for today. The truth is, it is for today and it is listed in the most doctrinal-master teaching book in the Bible, the book of Romans. If one were to believe that the gift of prophecy is not for today, it would be the only word in the whole most doctrinal book, along with the only gift within the list of basic fundamental gifts listed in the book of Romans. This would not apply today making it a word, as well as a gift, that would for that time period only be among the permanent gifts. This would be a very dangerous and false conclusion. With this said, it is very unfortunate that much of modern Christianity in the last three centuries has thought this way to a large degree. The truth is that many fear the truth that comes from this gift. We are living in the "me" generation and many believe they are not responsible for their actions. Jesus promises that the outcome of truth is freedom in Him, not a liberal mindset leading to mental prison. Yet man in his pride runs from truth with excuses. The spiritual decay of the world is getting worse and worse. The reason for this is that we are living in the end times of this age. The so-called true believing church is suffering today, to the point that 58% of the so-called evangelical church members are saying that there are other ways to get to Heaven without Jesus Christ. This is truly a lie from Hell! You may ask, "Why is this happening in the church today?" Because many people in the church today accept falsehoods. Here is how Paul put it:

But the Spirit explicitly says that in the later times some will fall away from the faith, pay attention to deceitful spirits and doctrines of demons. 1Timothy 4:1

Many so-called believers are not learning and listening to the truths of Scripture. It matters little if one knows Bible trivia that is not important, such as how many Wiseman were there that came from the east to worship the infant Jesus. Were there two or three or four or one hundred? Many so-called believers say they read the Bible, but yet 58% of them say there are other ways to Heaven. Wrong!!! The reason for this is that many so-called Christians are in denial of the gift of Biblical truth driven by the gift of prophecy, and they have no problem in despising it. This is because they fear the life-giving truth and they do not want to understand the truth that the Apostle Paul commands us to listen to, those that are the true interpreters of the Scriptures. Who are they? They are those that the Holy Spirit has given the gift of prophecy that is in need to be exercised today. Here is the command the Apostle Paul gave to the church about this gift.

Do not quench the Spirit; do not despise prophetic utterances. 1 Thessalonians 5:19-20

Keep in mind that the word utterance also means gifts. Oh, and as for the 58% so-called Christian believers that say that they can get to heaven other ways without Jesus Christ Himself, who is the only God-Man that was raised from the dead and ascended into Heaven, here is what Jesus says about that false way of thinking:

Jesus said to him, "I am the way, and the truth, and the life; no one comes to the Father but through Me." John 14:6

Service: This spiritual gift is not a speaking gift, but it is obvious that it is a helps serving gift. Some call this gift the helping gift. This is a gift that is a support gift in helping the weak. I know of a situation years ago where some of the believers got together to help a women and her daughter in repairing a very leaky roof. These men were not roofers but they had the know-how to get up on the roof and put a new roof on for them. The gift of service gives a person a supernatural capability in knowing what physical needs must be met in order to keep the function of the church in harmony. This gift is one of the permanent gifts listed in Romans 12:7 and in 1 Corinthians 12:28. This gift is a gift which usually responds to a temporary need to which the person with the gift acts in supporting that temporary need. I have heard of a person with this gift among a group of a hundred people in a fellowship group gathering room, and there is a guest speaker coming to the church in forty-five minutes and everyone is standing around waiting, but he or she with the gift of service sees that there is a shortage of chairs, so at that point the person starts by getting the correct amount of chairs and starts opening and placing them for all the church members and guests to be seated comfortably. This is one example of the gift of service in action. This is what Paul means in Acts 20:35 when he tells us to help those that are weak. The other thing that needs to be understood is that this servant gift is really the gift of ministering. This is the glue that keeps the church members joyfully together. We see in Acts 6:1-6 the strong need for this gift in the early church, where the Twelve Disciples heard a complaint in which the widows of the Hebrew group were not getting their daily amount of food. So the Twelve Disciples said to the church that they were to choose seven adult men with wisdom, filled with the Holy Spirit and faithful as well with the proper character, to take care of the task of serving tables. This was so the Twelve Disciples could devote their time to the Word of God. As I stated earlier, this is the gift that supports the needs of the church in a physical way to keep it joyful and harmonious.

Teaching: The spiritual gift of teaching is not based on talent, as most schoolteachers have, but is a supernatural gift from the Holy Spirit that gives one the ability to clearly convey and inform the Biblical facts along with a proper application of the facts. This gift is listed in the permanent list of gifts in Romans 12:6-8 and is stated in verse 7. This is definitely not a talent because talents are common to society at large. There are many topics and subjects that can be taught with one having the talent to teach because a talent is something a person has at birth. So, the conclusion is the talent to teach is not a spiritual gift. Also the talent of teaching a topic brings about the knowledge of a topic, but many times not the proper application of the information that was given. The spiritual gift of teaching is given to the person by the will of the Holy Spirit at the time that person accepted Jesus Christ as Lord and Savior. This is the meaning of being born again. When one accepts Christ, they are born again. This is the spiritual birth and this can be found in the Bible just by reading John 3:1-21. It is at this time of spiritual birth in which the Holy Spirit indwells this new child of God, and if He wills, within His indwelling permanent presence to give this new believer the spiritual gift of teaching, He will. The purpose of the grace of God is for His unmerited gift to be communicated and inform the church of the facts of Biblical truth. Then it also motivates and urges the church to apply these Biblical facts and truths in obedience to Christ for the purpose of glorifying God. If one has the spiritual gift of teaching, the teacher will have the ability to communicate Biblical facts to the learner. Then the learner, because of how the fact(s) are taught, can understand the truth or falsehood around the fact. From there, the student is encouraged to state this new understanding in their own words. Then the pupil can understand how the fact can be applied for their own betterment or others. Finally is the response of applying this Biblical fact. This is how the gift works from the proper way of one using their spiritual gift of teaching in communicating the facts, and the pupil being motivated to move forward with the application of the teaching, because of the supernatural way it was taught by a believer that received the gift by the Holy Spirit. Pastors are to be able also to teach (1 Timothy 3:2). If a believer has the gift of teaching, they need to concentrate on exercising the gift (Romans 12:7). The Apostle Paul also states that women are not allowed to be in authority by teaching over men (1 Timothy 2:12).

Exhortation: The spiritual gift of exhortation is the same as encouragement. This is the gift that brings comfort, counsel and understanding to the person in need. This gift is also listed in (Romans 12:8). The person with the gift has the supernatural capability to strengthen the weak and to be alongside of those who need help. They bring assurance to those that are tottering. They bring steadiness to those that need stability and console the trouble-hearted. The person with this gift is usually very gracious in the exercise of their gift. These are the people who are great at the one-on-one approach to comfort those that are sick and struggling with the complicated parts of their life. The Apostle Paul was such a person and he exercised the gift in so many outstanding ways. Paul was able to start churches with this gift. He also had a watchful eye in going back to those churches that he started, by encouraging them in their spiritual growth. This can be seen in Acts 14:21-23. The Apostle Paul, even after a most cruel experience from unbelievers, continued to exhort and encourage the new believers in Philippi. This can be seen in Acts 16:37-40. The Apostle Peter also wrote exhorting words to the elders of the churches of that day (1 Peter 5:1-2). As one reads the book of Acts, a person by the name of Barnabas was one who always encouraged believers, but not only was he gifted with the gift of exhortation, but his name means "son of encouragement" (Acts 4:36; 11:22,30; 12:25; 13; 14; 15). The person with the gift of exhortation is one who encourages others in a tangible way, as well as showing encouragement and concern in a loving way. One who is gifted with exhortation also has an impartial heart for the foreigner and those that are unfortunately unwelcome by many. Barnabas, for instance, welcomed Paul even though at one time before his conversion to Christ was a pursuing persecutor of the church. Hindsight tells us what a mistake it would have been if there was no one like Barnabas to accept Paul into the church. Why? Because the Apostle Paul wrote most of the New Testament that we have today. The person with this gift also has a supernatural capability in encouraging foreign believers as well as those non-believing foreigners to enter the faith. These are people from other nations that need comfort and encouragement, because these believers are cultured differently but they are still a part of the body of Christ. As for non-believers, they may have never heard of the Savior Jesus Christ and they also need salvation. The other thing that the person with this gift usually does is he or she persuades others to develop their spiritual gifts without any concern for their own position because their heart is for the will of God. Finally, a person with this gift is a person who understands human frailty and will give the person another chance if they did not succeed.

Giving: This spiritual gift is listed also in Romans 12:8 and is very often misunderstood. Some have thought that a person with this gift is a person who is blessed to earn a large sum of money and then gives it away. The truth is that the person with the gift of giving has a supernatural capability of knowing when to give to someone in need. It is not always money, but it is definitely included within the exercise of the gift. It can be food, water, shelter, etc. and you can even be one of the financially less fortunate and still have this gift. Jesus Christ tells us that even a cup of water in His name will be rewarded (Mark 9:41). Why didn't Jesus say money or food, etc.? Because a cup of water to most can be so minimal! Because He was telling us that the true need was more important. Not money, money, money as so many in this century think! If a person is suffering from thirst and is dehydrated, what good is money? In fact money, many times, is a cold, impersonal way of solving a problem and can make it worse. It is the need that the gift of giving ministers in the best way. I know a minister years ago that told me that a man came to his door and said he was hungry and cold so the minister gave him money for a couple of meals. Then he sent him on his way. The problem was that the hungry man took the money and went to the liquor store and then he was found the next morning after, getting drunk under a bridge to the local train tracks. The minister then found out about this and was very concerned and realized that money is not the cure-all, and that if a person with the gift of giving was handling this, they would have known and handled this situation better. Then about two weeks later, the minister hears a knocking at the door and there he was, the same man saying the same thing. But this time, the minister invited him in for a meal. But to his surprise, the man said no thanks. Well, then the minister knew that the man didn't have an empty stomach but had a desire for booze. The minister then decided to give him some of his clothes and then sent him off. If this minister truly had the gift of giving, he may have sent the man away in the first place after inviting him in for a meal. It is the need that is truly met with the gift of giving, not a desire. Now to those that think that money is out and not needed to give, this is not true also. The Apostle Paul urges the church at Corinth to take a bountiful gift of money and not to give in a sparing way, and not in a grudging manner, but to give joyfully (2 Corinthians 9:1-8).

This bountiful gift for the church of Jerusalem was because it had undergone a great deal of persecution and had many financial needs. This gift of money was for the poor believers of Jerusalem. After all, Paul said that each Christian is indebted to the early Jewish believers for the message of Christ to the gentiles. Paul said that gentiles need to support them with material type things (Romans 15:26-27). This is because the early Jews pointed them to a true God. This is the true spiritual gift of giving in action.

Leading: The spiritual gift of leading is also found in the book of Romans (12:8). One who has this gift has the supernatural capability of leading a church or a church group that understands who is the leader, and realizes that the leader's responsibility is not to lord over the church or group, but that the leader is to move the church or group forward in an organized and unconfused way. But within this the leader's true heart's desire is to Glorify God in his leading, but not to glorify himself. There are two good examples in the secular world of how this spiritual gift works. They are the captain of a ship and the airline pilot, and both are heading and leading a group of people for a major goal—getting to a destination safely. But if there is no leadership or there is disorder, something or someone will suffer loss. So it also is with church leaders — such as overseers like bishops or superintendents of churches, pastors, evangelists, prophets — only in the sense of foretelling the truths of the Scriptures and teachers. If these ministers are not allowed to fulfill their ministry, the church suffers. Not only in a local way, but in a universal way. This is unfortunate and one of the main reasons why the church is in a suffering overall state today. Leaders are important. In the book of Acts, Paul and Barnabas choose and assign leaders for churches (Acts 14:23). The word elder or leader is very similar in meaning. Paul also gave Timothy the qualifications for pastors, which many believe to mean a similar word to being a bishop, which is one who is an overseer of a group of churches (1 Timothy 3:1-7). The best example of a leader is, of course, Jesus Christ the Lord, as He became a servant even to the point of death on the cross to save many from their sins. The Apostle Paul tells believers to listen and obey their leaders (Hebrews 13:17). There is only one leader who is perfect and there are no others. But even so, those that lead and teach the proper Doctrines need to be obeyed. But if you are not knowledgeable to these master teachings or Doctrines, you could be in major jeopardy being lead the wrong way. Some churches say they believe the Bible, but do not believe or teach the most important Master Teachings called Doctrines in the Scriptures. Here is an example: if a church says they believe in God and the Bible which is His Word, and then teach or say things such as Jesus is the Son of God but He is not God, Run!!! This is a lie from Hell! If some church leader says or preaches there is no Devil or Hell, this is a very severe lie in every way contrary to God's Word, the Bible. The Master Teachings or Doctrines in the Bible must be taught in a church, or the believer needs to find a church that truly teaches the Bible from cover to cover, with the truth of the Master Teaching or Doctrines with no exceptions. These are the leaders that Paul wrote about. Those not believing in the correct things are not of God. In other words, it is bologna no matter how you cut it!!! The Apostle

John, in all three of his epistles, wrote about false teachers and teaching. The epistles of First John, Second John and Third John that are all in the New Testament will give you a better understanding about what leaders to avoid. All of the Major Doctrines are for each believer to know, so they can have the strong foundation we all need to be the kind of person God wants us to be, and having the true foundation of God's Word, within our hearts, mind, and life.

Mercy: This spiritual gift that is listed in Romans 12:8 is a supernatural ability to show compassion to those suffering in the body of Christ and others, and doing it with joy, pointing to the work of Jesus Christ and His realizing that He is in control over all things. The depth of compassion with this gift goes into the realm of the divine love of Christ for the person in need. The mercy of this gift is not an action and reaction that is a superficial emotional moment. This gift shows the person in need of the comforting, loving power of the Holy Spirit. It brings forth the action in the name of Christ and ultimately brings glory to God the Father. This person, again, is not on an emotional whim but must act with pity toward the person in need of mercy. Jesus Christ is the best example in the entire Bible and in all of history in showing mercy. He would feed five thousand (John 6:1-13) and heal those blind (Matthew 9:26-30), crippled (Matthew 9:6-8) and every other type of illness (Matthew 9:20-22). He would also heal the leper (Matthew 8:1-3), heal those that were demon possessed by expelling them (Matthew 9:31-33) and He even raised the dead by restoring them back to life (John 11:1-45). These were all acts of power as well as mercy. The Apostle Paul also tells us that this gift is to be with action as well as cheerfulness. This is a very important part of the gift of mercy. It is not always important to act on showing mercy, but it is cheerfulness that completes true mercy. When a person is sick or in the middle of a disaster, it is the cheerfulness that resonates hope and elevates one's entire being toward healing. It can bring one from sadness to thankfulness that things could be even worse. It even moves the believer that may be feeling fearful by reminding them they have a spirit of power and not to buy into a spirit of fear (2 Timothy 1:7). This is why the Apostle Paul said mercy needs to be done with cheerfulness, because if a merciful action is done in a gloomy downcast way, it does not allow the person in need to trigger hope. Hope is the second fiddle to faith and true faith in God always opens one's eyes for blessing.

Wisdom: The spiritual gift of wisdom is found in Ephesians 1:8; 17, and Colossians 1:9. This gift gives a person a supernatural ability to use, balance and apply knowledge. Here are some examples of wisdom in the secular world. A person can buy a canvas and brushes and knows all the names of the paints, but it takes some wisdom to paint beautiful scenery. One can have a great knowledge of words but it takes wisdom to put those words in the right order and form and to write a very convincing letter to a group of people from a different culture. In the Christian faith, those with the gift of wisdom are always ready and prepared to give an answer to the unbelieving world about those trying to attack and give arguments to demean the Christian faith. A great example of this is when Jesus Christ was asked a question to try to trap Him. The question was if He thought it to be right and lawfully proper to pay taxes to Caesar and here was His answer about what a person was to do:

...render to Caesar the things that are Caesar's; and to God the things that are God's. Matthew 22:21

This is a perfect example of wisdom: two systems that seemed to conflict, yet to Jesus they did not; in this case, one secular and one system of faith. Why? Because according to God both are needed to be rendered to. The next aspect of wisdom gives defense to antagonistic courts. This can be seen in the Scripture by the Apostle Peter and can be read about in the book of Acts (4:1-31; 5:27-32). Stephen also was given great wisdom to refute the Jewish leaders with a great defense that

Jesus Christ was the true Messiah. This great message, which was the gift of wisdom from the Holy Spirit, can be found in Acts 7:1-60. The gift of wisdom also is the application of finding a solution to situations that are problematic. This gift gives one understanding to the gifted person that all things are to be without partiality, with gentleness, peaceable and with purity (James 3:15-18).

Discernment: This gift can be found listed at the end of Paul's letter to the Philippians (1:9). The Apostle John tells the believer that the prerequisite attitude of discerning a person or matter is to know and believe that not every spirit is of God. The gift of discernment is the supernatural ability of knowing if a spirit is of God, or from the enemy who is the devil. The gift acts like inner spiritual radar, knowing the truth or knowing that what is happening or being said is a lie. The Apostle also goes on and says that every spirit is to be tested to know if it is of God or not. John goes on to say that there are false prophets in abundance in the world, so all spirits must be tested (1 John 4:1).

John tells us that if anyone tells us that Jesus Christ did not come in a bodily form, and it is because the Holy Spirit indwells the believer that they can easily discern that this is a false doctrine, and that Christ did come to this world in a bodily human form. Therefore the statement from the unknown spirit is false (1 John 4: 2-6). Discernment is never to contradict the Word of God, ever. Why? Because it is the tool that every believer is to test against. If a person were to claim themselves as a believer in Jesus Christ or say they are a Christian and then you were to ask them who is Jesus Christ to you, and they responded with something like this, "He is my friend or He is the greatest man that ever lived or He is a great historical figure", these answers are not of God. Let me go one step further, if a person responds to the question with, "He is God's Son", ok, this is true! But does that mean that you believe He is God? If the response is, "No, He is not God, but the Son of God", this answer can indicate one of two things.

Either the person saying that Jesus is the Son of God, but not God, is a very baby, uninformed Christian, or not a Christian at all. If this person with the correct teaching through the Word of God will not want to truly acknowledge that Jesus Christ is God, then this is a false spirit and this person is not a Christian.

Discernment is for the protection of the church. In this day and age of imbalanced positive thinking, all believers would be very wise in listening and taking to heart the believer who has the gift of discernment very seriously. Even the positive-thinking Apostle Paul says there is a strong "must" for discernment. He tells us that Satan goes around with the disguise of looking like he is an angel of enlightenment. So, one must realize that his followers will also appear as having the right way to God. But in the end, Hell is waiting for them (2 Corinthians 11:14-15).

This is how Satan works and counterfeits God's way. Every believer with the gift of discernment understands this:

God	Satan
Jesus is God and Christ	Antichrist
True Apostles	False Apostles
True Prophets	False Prophets
True Teachers	False Teachers
Sheep	Goats
Sheep	Wolves disguised as sheep
Wheat	Tares

Every teaching and spirit is to be discerned by the Word of God and nothing more or less. No horoscope, no fortune telling, no philosophy, no cult and no false religion or other religions are valid in interpreting the Word of God. Again, all Christian spiritual discernment is based on the Word of God and by the immovable Master Teachings, which are the True Doctrines from God's Word the Bible.

Faith: This spiritual gift is listed in 1 Corinthians 12:9. This spiritual gift is not the faith that saves a person, by them putting their trust and faith in Jesus Christ as Lord and Savior. Every believer in Christ has that kind of saving faith (Ephesians 2:8). I am talking about the spiritual gift of faith. This Gift is a supernatural ability given by the Holy Spirit to understand something that God wants to be done, even if at the time it may seem impossible for this certain thing to take place. Many times the odds are stacked up against this certain event from the start. Stephen, in the book of Acts, is an excellent example of this in Acts 6:8-15; 7:1-60. In these chapters, one can see the enormous power of Stephens's faith. He believed the impossible and it was possible. He believed that God wanted him to be the person to do wonders and he gave a most powerful defense for the Lordship and salvation only in Christ to the Sanhedrin, the very powerful Jewish leaders of that day. God heard the heart of Stephen, just as He did in the case of David when he killed Goliath in 1 Samuel 17:1-58. God honored their faith for the impossible to be made visible to many. The person with this gift can see and understand beyond others, and can see things that can appear to be totally hopeless, and yet this person will persevere and bring about a wonder that no one could have ever imagined or seen. This shows every believer that all things are always possible with the true God. God is not limited by our finite understanding. This goes for logic as well as creativity. Anything a single man or all the people of this world collectively can conger up is beyond inferior to a simple thought of God.

Evangelism: The spiritual gift of evangelism is listed in Ephesians 4:11. The first time we see the gift of evangelism in the Bible is by Philip in Acts 8:26-40. By reading this passage one can truly see the gift of evangelism in action. The gift is a supernatural capability to get the Good News out, and for the Holy Spirit to bring the unbeliever to the point of putting their true faith and trust in Christ for salvation, which brings them into the family of God. Philip is also titled as one of the Seven in Acts 6:3-5 and titled as an evangelist in Acts 21:8. If we look at the passage in Acts 8:26-40, we can see the most important aspects of a true evangelist. First, the person with the gift of evangelism is eager to bring the Good News of the Gospel of Jesus Christ to anyone in need. Nationality and culture are not barriers for them to bring the Good News, because the Good News is not to be held back and must be given to all people. We see Philip in Acts 8:26-27 moving urgently to bring the Good News of freedom over the power of sin, because he is motivated by the love of God to share about the death, burial, and resurrection of Jesus Christ, and he knows as a believer that by putting his faith in the God-Man Jesus Christ that he and anyone else receives eternal life. It is the evangelist that proclaims the Gospel with clarity as well as simplicity (Acts 8:28-35). The evangelist leads those in an effective way, resulting in a true conversion by bringing them to a point of making a sincere choice for Christ (Act 8:36-37). Then the evangelist follows through with some form of discipleship. This can be teaching more of the depth of who Jesus Christ is, but in this case it leads to water baptism. Let me just say that before this baptism there was discipleship taking place seen in Act 8:30-39. Philip was always prepared to proclaim the Gospel wherever he went. The evangelist can proclaim to one person or to thousands of people at any time. Numbers do not make a successful evangelist. The faithfulness to proclaim the Gospel is the key. Another thing is that the result is in God's hands if someone chooses not to accept Christ. The evangelist is not a failure, but they are a failure if they denied an opportunity to evangelize. It is the one who has heard the message of the Good News that is responsible. We can see this situation with the Apostle Paul in Acts 19:8-9 and also in the case with Felix the Governor in Acts 24:24-27.

Pastoring: Another word for this spiritual gift is shepherding. The word pastor is found in Ephesians 4:11. The pastor is an official office and position one has in the church. Jesus Christ is known as the Good Shepherd in John 10:11-17.

Jesus Christ is also known as the Chief Shepherd in (1 Peter 2:25). Because Jesus is the Chief, this means there must be under-shepherds called to pastor churches. The spiritual gift of pastoring is the supernatural capacity of feeding the flock the Word of God, as well as giving protective spiritual oversight. He is to gently guide, steer and teach those of his congregation to the major truths of the Bible by preaching the full Bible in all completeness. He is also to be able to teach his flock and disciple them, counsel them and discipline them. The pastor is to be fearless but not stubborn. He is to be immoveable about the truths of the Bible (such as Jesus Christ was born of a virgin, etc). It is the pastor's responsibility to make sure that his congregation is one of true believers. If one is not a believer in the congregation, he as a pastor is to take time in evangelizing that one to the point of accepting Jesus as Lord by teaching that person the truth of God's Word.

A true pastor is to lead his flock to feed themselves by encouraging them to study the Word of God for themselves so they can grow in the Lord even more. Yet the pastor should have oversight, making sure that no one is learning and also propagating any false teaching in pulling others away from the truth of God. You can see how the Apostle John handles this in (2 John 1-13). All thirteen verses show us the correct balance that should be in a church. This balance is of truth, love, and doctrine, which is the Master Teaching of God. John goes as far as to say that if anyone wants to preach false teaching of any sort, do not even greet him. That is how serious this all is. A true Shepherd is, yes, one who feeds the flock with the Word of God, but in no way is he to preach in a weak or milk-toast manner, making his preaching insignificant. He is to preach from the Bible, and not his own emotions just to keep everyone happy. He is commanded by God to preach God's Word (Timothy 2:15-19). This also means that a shepherd is not to read so many other books that the truth of the Word of God is crowded out and the flock gets misled, due to the pride of appearing as an intellectual and putting the Word of God aside. Every pastor needs to continue learning, but not to the cost of the Word of God feeding his flock. The Word of God is to be his authority at all times and nothing else.

20

THE MASTER TEACHING OR DOCTRINE OF TRUE BIBLICAL SALVATION

———❧❧❧———

First, one must ask, why does one need salvation? The reason one needs salvation is because everyone, from the time of Adam to the last person to be born through Adam, has a sin nature. The only one to be born and does not have, nor never could have a sin nature, is Jesus Christ the God-Man. It is only through Jesus Christ that one can obtain salvation from their sins (John 3:16-17). It is only through faith in the perfect blood sacrifice on the cross by Jesus Christ that one can receive forgiveness for their sins. And it is only through Jesus Christ's resurrection that one can obtain justification before God leading to salvation.

It is sin that separates one from God but it is only Christ who reconciles one to God. I have asked thousands of people on an individual basis, "Who put Christ on the cross?" Some say the Jews, some say the Romans and some say the Devil. Even though these answers are true, not one has pointed to the most important truth! The greatest answer is you did, I did, we all (even today) were the ones to put Christ on the cross. The reason being is that Christ paid the price for our sins even today, collectively and individually. We today, and all the rest of humanity, put the nails through His hands and feet. He died for us, arose from the dead for us and ascended into heaven to be with God the Father for us as well. All of this was to glorify God the Father in heaven. Do you believe that Jesus Christ would come for only you if He needed to save you from your sins? The answer is yes! This is why He is called one's personal Savior.

The Most Important Aspect Of Salvation Is That All True Believers Need To Know What Salvation Truly Means.

Note: All of the verses listed in these different aspects of one's true salvation need to be looked up and read in proper context of each Bible passage listed.

Grace: Grace is God's undeserving and unmerited favor and gift toward the whole human race. This is because man has rebelled against God by sinning. It is because of God's loving nature that He has reached out towards man, His greatest creation, in order to provide a way of escape from man's total spiritual depraved way. The only way for man to be accepted spiritually back to God and avoid Hell is through His Son Jesus Christ the Lord.

> For by grace you have been saved through faith; and that not of yourselves, it is the gift of God; not as a result of works, so that no one may boast. Ephesians 2:8-9

Looking at these two verses, one can see that God's grace is unmerited. It is a gift to man. We can see it is only by true faith in His Son Jesus Christ that one can benefit spiritually by God's grace. Then we can see that salvation is not by one's good works because that is a false way back to God. But God wants things His way, so no one is allowed to brag or boast. The reason is because no one can save themselves; only God can. Here is another verse about God's Grace:

> ...who has saved us and called us with a holy calling, not according to our works, but according to His own

purpose and grace which was granted us in Christ Jesus from all eternity. 2 Timothy 1:9

Other verses about God's grace are Psalm 84:11; 2 Corinthians 8:9; 2 Thessalonians 2:16; 1 Peter 1:10; Jude 4; Galatians 5:4.

Election: Election is God's choice of certain individuals to become His children. This choice that God has made has taken place before the foundation of the universe. Though this truth is taught in Scripture, it remains somewhat of a mystery to the finite mind of man.

> For those whom He foreknew, He also predestined to become conformed to the image of His Son, so that He would be the firstborn among many brethren. Romans 8:29

In this verse we can see that God, before the universe was created, knew those that would be His children and be destined to conform to His Son Jesus Christ. In Romans 8:33, the Apostle Paul goes as far as saying to us that no one has a right to attack those that God elected, and in Romans 8:34-39 he also says even under the worst of human circumstances, God's love for His elect is always with them no matter what. Some may say, "well if God has already made His choice of who will be His children, then how do I know where I stand in His predestined plan?" Here is a verse that many are familiar with and unfortunately many times, many in the public treat this verse in a very disrespectful manner (such as the media). But still this great verse gives us the answer to this troubling question.

> For God so loved the world, that He gave His only begotten Son, that whoever believes in Him shall not perish, but have eternal life. John 3:16

The key to this verse is God loves all to the point of giving His Son and anyone that puts their faith and trust in the work of His Son, Jesus Christ, will receive life eternal. So the person who does this and has a persevering faith in this salvation that God gave him must be one of God's elect. Here are some other verses about God's election (Mark 13: 20; Luke 18:7; 1 Corinthians 1:27; 2 Peter 1:10).

Effectual Calling: Effectual calling is God working towards us by the power of the Holy Spirit in giving one an understanding about their sin and spiritual depravity. From there, God illuminates and clarifies in the mind of the person by giving them a knowing knowledge of Jesus Christ, and from there God renews the individual's will. From this point, the Holy Spirit enables with loving persuasion to trust, accept and embrace Jesus Christ as the Lord and Savior of their life, according to the Good News of the Gospel of Christ's death, burial, and victorious resurrection.

I pray that the eyes of your heart may be enlightened, so that you will know what is the hope of His calling, what are the riches of the glory of His inheritance in the saints. Ephesians 1:18

In the verse above, the Apostle Paul is telling believers that God is the one who called them to be His children, and with this in mind Paul prayed that there is true heartfelt understanding to the point that they can see the rich and glorious inheritance in Jesus Christ.

But you are a chosen race, a royal PRIESTHOOD, A HOLY NATION, A PEOPLE FOR God's OWN POSSESSION, so that you may proclaim the excellencies of Him who has called you out of darkness into His marvelous light.1 Peter 2:9

The Apostle Peter in the verse above is telling every believer that God chose them as his race. Each believer has a priesthood to serve God. All believers are God's nation because we belong to God. All believers are to be bold in telling others about being called of God and how God has saved them by giving them this awesome, clear understanding of who God really is and His great love for the believer. Here are some other verses on the effectual calling from God: Romans 11:29; 1 Corinthians 1:26; Philippians 3:14; 2 Timothy 1:9; Hebrews 3:1; Revelation 19:9.

Faith: Faith is a gift from God, which applies total trust in God and belief in the facts and truths that are in His Word the Bible, and understanding that He is the Creator, as well as the Savior. One must realize that if one says they believe in God and their belief is not based on Bible truth, this belief is not from God but of man's idea of God. True faith in God is only based on God's truth in the Bible. Hebrews chapter 11 is considered the faith chapter of the Bible so the whole chapter needs to be read straight from the Bible. But if we look at the first verse of this chapter, it gives us a great definition of faith.

Now faith is the assurance of things hoped for, the conviction of things not seen. Hebrews 11:1

It is God who gives one the substance of fact-believing faith. Biblical faith is based on the fact of God's Word, the Bible. This fact points to Biblical hope. Biblical hope is not a gamble, like hope is in this world. Like, "I hope I pass the test in school." Biblical hope is different, it is like saying an event like Jesus Christ's second coming will absolutely happen beyond a shadow of any doubt. It is not just feeling it or sensing it. It knows it with conviction, no matter if things at the time appear visibly pointing in the opposite direction (this also applies to things that are non-visible). For instance, we cannot see God with our eyes, but a true believer knows that God is always much closer to them than their next breath. Why? Because the Word of God tells us that each believer is indwelled by the Holy Spirit who is the third person of the God-head.

For we maintain that a man is justified by faith apart from works of the Law. Romans 3:28

The Apostle Paul is telling believers that it is an absolute must to remember that it is only by faith in Jesus Christ, and nothing else, that saves a person from Hell. There is nothing that a person can do, like doing good things or good works of any amount or sort that will get them into heaven. It is only faith in Jesus Christ that justifies any person for eternal life. But after a person has truly put their faith in the Lord Jesus Christ of the Bible, then it is time they are to do good deeds or works to glorify God, not before. Here are some other verses in the Bible about the doctrine of faith: Galatians 2:16; Acts 26:18; Ephesians 2:8-9; James 2:17-20; Romans 5:1; Luke 17:6; Jude 3.

Repentance: Repentance is a change of mind, which starts and stems from the will of a person by recognizing and realizing that he or she has rebelled and sinned against God. At this point, the person realizes a need for salvation, due to recognizing his or her spiritual weakness and state because of their total spiritual depravity.

> Or do you think lightly of the riches of His kindness and tolerance and patience, not knowing that the kindness of God leads you to repentance? (Romans 2:4)

Some have a very hard time understanding that it is because of God's kindness and His patience that one understands from their own will that they are in need to change their minds about sinning. The natural reaction for the unbeliever is to keep on sinning and thinking it is okay because it is the way of life in general. But it is God who, in His time, makes a person understand that he or she is in need of a Savior because he or she is spiritually depraved, and it is only God the Son who can save him or her out of a condemned life of sin.

For the sorrow that is according to the will of God produces a repentance without regret, leading to salvation, but the sorrow of the world produces death. 2 Corinthians 7:10

The verse above explains to us the difference of repentance because of God's will and that it brings about eternal life, and no one ever regrets this life of the one and only loving true God. But the sorrow of the world is useless, because there is never hope from it and it leads to death. So sorrow leads the believer to repenting that gives life, but the sorrow of the world leaves out God's love through His Son Jesus Christ! Therefore, the world's sorrow always brings about death. Here are some other verses about the doctrine of repentance: Hosea 13:14; Matthew 9:13; Hebrews 6:1, 6:6; 2 Peter 3:9.

Conversion: Conversion is a "turning around" because a person has put his or her faith in the Lord Jesus Christ, and believing and accepting that He has fulfilled the perfect blood sacrifice to God the Father. Then at that point, the person is then simultaneously baptized by the Holy Spirit. Not by water in this case, but in a spiritual way. This places this new believer into the body of Christ.

For you first, God raised up His Servant and sent Him to bless you by turning every one of you from your wicked ways. Acts 3:26

The Apostle Peter in preaching to the Jews at the time of the start of the early church, said that Jesus Christ came for them first and that Jesus arose from the dead as He said He would. Then he encouraged them to turn around and leave their old sinful ways, as turning spiritually around is the beginning of conversion.

And the hand of the Lord was with them, and a large number who believed turned to the Lord. Acts 11:21

In this verse we can see that salvation was not just for the Jew but salvation was also offered to the gentiles (Acts 11:1), and God blessed the preaching to the point that a large group of gentiles converted by spiritually turning to God. Here are some other verses that show us or give us some aspect of the doctrine of conversion: Isaiah 2:2; John 6:44; Romans chapters 10 and 11.

Redemption: Redemption is the unlimited act of God through the Lord Jesus Christ by His making a full payment for the sins of the world. He is the perfect and only sacrifice that satisfies the demand of a righteous and Holy God.

> ...knowing that you were not redeemed with perishable things like silver or gold from your futile way of life inherited from your forefathers, but with precious blood, as of a lamb unblemished and spotless, the blood of Christ. 1 Peter 1:18-19

The Apostle Peter is telling us in these verses that the payment in full for all the sins of the world was not cheap. Nor was the payment made with precious earthly materials that will perish. The perfect payment was made by God the Father sending God the Son, Jesus Christ, to meet the righteous and holy demand for the payment of the sins of the world. This demand could only be met by a perfect, sinless person. It is only by the shed blood of Jesus Christ that anyone can have their sins forgiven and be able to receive eternal life.

(Speaking of Jesus Christ)

> ...who gave Himself for us to redeem us from every lawless deed, and to purify for Himself a people for His own possession, zealous for good deeds. Titus 2:14

The Apostle Paul is writing to Titus and telling him that Jesus Christ paid the redeeming price for even the worst lawless sinner. Even if this type of sinner believes and accepts Jesus Christ as their Lord and Savior for their most lawless sins, that person becomes God's own possession and child of God. Now that redeeming sinner is a believer and must persevere to doing good things, not lawlessness as before. Here are some other verses about the doctrine of redemption: Romans chapter 5, Galatians 1:4, 3:4; Ephesians 1:2; Revelation 5:9.

Reconciliation: Reconciliation is a restoration of peace between God and a person due to the fact that the blood sacrifice of the Son of God was adequate for the holy demand of God. This can only happen because of a person who believes in Jesus Christ as Lord and Savior. They are declared righteous through Christ the God-Man.

> ...and through Him to reconcile all things to Himself, having made peace through the blood of His cross; through Him, I say, whether things on earth or things in heaven. Colossians 1:20

This verse clearly tells us that the blood of Jesus Christ made peace for all true believers of this world. All spiritual debts were wiped away in heaven and on earth.

> ...namely, that God was in Christ reconciling the world to Himself, not counting their trespasses against them, and He has committed to us the word of reconciliation. 2 Corinthians 5:19

The Triunity (or Trinity) of God was and is working to bring peace to man through the shed blood of Christ to those who would and will believe. God overlooked man's sinfulness by knowing that only true peace, by believing, could happen by the demand of sinless perfect blood. It is only through the blood of Christ that this was met. It is only by the truth of the Word of God that a person can know and get this true peace from God. These are other verses that show us about the doctrine of reconciliation: Isaiah 53:5; Daniel 9:24; Romans chapter 5; Ephesians 2:16.

Propitiation: Propitiation is God turning away His wrath by the atoning sacrifice of Jesus Christ. The Son of God did this by the shedding of His blood, which satisfies God's wrath due to sin.

> …whom God displayed publicly as a propitiation in His blood through faith. This was to demonstrate His righteousness, because in the forbearance of God He passed over the sins previously committed. Romans 3:25

It was God's intention to show the world that He would turn away His wrath to any person who believed, by having faith, in His Son shedding His blood for that individual. This also shows us that God is loving, but He also is a righteous provider and that this sacrifice of His Son's blood would cover all sins.

In this is love, not that we loved God, but that He loved us and sent His Son to be the propitiation for our sins. 1 John 4:10

Many say they love God, but it is God our Creator who loved us first and sent His Son to be a sacrifice in our place. Knowing that God's sacrifice could never be fulfilled by anyone else except by His Son, God the Father turns His wrath away from anyone who believes His Son. Here are two other verses showing us about the doctrine of propitiation: Hebrews 2:17; 1 John 2:2.

Forgiveness: Forgiveness is the loving act of God's mercy in which He takes away the believer's sins because of the death of Christ.

> In Him we have redemption through His blood, the forgiveness of our trespasses, according to the riches of His grace which He lavished on us. Ephesians 1:7

Because of Jesus Christ and His blood sacrifice, the believer has been forgiven for all sins past, present, and future. This all comes about from the great richness of God's unmerited favor. This does not mean one is to go on sinning. But the believer is to show their love to God by preventing to sin at all costs.

If we confess our sins, He is faithful and righteous to forgive us our sins and to cleanse us from all unrighteousness. 1 John 1:9-10a

If a Christian sins, this believer is to confess this sin to God. This means the believer is to claim the sin as God calls it. It is not a mistake or an accident, it is a sin. If one steals or has lust in their heart for their neighbor's wife, then that is how one is to confess it as sin. Not something like, "I needed the money" or "it's a man thing". Then, after one confesses their sin to God, He wipes the slate clean so we can have power and more victory in our lives. But remember, God never rejects the believer, He always loves the believer but He always hates the sin. Here are some other verses that are in the Scriptures about the doctrine of forgiveness: James 5:15; Colossians 1:14; Luke 24:47; Acts 5:31; 26:18.

Justification: Justification is the action of God with the result of Him changing one's account and imputing righteousness to them because of their faith in Christ. This change of imputing of righteousness (or rightness) takes place by God the Father accepting the sacrifice of Christ, and man's repentant mind and heart from their sins by having faith in the Lord Jesus Christ's substitutionary death for that believer.

He who was delivered over because of our transgressions, and was raised because of our justification. Romans 4:25

This verse is written for and applies to the believer in that Christ died for the sins of the world. But to the person who believes in Him, that person is justified in the sight of God and it is only because of His Son's resurrection that a believer is justified. This means that a believer is declared righteous only because of faith in the resurrection of God the Son, Jesus Christ and His power over death.

So then as through one transgression there resulted condemnation to all men, even so through one act of righteousness there resulted justification of life to all men. Romans 5:18

Because of the sin of Adam the first man's sin, the whole world was denounced by God. It is because of that one sin that all people were born within sin that also gives them all a sin nature. It is only through the one righteous act of Christ's resurrection — which, of course, includes His death and burial preceding His resurrection — in which anyone on the face of the earth, who puts their faith and trust in Jesus the Christ, is declared by God the Father as justified and righteous. Again, only through Christ. Other verses on the doctrine of justification in the Bible are found here: Habakkuk 2:4; Acts 13:39; Romans 1:17; Galatians 3:11; James 2:14-26; Titus 3:7.

Regeneration: Regeneration takes place upon salvation by the Holy Spirit, giving a new birth. The Holy Spirit performs His ministry within the believer's life by making the person a child of God and teaching, guiding and convicting the believer of sin.

He saved us, not on the basis of deeds which we have done in righteousness, but according to His mercy, by the washing of regeneration and renewing by the Holy Spirit. Titus 3:5

Again, no person can do good works to get salvation, but it is only by faith and trust in Jesus Christ and in His work for that person that salvation is obtained. It is because of God's mercy. He cleans the offending person and gives them a new start. This new start is a brand new spiritual birth that gives everlasting life. This takes place when the Holy Spirit indwells the new believer.

Jesus answered and said to him, "Truly, truly, I say to you, unless one is born again he cannot see the kingdom of God." John 3:3

In this verse, the Lord Jesus Christ is speaking to a Jewish ruler at the time and explaining that it is very important to anyone who wants to have eternal life and get into God's kingdom that that person must be regenerated. This means having a true spiritual birth by being born from above. To understand this concept of the new spiritual birth, one can read about this in the full context of the Scripture found in (John 3:1-15). This new spiritual birth only happens when one puts their faith in Jesus Christ. Here are some other verses in the Scripture explaining the doctrine of regeneration: Matthew 19:28; John 1:12-13.

Adoption: All believers are adopted as children of God with all of the rights and privileges of membership in the family of God.

But as many as received Him, to them He gave the right to become children of God, even to those who believe in His name. John 1:12

In this verse we can see that, whoever puts their faith and trust in Jesus Christ as their Lord and Savior, it is by that type of faith that God accepts that person into his family, giving that adopted child all rights as all his other children. This also applies to those who may have never seen Jesus Christ, but to all who believe in Him — this means all the generations from His time (or the church age) to the end of time. If one has true faith in Him, not one person will ever perish.

"And I will be a father to you,
And you shall be sons and daughters to Me,"
Says the Lord Almighty. 2 Corinthians 6:18

This is a verse that tells us that if one puts their faith in God the Father who sent His Son Jesus and we accept His Son, God the Father will be our father, making us a son or daughter with equality. God is very firm about this and tells us this as a direct statement because He is a loving Father to the believer! The Bible has other verses in it that explain to us more about the doctrine of adoption: John 20:17; Romans 8:14; and the whole chapter Galatians 4.

Sanctification: Sanctification is the process of one maturing toward becoming more and more Christ-like. There are three stages in this maturing process. They are: being forgiven, growing to get victory over temptation and then glorification, which takes place at the moment one is brought into the presence of God before His throne.

For these whom He foreknew, He also predestined to become conformed to the image of His Son, so that He would be the firstborn among many brethren. Romans 8:29

This is a verse that shows us the maturing sanctification process. It shows us that God knows all about the person that would believe in His Son, Christ Jesus, so He provided forgiveness of sins. Then, before time began, God also has provided a way for His children to overcome temptation. This power is because of Jesus Christ and because of Him (Christ) sending the Holy Spirit to indwell each believer to give them victory over sin. Thirdly, the child of God is in the process of conforming to Christ and ultimately will be glorified when the believer gets to heaven (Romans 8:30). This can only happen because Christ, the God-Man, has gone before us in total victory in His death, burial, resurrection and His ascension. He is seated at the right hand of God the Father, which is the place of authority.

Now may the God of peace Himself sanctify you entirely; and may your spirit and soul and body be preserved complete, without blame at the coming of our Lord Jesus Christ. 1 Thessalonians 5:23

In this verse, the Apostle Paul is telling us that the believer is at peace with God and that God is working with each believer to give Him victory over temptation (1 Corinthians 10:13) within this sanctification process, and that we are to strive to be blameless in our spirit, soul, and our body for the coming of Jesus Christ the Lord. Other verses on the process of this doctrine of sanctification are: Hebrews 10:10; Ephesians 4:30; 2 Peter 3:18; 1 John 3:1-3.

Preservation: Preservation is the act of God by the Holy Spirit in protecting the believer — by sealing him or her as a child of God — through life and protecting them through physical death, leading them to heavenly glory.

He who has the Son has the life; he who does not have the Son of God does not have the life. These things I have written to you who believe in the name of the Son of God, so that you may know that you have eternal life. 1 John 5:12-13

These verses tell us that if one puts their true faith in Jesus Christ, that person has the Spirit of Christ within them, who is the Holy Spirit. If one does not believe the fact that Jesus Christ the Son of God is God, that person does not have eternal life. The Apostle John wrote this to the believer so they may know for sure that God is the protector of the believer's salvation and that the believer will know with all certainty that they have eternal life!

Now to Him who is able to keep you from stumbling, and to make you stand in the presence of His glory blameless with great joy. Jude 24

Faith in the Lord Jesus Christ protects the believer in all ways and also seals the believer for eternal life. In other words, the true believer has the mark of God on them and in them never to leave because of God the Holy Spirit. It is because of this that each believer will be able to stand in God's glory, with all sins forgiven, with great celebration from within in the great presence of the glory of God, and glorifying God. Other verses that explain more about the doctrine of preservation are: Ephesians 4:30; Romans 8:31-39; John 5:24.

Glorification: It is the act of God which refers to the ultimate state of bliss in which the believer is given a total state of spiritual, mental, and physical perfection before the throne of grace. It begins at the rapture (Revelation 4:1). Then this state of glorification continues throughout all eternity. This effect of glorification will also give each glorified child of God a glorified new body without a nature to sin, just like Christ.

When Christ, who is our life is, revealed, then you also will be revealed with Him in glory. Colossians 3:4

The Apostle Paul is telling each believer that Christ is the giver of eternal life and when Christ comes to get His child (children), the outcome will be glorification for the believer. God's love for all His children is for them to be like Christ and all true believers will be perfect in spirit, mind, and body because of the work of Christ, the God-Man, who is also called the first born of many brothers. This means that He has authority over all believers.

...and these whom He predestined, He also called; and these whom He called, He also justified; and these whom He justified, He also glorified. Romans 8:30

The Apostle Paul is telling us that God the Father is the one who started the process of our salvation from His predestined plan. From there, he tells those God predestined that the only way is by faith in His Son Jesus Christ. After this, God the Father justified those that accepted His Son and this makes them righteous only because of the righteousness of Jesus Christ. But God doesn't stop there, because the work is not finished. God will glorify each and every believer in His Son Jesus Christ. Other verses that show us about the doctrine of glorification are: Philippians 1:21, 3:20-21; 1 Corinthians 15:41-44, 1 Thessalonians 4:13-18.

Assurance: Assurance of a believer is based on the facts and statements in the Word of God. There is the inner witness of the Holy Spirit within the believer's heart, and because of this there is an outward evidence of a new life which is the effect of a change within the believer.

Therefore if anyone is in Christ, he is a new creature: the old things passed away; behold, new things have come. 2 Corinthians 5:17

The Apostle Paul is telling us in this verse that if a person has put their faith in the Word of God, who is Christ, this person is a new person because of Christ and because of this: this person has a new heart. It is this new heart that is the assuring witness of the Holy Spirit and it is because of this that the believer will bear fruit like love, patience, kindness, etc. (Galatians 5:22-23). It is wise to look these verses up to understand what it means for a believer to produce fruit.

For the good that I want, I do not do, but I practice the very evil that I do not want. But if I am doing the very thing I do not want, I am no longer the one doing it, but sin which dwells in me. Romans 7:19-20

The Apostle Paul, in these verses, is explaining about the battle that takes place within the believer between the new spiritual nature (due to the indwelling of the Holy Spirit), and the sin nature. This is like a civil war within the believer, and continues until the believer goes to be in the full presence of God by death or by the rapture to come. Paul tells us that we may want to do good, but we end up doing evil that we never intended to do. Then he tells us that if the believer is doing the evil thing he hates, it is not the true believer, but it is that wretched sin nature that is within the believer. It is this battle that rages in the believer that shows the believer that their assurance in Christ is real. There are other verses in the Bible that can help a believer to understand this doctrine on assurance of one's salvation in Christ: Matthew 7:20; Philippians 3:13-16 and to resist temptation: 1 Corinthians 10:13.

21

THE MASTER TEACHING OR DOCTRINE OF THE TRUE ORIGIN AND CONDITION OF MAN

———⟋⟍⟍⟋———

S ome people believe that man originated through a process called evolution. The theory of evolution, first and foremost, cannot be proven by pure science because according to those that believe in this theory, life on this planet has existed for billions of years. They will say that their tests—which are called Carbon 14 dating tests—that they have done on different fossils reveal that the world has been here for many millions of years and that man came about through a process. But for anything to be true, science, rather then fantasy or scientism (which is false science), testing must be done in a controlled experiment. This means that there needs to be an object to test against, like adding fertilizer to the soil of one potted plant and not to the other. This is a controlled experiment. Did the leaves get greener? Is the plant healthier? Did it have more blooms and are the roots stronger, or are both of the plants the same? This is a true scientific experiment, not some idea of illogic probability. The need for testing by observation under controlled circumstances is true and pure science. If not, it is false science. No one can claim that evolution is true because of the lack of human observation. But if one understands the major teaching or doctrine of inspiration, and authority of the Scripture, and how the Holy Spirit spoke and breathed the living Word through the writers of His Word, then we all can understand that God created all the heavens as well as the earth (Genesis 1:1). He created all things on the earth, including man on the sixth day with a mature appearance, as man may see those things that God created with age. By this I mean, when God created a tiger or the first man Adam, from the first day of them being created they appeared as fully-grown and with age; in fact, they were one day old. So which came first, the chicken or the egg? The answer is the chicken. But evolution would like you to ignorantly think the egg. If we could see the first man and woman created on that day we may say they looked Twenty years old, yet they were in reality only one day old. This is the case of Biblical creation and the answer to our origin.

The Creation of Man

God's creation of man was a deliberate plan and act of God. God planned for man to have dominion over all the creatures on the earth. Man is also God's greatest creation because God made man in His own image, with a will, intellect, and emotions.

Then God said, "Let Us make man in Our image, according to Our likeness; and let them rule over the fish of the sea and over the birds of the sky and over the cattle and over all the earth, and over every creeping thing that creeps on the earth." Genesis 1:26

This verse is very self-explanatory, but within this verse you will see words like "Us" and "Our", speaking of One God in a plural form like a cluster of grapes. There is one cluster and many grapes. This singular-plural form that is used is showing us the three persons in the God-Head. The Father, Son, and the Holy Spirit, who created male and female in His image with a soul-spirit.

God saw all that He had made, and behold, it was very good. And there was evening and there was morning, the sixth day. Genesis 1:31

God was very pleased with all that He planned and He also created and made. All things were in the state of sinless perfection at that time.

Man's Creation Was Direct, Special, and Immediate From God's Spoken Word

In Genesis 1:26, God says He will create man and in the next verse (Genesis 1:27) we can see that God created man in a special way in God's image. We can also see from this verse that God was very direct and to the point. From there we can see that God's creation of man was immediate and prompt. So, one can easily see and understand that man did not evolve from slime over thousands or millions of years. Also, man did not branch off from some form of primate like an ape or monkey. All these are false and all these non-factual statements are what the evolutionist teaches. Man is special because he is created in God's image. God promptly created man, and God, by His direct spoken Word, brought man into being. We can see all of this in the next verse:

God created man in His own image, in the image of God He created him; male and female He created them. Genesis 1:27

Next, the Word of God, the Bible, tells us how God made this first living man. God also named him Adam. We see this in Genesis 2:20. This is how God made the first man:

Then the LORD God formed man of dust from the ground, and breathed into his nostrils the breath of life; and man became a living being. Genesis 2:7

Again, the creation of man came about directly because God made the soil and the minerals of the earth, and artistically and scientifically, in proper proportion, made the form of the first perfectly-formed man. Then God did something very special with this form of a man; He breathed into this form of a man. Another way of saying this is God inspired His breath into man. This word "inspired" is also how God gave us the Bible. We call this the inspired Word of God (2 Timothy 3:16). Out of all the things God created such as animals, plants, planets, etc., it is only man that God has breathed into life. This is why all humanity is so special to God. After God breathed into this form of a man, life was immediately given and the form became the first living man called Adam.

Then God Made Adam the Man and a Female Companion Called Eve

There are two facets of God's creation of man. God made male and female differently. As we can see, God created the male, Adam, first from the earth then God gave Him life by God's breath (Genesis 2:7). The female was made in a totally different way. The Bible says that God put Adam in a deep sleep and then God took a rib from Adam and then healed Adam by closing him up. We can see this in Genesis 2:21. It was at this time God made a wonderful female called Eve. With the rib from Adam, God had all the making of a new person. God made a whole new person from a rib. Another thing is God made a different type of person in His image. He made a female from a male rib. God, with all His miraculous power, had all He needed to make this wonderful female to be with Adam. The rib came from the first man, who had God's breath in his being that gave him life. By this the first woman was given a soul and spirit, as well as a will, intellect and emotion as Adam, but in a female way.

Just a side note: Every person that has been born from the time of Adam and
Eve has gotten their soul from their parents. This is why the Author believes
that cloning may seem successful with the animals but is a very dangerous
science in attempting to clone humans. The reason being is that if a person, at
the time of conception, receives a soul from their human parents through the

proper reproductive process from a sperm and an egg.
Cloning a person would
leave the cloned person without a complete human soul,
but would be replaced by
or possessed by a spirit that doesn't originate from God.
This will be disastrous for the sake of the existence of
humanity in every way.

In the book of Genesis, the first book in the Bible, we can
see that God made this wonderful being called woman. Here
is the evidence:

The LORD God fashioned into woman the rib which He
had taken from the man, and brought her to the man.

The man said, "This is now bone of my bones, And flesh
of my flesh; She shall be called Woman, Because she
was taken out of Man." Genesis 2:22-23

God's Pattern for Man's Creation As Was Stated Earlier

God created man in His image and as well by His likeness.
We can see this in Genesis 1:26-27; 5:1-3; 1 Corinthians 11:7;
James 3:9. This means that man has a will, intellect and emotions as well as a soul-spirit. It is God who gives man a spirit,
but being made in the image of God goes further than that.
God gave man intelligence and the power to make decisions.
In fact, the power for man to make one's own decisions is
the greatest natural gift that God has given mankind. God
has created man to make decisions as a way to glorify Him,
but all things are needed to be in accord with His will. God
encourages the first couple, Adam and Eve, to multiply in a
fruitful, loving way and to have children like them. In fact,
God commanded it! The reason was to fill the whole earth
and rule and manage it. God gave the earth to man so that
he can be over all its creation (Genesis 1:28). God also told
them to work the earth to get food from trees and plants for

nourishment (Genesis 1:29). So it is God who has given man the power to make decisions in responsible innocence. We can see this in this next verse.

God blessed them; and God said to them,

"Be fruitful and multiply, and fill the earth, and subdue it; and rule over the fish of the sea, and over the birds of the sky and over every living thing that moves on the earth." Genesis 1:28

God Created Man to Have a Close Relationship with Him

God created man to have a personal relationship with Him. God also made man as a couple, Adam and Eve, to have a relationship with each other as well as with Him (Genesis 2:23). God never intended to create the world and then leave man alone as so many have thought through the centuries. God intended that Adam and Eve would multiply, have children and then those children would also have a close relationship with Him. God still wants a close relationship with all humans today, but if one doesn't believe in His Son, Jesus Christ, this relationship cannot and will not happen for the simple reason that sin has entered into the world.

Then the Lord God took the man and put him into the garden of Eden to cultivate it and keep it. Genesis 2:15

God supplied all the needs for man, and He also wanted man to benefit from his own decisions and proper choices that God gave him in the proper boundaries. God also wanted man to benefit in cultivating the garden by its beauty, joy, peacefulness and tasty nourishment from the fruit of the garden. God also protected the first male and female by telling Adam not to partake of only one of the trees. This tree was the tree of the knowledge of good and evil. If man partook of this tree, spiritual death would take place. This can be seen in Genesis 2:16-17. God also gave man the responsibility to name the animals that He formed. All the birds, and all the other animals, such as cattle, etc. God brought them to Adam and Adam named each and every one of them (Genesis 2:19-20). One must truly understand what this means: God brought all the animals to Adam, and Adam named them. In the insect world, which is the science of entomology, there are over 50,000 species of beetles (and at that time there could have been even more species of beetles, but today some may be extinct). Adam and Eve must have been so much greater in intelligence than we are today, because of the true purity in their life before they sinned. The thing I am trying to point out is that if Adam could name 50,000 species of beetles, his IQ must have been through the roof!

Just think about it! If Adam could name 50,000 species of beetles alone, his vocabulary capacity must have been enormous. There is not one man or woman today even with the ability of having a vocabulary of 25,000 words. But here is Adam, naming all different species, which is far greater then the human mind could even comprehend today.

The man gave names to all cattle, and to the birds of the sky, and to every beast of the field. Genesis 2:20

It is very unfortunate that man ever had to fall into sin against God.

God Has Made Man with the Ability for Transmission to Reproduce by His Being by Natural Generation

But what does this mean! We all know that animals can reproduce, but they are not made in the image of God according to the Scriptures. Because God breathed into Adam and gave him life, this gave the first man, Adam, a soul-spirit, with a will, intellect and a full range of emotions. This is because of God breathing into Adam with His breath. It gave Adam (man) an immaterial form of life within Adam's (man's) physical material form of life that is his body. It is by God's plan that all men and woman have this immaterial part that is the essence of being a human life, from God through Adam. Every human being who is a Christian or non-Christian has gotten their soul from their biological parents. This only has one exception and that is Christ Jesus, who is the Son of God. The reason for this is that the conception of Christ Jesus took place by God the Holy Spirit overshadowing Mary's sin nature that gave birth to a pure God-Man, who is totally sinless and could never sin. As mentioned earlier, Adam and Eve's sinful rebellion against God and humanity has placed humanity into a fallen state from that point on. So man's sin nature, along with his soul-spirit with a will, intellect, and emotions, has had a need and still has a need for a Savior who is Christ, and can only be Jesus Christ. Adam and Eve transferred their immaterial nature to their children, and we can see this in the next verse:

When Adam had lived one hundred and thirty years, he became the father of a son in his own likeness, according to his image, and named him Seth. Genesis 5:3

So Adam and Eve were made in the image of God (Genesis 5:1-2). Then Adam and Eve's children were made in the image of Adam, which includes Eve (or Man) as is found in Genesis 5:3. So, all of man is made in the image of God. Some may have trouble with this logic, but after the great flood that most all know about or at least have heard about, meaning Noah and the Ark that he built, God said this to Noah:

Whoever sheds man's blood,
By man his blood shall be shed.
For in the image of God
He made man. Genesis 9:6

From this verse we can see:

1. How precious man is to God.
2. That God doesn't take sin lightly.
3. Blood is required for life according to God.
4. God made man in His own image.

5. This image of God continues from generation to generation.

We can even see this in the New Testament, where it tells us that the great Old Testament prophet had a great-grandson by the name of Levi. But this part of Scripture tells us that before Levi was born, he was within his father Abraham (Hebrews 7:9) meaning great-grandfather Abram (Genesis 14:18-20). Then, in the front part of Hebrews 7:10, it tells us that Levi was within the parts or loins, meaning the immaterial part of the man being transferred from generation to generation, as well as the material physical part of man which we call today DNA.

A Deeper Look of the Nature of Man, Male and Female

The Scripture shows us that man is a bipartite unity of a material and non-material nature. We can see this in Genesis 2:7 at the creation of man. Jesus Christ tells us that the part that man needs to be concerned about between body and the soul is the soul. This is because God is the judge of the ongoing, everlasting part. This is because of one's need to have a faith in Christ as Lord and Savior to receive the outcome of everlasting life. But if a person has lived a life of rejection of Jesus Christ, the only alternative is to be separated from God and the bliss that He has to offer for eternity and that means being placed into the torment of Hell.

> Do not fear those who kill the body but are unable to kill the soul; but rather fear Him who is able to destroy both soul and body in hell. Matthew 10:28

The Apostle Paul also shows us that man is made up of this bipartite unity by mentioning the three components of man. Two of which are together and work together, which are the non-material part of man (called the soul-spirit part) and then the material part (which is the body). Paul goes on to say that God's goal is to give the believer peace and that He sets the believer apart so that He (God) will protect their entire spirit, soul and body for eternity.

> Now may the God of peace Himself sanctify you entirely; and may your spirit and soul and body be preserved complete, without blame at the coming of our Lord Jesus Christ. 1 Thessalonians 5:23

The Apostle James also tells us that physical death occurs when the spirit is absent from the body. This can be seen in James 2:26. Then the Apostle Paul takes this to another level as he tells us that when the believer dies in this life and their body is still on earth, the believer's immaterial part is safe and at home with Jesus Christ. This can be seen in 2 Corinthians 5:6-9.

The soul-spirit is central to one's spiritual and emotional experiences. But the difference with a man, as in comparison to an animal, is that man was created in the image of God. Many times in Scripture the soul and spirit are used interchangeably while reading through the Bible. As for the spirit, the Apostle Paul tells the believer that they do not have a spirit of fear or timidity:

> For God has not given us a spirit of timidity, but of power and love and discipline. 2 Timothy 1:7

Then the Apostle continues to tell the believer that they have a spirit as one, who is an adopted son with all the rights of a natural son. That son is able to call out to God with the loving title of "Daddy" as their loving Father. This is found in Romans 8:15. Then in the next verse, the Apostle Paul tells the believer that the Holy Spirit gives witness within the believer's spirit, letting them know that they are truly a child of God. Here's the verse:

> The Spirit Himself testifies with our spirit that we are children of God. Romans 8:16

Some may think the spirit of a man is the only thing that goes to God! But the soul also goes to heaven to be with God upon bodily physical death. We can see this because the Apostle John states that he saw souls in heaven and wrote this in the book of Revelation. The souls that John saw were the souls of those believers that died as martyrs, meaning those that died for the cause of Christ.

> ...I saw underneath the alter the souls of those who had been slain because of the word of God, and because of the testimony which they had maintained. Revelation 6:9

The next thing we all must understand is that man is not a spirit, but that man has a spirit. We can understand this by looking up these additional verses: Numbers 16:22; 1 Corinthians 2:11.

The Material Part of Man Consists of the Human Body as We All Know

If a person is a believer, they will receive a glorified body when the Lord Jesus Christ comes to get His believers, which is His church (Philippians 3:20-21). To the unbeliever they will not receive a glorified body, but will be raised and judged for their sin by the Lord Jesus Christ and be cast into Hell (Revelation 21:8). This will be covered more in detail when we get to the doctrine and major teaching of future events, also called eschatology.

The Fall of Man Due to Sin

When we look at Genesis 2:16-17, we can see the only boundary that God gave to Adam, and there was only one, was not to eat from a tree in the beautiful garden of Eden. The tree was the tree of knowledge of what is good and evil. God even told Adam that if he ate from this tree that Adam would be separated from God and die. The greatest natural gift that God has given to all humanity is power to make our own choices. This means that God gave humanity a free will. Well, we see in chapter three of the book of Genesis that Eve was deceived by the shining one; the serpent is the devil who is the enemy of God and all mankind. But because of Eve being deceived, Adam went along with it in a deliberate act against God. This is the fall of man. This is the first sin man committed against God. It was at this point that man acquired a sin nature, and at that point man was spiritually separated from God, that led to death. There are many other Scriptures in the Bible that tell us about the fall of man. Here are just a few:

(Romans 5:12-21)
Tells us that Jesus Christ is the only legal cure for this penalty of sin.

(1 Corinthians 15:1-22)
Tells us that faith in Jesus Christ and His resurrection is the only way to everlasting life.

The Fact and Results of the Fall of Man Due to Sin

Adam was responsible for the fall of man, even though Eve was deceived first. It was Adam who was created first, and Eve from Adam, so in this case the origin of this sin was Adam (1 Timothy 2:12-15). In these verses we can see that Eve laid out the un-royal red carpet to the fall and Adam took the walk. That is what brought the fall onto the whole human race. We can see this in Genesis 3:1-6. Then in Genesis 3:7-13, we can see the guilt of Adam's sin, and that is in Genesis 8-9, God who already knows of Adam's sin, even before He called out to Adam. This is seen in Genesis 3:9. We know that God held Adam responsible for the first sin even though Eve was deceived, because the all-knowing God called to His first created human, Adam. Then God gave out the consequences for this sin to all involved. It needs to be noted that because God is Holy, and He is all truth as well as loving, the consequences had to happen for the sin of man because God is not a liar.

The First Consequence Because Of Sin

God placed a curse on the serpent. God said to this shining, crafty, fork-tongued beast that he was to be considered the lowest in all in the animal kingdom. Then God forcibly humbled the serpent and said he would crawl on his belly as the reptilians do today. The serpent was lowered to the point of eating dust. We can say that God made the serpent as low as dirt. There are many kinds of dirt. The serpent was never to recover, but to remain in the lowest out of all the dirt positions, full-bodied over the dirt and eating dirt (Genesis 3:14). At this point God is speaking to this shining one, for this is what the word serpent means, the shining one. This is because God cannot be fooled; He knows that the devil was this tempting serpent, and therefore is the enemy of God as well as the unholy angels. Both are also the enemy of man. Then in the next verse (Genesis 3:15), God protects the human race by putting an antagonistic hostility between the serpent and the woman (Eve). This is why most women do not like snakes, lizards and most other reptiles even to this day. In the next part of the same verse of Genesis (3:15), God took care of the physical protection from the serpent even though Adam should have protected Eve from being deceived. God goes much further and gives a first prophecy from the point of this enmity. Let's look at this prophecy from God:

...and between your seed and her seed;
He shall bruise you on the head,
And you shall bruise him on the heel. Genesis 3:15

First we must realize that God is talking to the devil, who is the serpent in this situation. Then God is telling him (the devil) that there will be a battle between the evil seed of sin he planted into humanity. Then God goes on in the next statement and tells the serpent that this human (meaning Jesus Christ the God-Man) will ultimately destroy this devilish serpent by destroying his power source, which is his evil head. In the next statement God says that the devil will bruise this man (who is Jesus Christ) on the heel. This is a prophecy that is telling us about Jesus' death, burial and resurrection thousands of years before the Lord Jesus Christ came. This man that is the God-Man, Jesus Christ, will come to save humanity from their sin.

The Second Consequence: God will bring about suffering to the woman in childbirth

> To the woman He said,
> "I will greatly multiply
> Your pain in childbirth,
> In pain you will bring forth children;
> Yet your desire will be for your husband,
> And he will rule over you." Genesis 3:16

First, as was mentioned earlier, God held Adam responsible for the fall of man. But, God responds to the situation in the pattern that the problem occurred. First, God gives judgment to the serpent. Then, God gives judgment to the woman and then to the man. This obviously is a good pattern in handling family problems for us as humans; it corrects the irresponsible source that deserves the response in order (Genesis 3:14-19). God tells the woman that to bring forth children from this point there will be suffering involved. It is possible that Adam and Eve had other children before the fall of man and before sinning. Suffering has a way of making us feel like we are not in charge of our life and that we need help from someone near us. Eve didn't stay near Adam and this left an opening for trouble to enter into their relationship. But we must also understand that after one goes through suffering, many times it brings about great joy, wonder and beauty, when we truly look for the results that it brings when the suffering is over.

This is why in verse 16, God tells the woman that He will bring about suffering with the joy of childbirth. It is also very possible that when God created the universe and man that He had great joy, and the fall of man brought about a strong feeling of grief. In the last part of this verse God tells the woman that the woman is to be in a state of longing and yearning for her husband and that he will be the one to give order, guidance and hold to proper boundaries. This may not sound like the modern woman, but this form is to protect the marriage, the wife and the children in society. God set this plan because it is the most responsible and also the safest way, being that sin entered the world.

The Third Consequence

The man, Adam, is the one responsible for sin entering into the human race. Therefore, Adam is considered the federal head or the head of all of the human races and nationalities. Right down to the single person. From the time Adam became responsible for sin entering into the world, frustrated labor has occurred and death entered into humanity. We can see this in (Genesis 3:17-19, 5:5; Romans 5:12-14). Here is an example of how God upheld His Word to Adam:

Then to Adam He said, "Because you have listened to the voice of your wife, and have eaten from the tree about which I commanded you, saying.

'You shall not eat from it';
Cursed is the ground because of you;
In toil you will eat of it
All the days of your life." Genesis 3:17

The Scripture tells us also that shame and fear entered into the world because of sin (Genesis 3:7-10). Then, because Adam was sinful, God separated the man and woman from Him by impelling and forcing them out of the garden of Eden in which

God made by His creative power to give them bliss (Genesis 3:22-24). We can also see that death occurred because of Adam.

Therefore, just as through one man sin entered into the world, and death through sin, and so death spread to all men, because all sinned. Romans 5:12

So what is the cure? Who is the One who can save any sinful human from eternal separation and death? Here is the answer to both questions in one verse.

...so that, as sin reined in death, even so grace would reign through righteousness to eternal life through Jesus Christ our Lord. Romans 5:21

So the cure is God's grace, which is His favor and love toward humanity in an undeserving way. This means we can't work to get God's grace but God's grace is His gift to us. Jesus Christ is the One and Only One to cure the problem of death. He does this because of His righteous perfection as being fully God and fully Man. He is the One who can give everlasting life to any person, by that person putting their faith and trust in Him, by that person believing in His death, burial, and resurrection, which is Jesus Christ's victory over death for the sake of the believer.

22

THE MASTER TEACHING OR DOCTRINE OF SIN

The word sin is not something that is to be taken lightly, as mentioned earlier; it was one sin that put mankind into a state of frustration, suffering, struggling and death. The first to ever sin against God was an angel by the name of Lucifer who, after he rebelled and sinned against God, was then called Satan (Ezekiel 28:11-19). It was this Satan that appeared as the shining serpent to Adam and his wife Eve, that troubled both of them by deceiving Eve and tempting Adam to rebel against God. Because God is a Holy God, death had to occur due to their sin (Romans 6:23). Yet it amazes the author that humanity in general thinks so lightly of the word "sin" in this world, as well as their own personal life. God hates sin, but still loves the sinner. The word sin is synonymous with evil, wickedness, lawlessness, transgression and trespassing, etc. But humanity tries to cover the word sin with less threatening words like mistake, problem, emotional problem, psychological problem, and so on. I am not saying that there are lovely people out there without emotional and psychological problems, but there are many times people try hard to do the correct thing in life, but they are in a toxic family environment that can cause emotional and psychological problems in their life. But that does not mean that they are wicked, evil, of sinning. To go further with this word sin, there are some people who sin and call it a mistake and then joke about it. Then there are many who know that they are offending God by sinning, and couldn't care less and have no concern or remorse at all.

The definition of sin is lawlessness. This can be found in 1 John 3:4. It is also missing the mark or standard that God has set for humanity. This is similar to someone missing a target or missing the mark. Sin has been committed by all. This means all, including every single person: those in the highest Christian positions, and all other religious positions from the beginning until the end, and all the rest of humanity in between. The only One exception is Jesus Christ, who is the God-Man; He is fully God and fully Man. He is the one and only who could never, ever sin. It is Jesus Christ who is the only remedy for one's sin, giving eternal life. There are two basic words that come to mind about the types of sin. They are transgression and trespassing.

The Word Transgression is One Type of Sin

Transgression takes place when one does not do something that they need to do. Ignoring responsibility to do right to man and self, but especially to God. One example of a transgression is not paying a bill when you have the money to pay it. Another example is that if one were to see a truly starving person and not give them food to save their life. Another is not telling others about the true God of the Bible even though they are seeking for the true God. So this is sin that takes place when one knows the thing they need to do, but they choose not to do it. We can see this in James 2:1-9. From here, let's center in on the word transgression from the Scripture in this passage:

But if you show partiality, you are committing sin and are convicted by the law as transgressors. James 2:9

When one, as a true believer, understands that there is a need (as in the verses stated in James 2:1-13) in the sight of God that a poor man be known as just as important to God as a rich man. The poor need to be given dignity and no one is to set themselves up as a judge and make a partial choice for the rich over the poor or the poor over the rich. A very good example of a person who did not transgress and sin is the Good Samaritan in the Gospel of Luke (10:30-37). One other example of transgression is that all believers are to read and study the Scriptures on their own. How else can one know and understand God! Each and every believer is to have a close relationship with God. Reading and studying the Bible alone, with prayer, is an essential to have a good relationship with God. To not do this is committing the sin of transgression.

The Word Trespass Is another Type of Sin

Most people know what it means to trespass. I remember a cartoon as a child in which an old man put up a sign that said no trespassing, and here comes a trespassing hunter, and you can just imagine what the old man did to the trespasser: "KABOOM". Well, right away as a child I understood what to trespass meant. It means to go over a boundary. God's Word tells us of the boundaries we all need to keep in order not to sin. The Ten Commandments are a good example of boundaries that God wants us to uphold, and the believer knows that it is only by the power of God one can keep these commandments. Another example of a trespass is when the Apostle Paul in 1 Corinthians 5:1-13 has heard of a man in the early church doing an immoral act with his father's wife, and the church thought it was a big joke! But in reality, to the Apostle and to God, it was a trespassing sin against God. Other kinds of trespasses are: drug abuse, drunkenness, idolatry and even taking a Christian brother to court. This can be seen in

1 Corinthians 6:1-11. The book of Ephesians tells us that the true believer is not to trespass as he or she did before believing in Christ as Lord and Savior. This can be seen in Ephesians 2:1-3. The Apostle Paul also tells us that if you are a believer, you need to help a person by picking them up from their trespass in a firm, but kind, manner. We can see this in the next verse:

Brethren, even if anyone is caught in any trespass, you who are spiritual, restore such a one in a spirit of gentleness; each one looking to yourself, so that you too will not be tempted. Galatians 6:1

It was a man's sin against God that brought about a great distortion of His divine image. But not its total destruction. God created man to be shame free, guilt free and to not suffer or struggle in any way physically, mentally or spiritually. Because sin entered into the world, one will experience sickness of all sorts, either by oneself, or the powerlessness of a sick loved one not healing. Death is not from God; it is an affect of man's choice to sin. God tells us in His Word that if one man takes the life of a person, which at one time in the total innocence of humanity could not even be thought of or conceived of, God said that that person's life was to be taken.

Whoever sheds man's blood,
By man his blood shall be shed,
For in the image of God
He made man. Genesis 9:6

In the book of James (3:9), we are being told that man is so totally sinfully depraved, that we bless our God with our mouth and with the same mouth we curse man. Yet, man is made in the image of God. Here is the verse in mentioning the tongue:

With it we bless our Lord and Father, and with it we curse men, who have been made in the likeness of God. James 3:9

The verse above gives us a perfect example of the magnitude and deep-rootedness of the effect and infection of sin that all mankind has suffered from.

The Inheritance of the Sin Nature

Because of the sin of Adam, sin entered into our perfect human nature. Man is still made in the image of God. It is also true that man is the average size of all things in the creation, from the largest star to the smallest atom. Man is made of trillions of cells and all of these cells know where to go to form a brain, eye, etc., to ultimately form a whole human body. Modern science unfortunately tells us that this is all by chance. But any truly intelligent person, even a young child, can understand that there was a greater being (God) who started the whole process of creation and life. To go further, God created a human that is made in His image. But this human being rebelled and went against God's boundary, and a nature to sin was born and entered into this perfect human nature.

Realize that God gave man a free will and the power to make choices, but it was the one choice that God said He would not allow. Because of that choice, man became polluted by sin as Adam and Eve had children with their polluted nature and passed it on to their children, and their children's children, and so on to our current condition today. This is why we have the condition of death 'till this day.

> Therefore, just as through one man sin entered onto the world, and death through sin, and so death spread to all man, because all sinned. Romans 5:12

This verse shows us the origin of sin entering into the human race. Adam sinned because Eve was deceived. They opened themselves up to and received a nature to sin. They had children and they received their sin nature at conception, and so on to this day, and we (all humanity) have received our sin nature from our biological parents, and our parents from our grandparents. At conception a baby receives their sin nature from their parents and there is no escaping it. Babies may not have sinned in their infancy but they all still have a sin nature. The reason for this is simple: because they were born from sinful parents. Even if it were possible for a person not to sin, they would still be born into sin and have a sin nature and therefore would still be in need of a Savior. That Savior would still be Jesus Christ.

In the event that one may think that God would hold an unborn child responsible, or a young child, or even an adult who doesn't have the mental capacity to understand that they were born with a sin nature, we must realize that God knows all things. Therefore He also knows the age, as well the ability and capacity that a person has to understand their need for a Savior from their sins. The Bible teaches that the penalty for sinful man is eternal separation and death. We can again see this in the next verse:

> For the wages of sin is death, but the free gift of God is eternal life in Christ Jesus our Lord. Romans 6:23

In the beginning of this verse, we see that the outcome of sin is death and that death is the state of conscience eternal separation from God in the Lake of Fire or Hell. But what happens in the situation of an unborn or infant, or even an adult without the capacity for understanding their need for a Savior from their sin? In this case we can refer to the Old Testament book of Job (3:11-16). In Job 3:11-12, we need to understand that Job was in a state of extreme anguish. If we jump ahead and read verses 14-15, Job mentions adults who had a full life and where God appeared to bless them, giving them rest in their lives because they were waiting for the Savior to come. We can see that this rest Job is speaking of is found in verse 13. But again, Job mentions and connects those who had a righteous life, by looking forward to the Messiah and Savior in Old Testament, with those who didn't even have an opportunity to have a live birth. These children could have been aborted, stillborn, and to go one step further there are some others that are unfortunate. These are the ones who have a live birth and grow to full adults and yet would never have the mental capacity to understand their need of a Savior. According to these verses in Job 3:11-16, it appears that God has a special type of understanding love for them to give them a place of eternal resting life.

All humanity needs to know that it is only by God's grace that a man's sin can be forgiven through faith in Jesus Christ. One, on a personal basis, must receive the Lord Jesus Christ and believe that it was He who died in their place by the shedding of His blood to the point of death for the forgiveness of sins, and it was He who arose from the dead to justify the believer, giving the believer an everlasting life of bliss to come.

23

THE MASTER TEACHING OR DOCTRINE OF ANGELS

The Bible tells us that God created the angels. Angels are spiritual beings that can appear in a physical form, and yet are not physical. There are different ranks of angels and they are superior to man in many ways. There are un-fallen angels that are holy and spotless, that God created in their original state, and then there is another separated group that was and is rebellious to God. These are called the fallen angels or demons.

It is quite amazing to me that man believes there is life in outer space, and looks into space for some type of physical creature like an alien, or Martian from Mars, etc. But there is no true scientific evidence that there is any physical life in outer space. The person who puts all stock in the physical will be disappointed. The Bible tells us that there are millions upon millions of angels around us here on earth and in space. So is there life in outer space? The answer is yes! They are spiritual beings. Angels are in the highest heaven (this is the place of the first heaven) ministering to God. Then there are angels in outer space in the second heaven. Then, finally, there are angels in the lower heaven or the sky of the earth, and on, as well as in, the earth.

All the holy, spotless angels are ministering for God. The fallen angels that sinned are called demons and are always, in every way, working contrary to the will of God. Lucifer was at one time the top-ranking angel who first committed the sin of pride against God. God then took Lucifer, who also is called Satan, and threw him out of heaven along with a third of the angels which are called demons. So, where are the unholy evil beings? They are in the second heaven, which we call space, and the heaven that is earth's atmosphere. Yet man, in his foolishness, is looking, looking, looking into space in search of some physical life in outer space. There are thousands upon thousands of UFO sightings from people not having much to do, believing that they have seen other beings. These are counterfeit and delusional signs in the sky that God tells us would happen in Isaiah 66:4 and 2 Thessalonians 2:7-12. Here is the main verse of explanation:

> For this reason God will send upon them a deluding influence so that they will believe what is false. 2 Thessalonians 2:11

We must keep in mind that the devil, also known as Satan, is the most deceptive being of all, and that his goal and desire is to slow down, deceive, distract and turn people away from the will of God. Most of all, he does not want glory to go to God and he also would prefer that a person put their faith in a false god and never come to faith in Jesus Christ. The enemy wants, most of all, to turn others away so that there is no faith in Christ Jesus and His shed blood. This is because Christ took the place on the cross for all sinners of humanity who place their faith in Him. Jesus Christ is the only Son of the only living God. This is the spiritual war that is going on to this day until the Lord Jesus comes and sets up His kingdom here on earth. Let me remind you that we are all in this spiritual war. The question is who are you with? God's holy un-fallen angels are still faithfully doing the will of God by guiding, protecting and delivering those of God's elect (believers) because of their love and obedience to God.

Where Did the Angels Come From

The angels, as well as all other beings and things, were created by God. God created all spiritual and non-spiritual beings for His purpose. The purpose in this is that God is to have all the honor and glory (Nehemiah 9:5). Looking at the next verse in this chapter of Nehemiah, we can see that God is the maker of all things.

You alone are the LORD.
You have made the heavens,
The heaven of heavens with all their host,
The earth and all that is on it,
The seas and all that is in them.
You give life to all of them
And the heavenly host bows down before
You. Nehemiah 9:6

But where is Jesus Christ in the time of creation? Because Jesus is God, He was the major focal point of all creation. He is the rescuer from darkness. He is God the Son, the second member of the Godhead. He had and has all authority over all creation. That is why He is called the firstborn of creation, as well as the firstborn from death, because He conquered death. We can see this in Paul's letter that is in the Bible in Colossians 1:13-15. The next verse tells us that Jesus Christ as God the Son created everything, including the angels, and it also shows us His power and authority over all He has created.

For by Him all things were created,
both in the heavens and on earth,
visible and invisible, whether thrones or
dominions or rulers or authorities-all
things have been created through Him and
for Him. Colossians 1:16

Now that it is established that God created the angels, let's go deeper in our understanding of the Biblical truth of angels.

There are Different Ranks of Angels and Angels are great in Number

The Bible tells us of the different ranks of angels, such as the Cherubim listed in Exodus 37:9 and Ezekiel 10:8. There is another rank of angel called Seraphim. This is found in Isaiah 6:2, 6. The Bible tells us some of the names of some of the highest-ranking angels, such as Gabriel in Daniel 8:16 and Luke 1:19, 26. Then there is Michael, who is called an angelic prince in Daniel 10:21 and he is also called an archangel. We see this written in the letter of Jude in the New Testament.

But Michael the archangel... Jude 9a

As you can see from the Scriptures in the Bible, there are different ranks of angels. It is also most likely that there are other ranks of angels also not mentioned in the Scriptures, but one thing is for sure, there are a great many angels in great numbers. When we read through the Gospel of Matthew in Chapter 26, we can see how the Lord Jesus Christ was coming very close to the time of His crucifixion, and how Judas and the spiritually blind officials were setting the stage to have Jesus crucified. As this gang of officials went to get Jesus Christ to take Him through a process of false justice of their court system, Peter, the disciple who became the Apostle Peter, took out His sword and cut off the ear of the slave of the High Priest in defense of Jesus. Then Jesus healed the slave's ear and He rebuked Peter for doing that in His defense. Jesus tells us that if He chose to call upon His Father for help, He easily could have; for His own defense that God the Father would have sent twelve legions of angels. But how many did He say He could ask for? The answer is more then 72,000 angels. We get this answer because there are 6,000 troops in a legion. Here is how Jesus said it:

> Or do you think that I cannot appeal to My Father, and He will at once put at my disposal more than twelve legions of angels? Matthew 26:53

If 72,000 angels is not enough for you, how about millions multiplied into billions. When the Apostle John was brought up to the highest Heaven before the throne of God in Revelation 4:1-2, he witnessed this innumerable number of angels worshipping the Lamb of God, who is the Lord Jesus Christ.

Then I looked, and I heard the voice of many angels around the throne and the living creatures and the elders; and the number of them was myriads of myriads, and thousands of thousands. Revelations 5:11

When we look at this verse, we must understand that the cultural language of the time didn't have the words millions or billions. But we can see how John described the counting of the holy angels in a multiplex manner, basically saying there were great numbers by great numbers, and thousands by thousands, potentially multiplying into the billions or more of angels. One must also realize, in Heaven there are no limits as we are accustomed to on earth, such as time, space, gravity, etc. John was in heaven and he was not limited to what he could see. Here are some other verses about the rank and great number of angels: 1 Thessalonians 4:16; Hebrews 12:22; 1 Peter 3:22.

Angels Have Superior Abilities Compared To Man

Holy angels are God's servants that always obey God to the greatest extent in serving Him. They are powerful and mighty. Their intelligence is superior to man's, and they are swifter than any created being on earth, and swifter than all other things known to man. Because they have been created by God and are His servants, they rarely appear to man and are not to be worshiped. It is only God who deserves worship, no one else. For the true believing Christian, God has given the angels the responsibility to guard those that are of God's elect (His true believers).

For He will give His angels charge concerning you,
To guard you in all your ways. Psalm 91:11

I believe that angels start to minister to individuals from the time of conception, and at the time of death, they are the guards and protectors of a believer's soul into the entrance of Heaven, as we can see in the verse above. It basically tells us that God's will protects the believer in every way, here and beyond, into the presence of the Lord. Angels are so superior to man that they have the power to do things that humans can't logically understand. In the book of Acts, as the Apostle Peter and the other Apostles were in Jerusalem preaching and teaching to bring the Gospel forward and healing the sick and the afflicted, the high priest of the temple and those with him became envious of the Apostles and physically assaulted Peter and the other Apostles and threw them in jail. That same night, the Lord sent an angel to free the Apostles by opening the prison door and getting them out. Then the angel told them to go and preach the Good News of the Gospel in the temple. At that time, the high priest called for a major meeting and then gave an order for the Apostles to be brought in. Now the jail cell was tightly locked and also well-guarded all night, but when the cell was opened to take the Apostles before the high priest and the council, the cell was empty. This is the power and the intelligence of God's angel in getting them out of the cell for the sake of the Good News (Act 5:12-25). Here are the key verses for this topic:

But during the night an angel of the Lord opened the gates of the prison, and taking them out he said,

"Go stand and speak to the people in the temple the whole message of this Life." Acts 5:19-20

Here are some other verses about how superior angels are compared to man: Psalm 103:20; Isaiah 6:2; Daniel 6:22; 2 Kings 19:35; Luke 20:36.

All Angels Are Subordinate to God

We can see that God the Father tells us that Jesus Christ is God and not to mistake Him for an angel; therefore, all angels are subordinate to God the Son. But the key verse in showing us that Jesus Christ is the King, Lord, and Messiah (Christ) and that He is God is in the next verse. God the Father speaking of God the Son:

But to which of the angels has He ever said,
"SIT AT MY RIGHT HAND,
UNTIL I MAKE YOUR ENEMIES
A FOOTSTOOL FOR YOUR FEET?" Hebrews 1:13

This verse above tells us that God the Father would never make this statement to an angel but that He made it to His Son Jesus Christ. Then in verse 14 of this chapter, we see that all the Holy Angels are sent by God to minister and to help those that are elect to inherit the gift of salvation. Speaking of the Holy Angels:

Are they not all ministering spirits, sent out to render service for the sake of those who will inherit salvation? Hebrews 1:14

Humans are never in any way to worship angels! One can just imagine how beautiful and awe-striking they are. The Apostle John was in such great awe that he dropped down on his knees at the sight of an angel and even started to worship one. The angel then told this great Apostle to get up and stop, and not to worship him. Here is the verse to show us this wrong type of worship:

Then I fell at his feet to worship him. But he said to me, "Do not do that; I am a fellow servant of yours and your brethren who hold the testimony of Jesus; worship God. For the testimony of Jesus is the spirit of prophecy." Revelation 19:10

Not only does this verse tell us that humans are not to worship angels, but also that other believing humans, like apostles, popes, priests, pastors, etc., are to be servants in worshiping and glorifying only Holy God. Therefore, no human is to ever be worshipped, not even a pope. The other interesting thing about this verse is that all true prophecy always points to the saving work of Jesus Christ. Biblical truth is to always point to Jesus Christ the Lord over all.

It was prophesied in the Old Testament that the Messiah would come through the line of King David, and also that He would suffer and die on the cross and raise from the dead and save His people from their sins. Jesus Christ came and fulfilled all these prophecies and many, many more, and there are still more to be brought to fulfillment. All true prophecy is related to Jesus Christ and only Jesus Christ, no one else. What is meant by this is that there are many false predicting prophets today. They may say things unrelated to Jesus Christ and claim there are false events that are going to come. Do not be deceived; this is only to distract you and claim these unbiblical events as true prophecy. Here is an example: someone predicts that on July 8th of this year the world will come to an end. This can be from a false spirit or even a scientist. If this is a true prophecy, the Word of God would tell us that this date would be the end of the world! The Bible tells us that the Lord Jesus Christ will come again very soon but it never tells us what day or what hour in history He will come. If we look at 1 Thessalonians 5:1-11 we can see this:

> Now as to the times and the epochs, brethren, you have no need of anything to be written to you. 1 Thessalonians 5:1

So you see a person predicting the day or end of the end of the world is a lie. True prophecy is Biblical and points only to the work of Jesus Christ and we only get this in His Word, the Bible.

The Characteristics of Angels

There are many distinguishing characteristics and qualities to God's Holy Angels.

Their Appearance Is Beautifully Awe-Inspiring

All angels that are mentioned in the Bible appear to have male characteristics and the Bible states these Holy Angels as male. In the Old Testament we see an angel that looks like a man, dressed in pure white linen, and around his waist he has a belt made of the purest of gold. His body was similar to the glimmering of a diamond. He had beautiful and powerful, flaming eyes and as for his appendages, they were glimmering like highly polished brass. In all this power and beauty, his words were powerful and understandable. This is found in Daniel (10:5-6). The Apostle John states the appearance of an angel when he was in Heaven. He truly saw an awe-inspiring angel. Here is a list of some of these magnificent qualities about this one angel that John saw:

1. The angel was powerful.
2. He went down to the earth's atmosphere.
3. His clothing was in the appearance of a cloud.
4. A rainbow was emanating from his face. This means the rainbow was around his face, and as he moved, the rainbow moved with him.
5. The angel's face was like that of our Sun, very bright, warm and revealing.
6. The angel had feet that were stable and pure.

We can see all of these in the next verse:

I saw another strong angel coming
down out of heaven, clothed with a cloud;
and the rainbow was upon his head,

264

and his face was like the sun, and his feet like pillars of fire. Revelation 10:1

In the book of Matthew, chapter 28, it tells us about an angel that descended to the earth after Jesus Christ arose. As this angel came to the place were Jesus Christ was buried, an earthquake occurred. Then he removed the stone that was very secured over the tomb where the risen Christ was buried, and authoritatively sat on the stone that the Jewish leaders had placed over the tomb that Christ was buried in (Matthew 28:2). Here is what this angel's appearance looked like from Scripture:

> And his appearance was like lightning, and his clothing was as snow. Matthew 28:3

I believe this angel gave an appearance of God's Holy Power. The appearance of some great being who can talk, and yet have an appearance of lighting, is unfathomable. Also this angel was probably wearing purely white linen. This is symbolic of the angel's purity, as well as his earthy ministry to the believer.

Angels Have Superior Intelligence to Man

If you were to take all the knowledge, from the beginning of time to the very last day before the Lord Jesus Christ's return, this would in no way exceed the intelligence of the holy angels. The Bible numerous times tells us and shows us about the superiority of the holy angel's intelligence as in comparison to man. Here is a verse:

> ...But my lord is wise, like the wisdom of the angel of God, to know all that is in the earth. 2 Samuel 14:20

As was mentioned earlier, Jesus Christ was born of a virgin. The virgin's name was Mary. The conception of Jesus Christ can be seen in the Gospel of Luke (1:26-38). If we discern correctly the words of the angel Gabriel in Luke 1:26-38, because Mary was a virgin, how could this holy angel know that the Holy Spirit, the third person in the Godhead, was to conceive in Mary the Child that is to be fully God and fully Man? The angel Gabriel goes further in saying the Holy Spirit will also overshadow her. But what is meant by overshadowing Mary? This means that she (Mary) had a sin nature and that the Holy Spirit was going to overshadow her sin nature. This was all for the purpose of giving birth to a perfectly sinless Christ Child whose title would be the Son of God. The angel explained to Mary the plan and procedure of how this blessed miracle would happen, from the conception to the outcome. This defies human logic and science to this day. This is the superior intelligence of just one of God's holy angels:

The angel answered and said to her, "The Holy Spirit will come upon you, and the power of the Most High will overshadow you; and for that reason the holy Child shall be called the Son of God. Luke 1:35

Here are some other verses that show the superior intelligence of the holy angels: Matthew 13:41; 16:27; 24:30-31.

Angels are Mighty and Powerful

The Bible is very straightforward about the power and might of angels. Angels are not like humans, in that a human may attempt a goal or project, but because they are limited in their physical being, they may not be able to accomplish it. A good example is that of a weightlifter. The weightlifter may have the power to lift 400 pounds overhead, but even in his desire and love for the sport of weightlifting, he will never be able to lift 1,000 pounds overhead. It doesn't matter who encourages him or what he does, he will never lift 1,000 pounds overhead. Angels on the other hand, are not limited. If God tells them to do something, the angels in their might and power will perform the will of God and get the task done in the most instantaneous moment. They don't get tired or unfocused, and they don't get injured. They get the will of God done!

> Bless the LORD, you His angels,
> Mighty in strength, who perform His word,
> Obeying the voice of His word! Psalm 103:20

Holy angels are mighty and will be given the task when Jesus Christ the Lord returns. It will be the Holy angels that will be with the Lord Jesus and they will be responsible for justifiable punishment to those that have made believers suffer for their faith in the Good News of the Gospel. These angels are said to come in a flaming, glorious fire. This is found in 2 Thessalonians 1:3-8:

> ...and to give relief to you who are afflicted and to us as well when the Lord Jesus will be revealed from heaven with His mighty angels in flaming fire. 2 Thessalonians 1:7

The mighty angels of God will also gather all people that will have become believers after the church was raptured during the tribulation (also known as the Great Tribulation). This is to be read from Matthew 24:29-31.

Angels are Very Swift

In fact, when one reads the Scripture, they are the fastest of all created beings. In the Old Testament book of Daniel (9:20-23), we see this great prophet of God in prayer. Just as Daniel was at the beginning of his prayer for understanding, the Angel Gabriel in the appearance of a man went to Daniel in a vision and answered his prayer. This was extremely swift because angels are not limited by time. I'm sure that angels can move faster than the speed of light, which is 186,000 miles a second. Their speed and swiftness is incomprehensible. Here is the key verse that shows us how swift and quick an angel can move, this is what the angel Gabriel said to Daniel:

At the beginning of your supplications the command was issued, and I have come to tell you, for you are highly esteemed; so give heed to the message and gain understanding of the vision. Daniel 9:23

From that point on, the angel revealed the course of events called the "seventy weeks", and how the Messiah would come and die, and then after this the events that would lead to the end of this age. This can be read in Daniel 9:24-12:13.

Characteristics of God's Unfallen Holy Angels

They are Holy and Spotless
The word holy means that they are separate from any type of sin and they are sacred for God's service.

They said, "Cornelius, a centurion, a righteous and God-fearing man well spoken of by the entire nation of the Jews, was divinely directed by a holy angel to send for you to come to his house and hear a message from you." Acts 10:22

Other verses on the holiness of God's angels are found in Matthew 25:31; Luke 9:26; Revelation 14:10.

They Are Humble
This means that a holy unfallen angel of God doesn't allow himself to be provoked and only loves to serve and honor God in every way possible.

But Michael the archangel, when he disputed with the devil and argued about the body of Moses, did not dare pronounce against him a railing judgment, but said, "The Lord rebuke you!" Jude 9

If we read Isaiah 6:2 and 2 Peter 2:11, these verses show us that God's holy angels are humble.

They Are Obedient
God's holy angels are obedient only to God. They are not obedient to any other. This is why it is not only wrong for one

to pray to an angel (because only God should be worshiped and glorified), but because God's holy angels are only obedient to God's will and no one else, it is fruitless and sinful to pray to any angel. This is because he will only obey God not man.

> Bless the LORD, you His angels,
> Mighty in strength, who perform His word,
> Obeying the voice of His word! (Psalm 103:20)

Jesus Christ gives reference of the obedience of God's holy angels in the Lord's Prayer in Matthew 6:9-13. In verse 10 of the Lord's Prayer, it tells us of their holy, angelic obedience where the Lord Jesus says to the Father:

> Your kingdom come.
> Your will be done,
> On earth as it is in heaven. Matthew 6:10

This verse spoken in Scripture shows us that God's holy angels are always obedient to do God's will.

The Ministry of God's Holy Angels and Their Ministry of Guidance

God's holy angels in the Old Testament and New Testament have guided many by the great impression of their words of peaceful encouragement more so then their appearance. In their guidance, at times, they will also announce to the person or persons they are speaking to as an answer of God's fulfilled prayer. For instance, in Luke 2:10-12 we see an angel stating that in King David's city the Messiah is born (verse 11). Then in verse 12, we see the angel announcing an unusual fact about how to recognize this true Messiah in that He would be born and found in a manger and that He would be wrapped in pieces of cloth.

But the angel said to them, "Do not be afraid; for behold, I bring you good news of great joy which will be for all the people;

for today in the city of David there has been born for you a Savior, who is Christ the Lord.

This will be a sign for you: you will find a baby wrapped in cloths and lying in a manger." Luke 2:10-12

Verse 10, is the statement of encouraging guidance.

Verse 11, is guidance by history and prophecy.

Verse 12, is the evidence of this historical prophecy fulfilled that Jesus Christ the Lord is truly born and how He was to be found.

Before the New Testament was completed, angels would appear. But being that the true believer is indwelled with the Holy Spirit today and the canon of the Scripture, the Bible, is complete, all believers can understand God's guidance through the Holy Spirit's guidance. This goes also for the appearance of holy angels because every type of guidance is to be discerned through the Word of God, not by what we see. We have a very good example of this in Acts 8:26, where we see how Philip the evangelist was told by an angel to go to the south on a desert road. The angel didn't tell him why, but to just get going! In this verse it doesn't say that Philip saw an angel, but he heard an angel. Don't mistake this with someone claiming to hear random voices! This is not the case at all. All things for believers today are to be discerned through the Word of God. This is why it is so, so, so important to know the Word of God. Otherwise, false guidance can be false emotionalism, or even greater, deception, which is quite dangerous for the individual and others.

In this passage of Acts 8:26-40, we can see that this holy angel spoke to Philip and he heeded the words of this holy angel, and a eunuch from Ethiopia was saved because of Philip's teaching and evangelizing to him about the Lord Jesus Christ. Here is the key verse for this topic:

But an angel of the Lord spoke to Philip saying, "Get up and go south to the road that descends from Jerusalem to Gaza." [This is a desert road.] Acts 8:26

Some other verses that show us the ministry of guidance from holy angels to believers (Acts 10:1-7).

Their Ministry of Protection

The Old Testament has many examples of angels protecting believers. The prophet Daniel had a situation were he was trapped by the King's commissioners, stating that Daniel was a law breaker because he gave all his heart and loyalty to God first. It was these governing commissioners that proposed a law to the king in that he was to be worshipped as a god. Yet Daniel resisted this law because all his love and loyalty was for the true God. The king was respected by Daniel, but the corruption of the commission tried to find grounds against Daniel and convinced the king that Daniel was a law breaker, and that he should be put to death by putting him in the lions den. This all can be found in the book of Daniel (6:1-28). It was the God of Israel that protected Daniel from all the lions in the lion's den by sending an angel into the lions den to protect Daniel from this perilous situation. Here is the testimony of Daniel:

My God sent His angel and shut the lions' mouths and they have not harmed me; inasmuch as I was found innocent before Him; and also toward you, O king, I have committed no crime. Daniel 6:22

Jesus Christ, in Matthew 18:1-10, is teaching His disciples that they were not to be concerned about their status here on earth or in heaven. He used the example of a child and that as believers we are to go to Jesus in a childlike way. A child depends on their parents to fulfill their needs as it is Jesus

Christ who is the only one that can save us. We can do nothing to save ourselves so they had no need of asking for their status in heaven. As Jesus is teaching this concept to His disciples, He explains that God is very concerned about everyone, even those who have no status here on earth, such as the children, and that the angels are constantly ready to protect the little children. Angels are just waiting for God the Father to say something in the protection of the little children. Likewise, God is always protecting those that love Him by the protective ministry of the holy angels.

See that you do not despise one of these little ones, for I say to you that their angels in heaven continually see the face of My Father who is in heaven. Matthew 18:10

Here are some more verses about the protective ministry of God's Holy Angels: Psalm 91:11; Isaiah 63:9; Genesis 28:11-15; Exodus 14:19,23:20; 2 Kings 6:15-17.

Their Ministry of Comfort

Being that Jesus Christ is fully God and fully man, when He was on this earth Satan tried to trouble Him in every way, especially in trying to use His humanity as the God-Man (Jesus Christ) against Himself so He could corrupt Himself. But because Jesus Christ is fully God and fully Man, Jesus Christ could never sin or fall to the devil's corrupt power in any way. But the devil did all he could to make Jesus fall in His humanity. Jesus was without food for forty days and nights and also in the discomfort of the wilderness. After each time, the devil wasted his effort on Jesus and Jesus rebuked him with the verses from the Old Testament and basically told the devil to get lost. This can all be seen in Matthew 4:1-11. It was after the failure of the devil that angels came to bring comfort to the Son of God in His humanity. The angels did this by ministering to Him. This could mean all kinds of good things, such as food from heaven (called manna), praise, worship, etc. Yes! Even angel's comforted the God-Man Jesus Christ. Here is the verse that shows us this:

Then the devil left Him; and behold, angels came and began to minister to Him. Matthew 4:11

That was not the only time the angels comforted Christ. If we look in the Gospel of Luke (22:39-47), we see that before Jesus Christ was betrayed by Judas with a false kiss, He was at the Mount of Olives with His disciples to pray. Jesus, a good number of yards away, started praying to His heavenly Father, asking the Father if there was any other way to save sinners except that He be crucified. Jesus also said that if the Father was not willing, He would do the Father's will and accomplished it in every way. It was after this that God the Father sent an angel to comfort Christ in the worst impending trial of His life. Here's the verse:

Now an angel from heaven appeared to Him, strengthening Him. Luke 22:43

If Jesus Christ, being fully God and fully man, was comforted by angels as well as the prophets and the apostles, God can still send us angels to comfort His believers today. We may not see them, but God loves His children and knows how and when to comfort them. When we ask Him and even when we don't ask Him, He is always faithful to comfort His own. Here are other verses that will shed light on the comforting ministry of angels: Genesis 16:7-13, 28:10-12; 1 Kings 19:2-8; Acts 27:23-24.

Their Ministry of Deliverance

King David mentioned angels numerous times in the Psalms as defenders and protectors of God's true believers. Yes, those that honor God are protected and delivered out of their troubles according to God's perfect will. We can see this from the statement of this King and Prophet, David, in Psalm 34:1-7. Here is the verse that tells us of God's rescuing deliverance:

The angel of the LORD encamps around those who fear Him. And rescues them. Psalm 34:7

In the book of Acts we can see this ministry of deliverance by God's Holy angels in the situation of the Apostle Peter being thrown in jail for a second time by King Herod. We can see this incident in Acts 12:1-17. The Apostle Peter was closely guarded by four small groups of soldiers and placed in jail and held by two chains, stuck in between a guard on his left and one on his right, and had other soldiers guarding him at the door of the jail cell. Peter was in total lockdown. Pretty tight, wouldn't you say? Not for God and His power working through the deliverance ministry of His angels! Here is the key verse:

And behold, an angel of the Lord suddenly appeared and a light shone in the cell; and he struck Peter's side and woke him up, saying, "Get up quickly." and his chains fell off his hands. Acts 12:7

Basically, this holy angel told Peter to get ready because he was going to get him out of the jail and he did. This is seen reading the rest of this passage in Acts 12:8-11. Here are some other verses on the ministry of deliverance by God's holy angels: 1 Kings 19:5-7; Acts 5:19.

Their Ministry Of Judgment

Because God is a holy loving God, He is also a just God. His holy angel's are like the police that enforce God's judgment. Therefore, God's holy angel's have a ministry to enforce judgments. This topic of God commanding His judgments is very uncomfortable for many to understand, but it is still a fact that those who reject God's Son, the Lord Jesus Christ, will be judged for their sins and suffer eternally. If you are a believer, you are not to fear God's eternal judgment. The reason is because your sins were judged on the cross with Christ. The judgment that falls on the non-believer, one who is not in Christ because they have rejected God's forgiveness in Christ, is a form of God repaying the ungodly for afflicting the believer. This can be seen in 2 Thessalonians 1:6-10. In verse 6, the Apostle Paul tells us why a loving God will come and send His holy angels to minister judgment:

For after all it is only just for God to repay with affliction those who afflict you. 2 Thessalonians 1:6

Then in verse 7, we can see that Jesus Christ will be seen from heaven with His holy, fiery-looking angels to bring this judgment to the hardhearted unbelievers.

Angels have already administered judgment as far back as in the book of Genesis. One example is in Genesis 19:1-29, with the doom of Sodom and Gomorrah. An angel even administered judgment on Israel, but God stopped the Angel from destroying Jerusalem (2 Samuel 24:1-17). Just how severe can an angel's judgment be? For this, we can see how powerful and swift one of God's holy angel's ministering judgment was.

Then it happened that night that the angel of the LORD went out and struck 185,000 in the camp of the Assyrians; and when men arose early in the morning, behold, all of them were dead. 2 Kings 19:35

This angel of God took this enormous amount of enemy soldiers out with one quick strike. The reason is, God was defending His City, also known as the City of David. This shows us the power of the ministry of God's holy angels.

The Corruption and Evil of Fallen Angels

The leader of the fallen angels is the devil, the total enemy of God and of all godliness. Therefore, he is the enemy of all mankind who was made in the image of God. Along with that, the devil also tries to stop the believer's spiritual growth toward the One and only true God. He is the enemy of life. Another word for the devil, as you may know, is Satan. Many people know these names for him but what a lot of people do not know is that he was a holy angel at one time. His name then was Lucifer, which means "son of the morning". This angel by the name of Lucifer was of the highest ranking of the angels. He was a cherub in rank. In the book of Ezekiel (1:5-14; 10:8-22), we see other cherubs ministering and glorifying the Lord God after the fall of Lucifer. In fact, it was Lucifer who was the closest to the triune God (the Father, the Son and the Holy Spirit) before Lucifer committed sin—and a great sin at that! It was the sin of pride! This angel sinned and thought in his pride that he was going to make himself greater than God. This can be seen in Ezekiel 28:12-19, and Isaiah 14:12-14. Just in the passage alone we can see the epitome of pride in this fallen unholy angel, who is now titled Satan:

How you have fallen from heaven,
O star of the morning, son of the dawn!
You have been cut down to the earth,
You who have weakened the nations!
But you said in your heart,
"I will ascend to heaven;
I will raise my throne above the stars of God,
And I will sit on the mount of assembly
In the recesses of the north.
I will ascend above the heights of the clouds;
I will make myself like the Most High." Isaiah 14:12-14

Because this cherub, who was the highest in rank and position, sinned in the worst manner of pride, God took Lucifer who became Satan and all the angels that sided with his wickedness and cast them out of heaven. Therefore, it is God who will judge them for their fatal, eternal sinful error. This will all happen in God's time for it is God who allowed this, but it is God who is in control of all things at all times. The small letter that Jude wrote to the Christians found in the New Testament says:

And angels who did not keep their own domain, but abandoned their proper abode, He has kept in eternal bonds under darkness for the judgment of the great day. Jude 6

If a person is a true believer in Jesus Christ, they need to persevere in the faith. Believing in Christ is not just a position as His child, and then run off and not grow. But healthy children grow and don't stop growing. After all, they are a child of God. Why wouldn't they want to grow stronger and deeper in faith? Here are some other verses about this topic: Jude 9; 1 Timothy 3:6.

The Fate of Both Satan and the Fallen Evil Angels

Because of the rebellion of Satan's pride and those fallen angels called demons, God has a severe terror awaiting them. This will be sudden, painful, destructive and punishing into the lowest and most confining place. This is what God has been waiting for. He is waiting for the right moment, so He will be able to cast these destroyers of life into Sheol. Some may not be familiar with this name, but a more universal name is Hell. Here is what the Bible says is waiting for the devil:

Nevertheless you will be thrust down to Sheol,
To the recesses of the pit. Isaiah 14:15

It has always amazed me that some call themselves Christians and say there is no such thing or person as the devil or Satan, or even the bad place called Hell. Well, if that was not true, what need would there be for the Savior Jesus Christ to die for our sins and to be buried and resurrected for the believer? In fact, if a person says that the devil doesn't exist, or even Hell for that matter, they are in denial of the Word of God and cannot be a true Christian. Let us look and see what the Apostle Peter has written about this under the inspiration of God the Holy Spirit.

For if God did not spare angels when they sinned, but cast them into hell and committed them to pits of darkness, reserved for judgments. 2 Peter 2:4

As we can see from this verse, there are evil angels called demons of whom the devil is the leader, and there is a Hell and there is no way around disbelieving this. In the Gospel of Luke (10:17-18), we can see two real and truthful things in verse 17. We see the mention of demons subject to the name of Jesus, showing us that demons, who are fallen angels, do exist. In verse 17, Jesus Christ tells us that He actually saw Satan get thrown down from heaven. If one goes to Revelation 20:1-15 in the Bible, you will see the final doom of Satan and the enemies of God in the fiery lake being described, and that the believers are written in God's book of life.

Here Is the Character of Satan and His Demons and Some of the Evil One's Names:

Belial, means lawlessness
Beelzebub, means the ruler of evil spirits
Apollyon, means the destroyer
Satan, means adversary
Devil, means slanderer

Just by looking at the names and meanings of the names of this enemy of God, we get a good idea of the hate he has for God and God's creation.

Satan's Wickedness

Just by understanding the names of Satan, we can see that he is not of God and that he truly hates mankind so much that he even hates those blind and wicked people that love and worship him as their god. One of the most wicked things that Satan does is that he steals the Good News of God's Kingdom away from someone so that they do not accept the one and only true God and Savior, who is the Lord Jesus Christ. He, the devil, does this to steal glory away from God and so one will not receive eternal life. Here is what Jesus says about this in His own words to us:

When anyone hears the word of the kingdom and does not understand it, the evil one comes and snatches away what has been sown in his heart. This is the one on whom seed was sown beside the road. Matthew 13:19

From God's view of all things, this stealing that Satan does to God is one of the worst of the devil's schemes of wickedness. One thing that we must all understand is that God deserves all the honor and glory because it was He who gave us life. Therefore, it is God only who should be in our heart and mind at all times. It is God who commands us to love others, even our enemies. But many people are also blinded by Satan, in that they believe that all people are true children of God. This is not true. This is another very deceptive, great lie of wickedness from the devil. Again, here is what Jesus Christ, the one and only Savior of the world in heaven and on earth, said about those who did not want to accept, receive and believe in Him as Messiah and Savior.

"You are of your father the devil, and you want to do the desires of your father. He was a murderer from the beginning, and does not stand in the truth because there is no truth in him. Whenever he speaks a lie, he speaks from his own nature, for he is a liar and the father of lies. But because I speak the truth, you do not believe Me. John 8:44-45

Very powerful words from God the Savior! Do you think that Jesus hated these men He said this to? The answer is no, He loved them enough to tell them that Satan had them in his wickedness and He wanted them to wake up and turn to Him, Jesus, who is the King and Lord of all. What Jesus did hate was their sin, the lying and their pride. They stubbornly thought their own way and not God's way. This is the work of wickedness of the devil known as Satan. Jesus also tells us that it is God who can keep us out of evil. This can be seen in the Lord's Prayer in Matthew 6:13. We are also told that the person who habitually enjoys sin and has no concern for their evil deeds of sin is of the devil. This is how wicked Satan works through some, even to the point of murder (1 John 3:8, 12).

Satan's Hateful Power

He, the devil, blinds the unbeliever. The Apostle Paul gives us two examples of Satan's hateful power. As we all know by now, Paul was given a mission by God to preach the Gospel to the whole known world at the time. But even Paul understood about the hateful power of Satan. We can see one example of how the devil blinds the hearts and minds of unbelievers in Acts 26:16-20. Paul basically is saying that he did nothing wrong, even down to the customs of his Jewish people. Even the Romans said he was guiltless, and yet still the Jews called for his death, and there he was in front of his people in Rome in chains and guiltless. Why? Because even though the Jews were waiting for the Messiah and He came to His people, Satan blinded the Jewish leaders of that day and put Jesus to death. Paul was experiencing just a little of what Jesus Christ went through, even to the blinding power of unbelievers trying to put Paul, this Great Apostle, to death. This is what Paul said about this experience He had in Jerusalem:

...Brethren, though I had done nothing against our people or the customs of our fathers, yet I was delivered as a prisoner from Jerusalem into the hands of the Romans. Acts 28:17

Satan Can Hinder Believers from Service

If you are a true believer, and if you have ever had a great eagerness to bring the Kingdom of God forward by doing God's will (Matthew 28:19-20), there is a great probability that you have encountered hindrances from the enemy, the devil, as the Apostle Paul did in 1 Thessalonians 2:17-20. But one must always remember that God knows the loving desires of your heart. Acting to the point of the enemy's hindrances still counts in the sight of the true God.

For we wanted to come to you–I, Paul, more then once-and yet Satan hindered us. 1 Thessalonians 2:18

Satan is Very Very Subtle

The meaning of the word subtle gives us an understanding that projects a sense of "under" or "beyond the understanding of a base level of something". Such as when one looks up through a telescope to see a planet, one cannot see the ground one is standing on or anything below the telescope for that matter. In the same way, Satan is very subtle in many ways to cause one to fall into sin, which creates a lack of glory to God and which causes harm to oneself. Just think of smoking cigarettes. They are costly, habitual, cancer-causing and not truly pleasing if one is truthful to admit it! And not only does smoking affect you, but also those around you. All in the realm of minor irritation, and up to and including physical death. But all of this is very, very subtle. This is how the devil works. If we look at Matthew 4:1-11, we see that Jesus Christ was fasting for forty days and nights in the wilderness and was very hungry, to say the least. Jesus was in a state of physical weakness, and here comes Satan to trouble Jesus to see if he (Satan) perhaps could make a suggestion using the Word of God incorrectly so that Jesus would hear it and act on it. We can see this in Matthew 4:4-11. But Jesus rebuked Satan correctly with the Word of God and then Satan left. This is proof that Jesus Christ is God in a fleshly body and could never sin because He is God. This passage is also a warning to all of us, and shows us how easy it could be for us to fall into sin in our weakest moments, being tempted by the devil and his demons.

Satan is very subtle; to the point that if we as humans have a great success, he could tempt us to sin and we could fall. Satan tried this with Jesus Christ the God-Man. As we can see, Jesus was very aware of this and the outcome is that Jesus defeated the devil's attempt in troubling the Lord Jesus Christ as if He could sin.

After Jesus Christ fed the five thousand men (plus women and children) with leftovers to spare in John 6:1-15, we can see the crowd looking and seeing this great miracle as a sign that Jesus was the Great Prophet that they were looking for.

So, Satan used this opportunity to subtly stir them up and have them try to forcefully make Jesus their king. The crowd was so tempted that they wanted to make Jesus king by force. But Jesus got away from this situation because He knew He was first to be crucified, raised from the dead and ascend into heaven and then come back as the King of all Kings. Satan wanted to throw the order of God's plan out of order, so man would not have a Savior. Here again, we can understand the devil's subtle trick that again did not work!

So Jesus, perceiving that they were intending to come and take Him by force to make Him king, withdrew again to the mountains by Himself alone. John 6:15

Satan is so subtle that he has even infiltrated people here on earth. Some people are claiming that they are doing God's will, and some even go as far as claiming that they are equal to Christ's original apostles and therefore deny the Word of God and are false. One can see this in 2 Corinthians 11:10-15. Anyone who claims to be any servant of God and denies the Bible as the true Word of God is a liar and is taking part in the lying wonders of Satan.

No wonder, for even Satan disguises himself as an angel of light. 2 Corinthians 11:14

But there is even a greater lying type of wonder to come. He is called the lawless one, evil to the core of Satan himself, also known as the antichrist. One can read about this one who is called the antichrist in 2 Thessalonians 2:1-12. He is to appear after a falling away from Jesus Christ, and I believe we are currently in the falling away or we are very close to it. The antichrist will be so wicked that he, in every way, will put himself in the place of God. He will achieve all this in a very subtle, lying way by the power of the enemy who is Satan. The Apostle Paul tells us about the antichrist and the power he will have to achieve this blasphemous wickedness:

...that is, the one whose coming is in accord with the activity of Satan, with all power and signs and false wonders, and with all the deception of wickedness for those who perish, because they did not receive the love of the truth so as to be saved. 2 Thessalonians 2:9-10

Satan and His Hateful Work

Because Satan rebelled against God and God threw him, and about one third of those angels that sided with this evil one out of Heaven, Satan and his demons have tried in every way to take glory away from God the Creator by trying to turn man away from God. Here are just a few of his (Satan's) tactics:

He is A Tempter

How does he tempt mankind? Through the pride of this world. This means the worldly overall system that is to the demise of mankind. We can see this in 1 John 2:15-18. The Apostle John tells us that a love for the world system is not of God. He even goes as far as telling believers that a person who loves the ways of this lustful world, by one's desires, or by what one sees and believes, that this is not of God because one's heart and eyes are to be looking to God's perfect will. Otherwise, the outcome is pride. One then says I wanted this position, possession or power, and they leave God out of their life, and this leads them forward to the destruction of one's own soul as well as those around them. This is what believers are to do according to the Word of God written by the Apostle John:

The world is passing away, and also its lusts; but the one who does the will of God lives forever. 1 John 2:17

Look to God, not to the world system that Satan works through to destroy. Satan tempts in our human need and weakness to sin (Matthew 4:3). Only Jesus Christ never sinned.

We are to call on Jesus the God-Man to overcome the power of temptation. Satan tempts by keeping one's mind in blind darkness so they cannot recognize the light of the world who is Jesus Christ, God the Son. We can see this in the Gospel of John (1:1-14). Every person that hears the Word of God, which is the Light, is responsible to accept God's Light. But because of the darkened heart of man's pride and the tempting work of Satan, they in their foolishness reject the truth of the work of Jesus Christ the Savior, and because of this they are lost. But to the one who accepts the saving Light who is Jesus Christ and His work, they receive everlasting life. Here is the verse of man's responsibility to God:

There was the true Light which, coming into the world, enlightens every man. John 1:9

So you may say "okay, one has accepted Jesus Christ and all is okay right!" Well, yes, if there is perseverance in their faith in Christ, all is okay. We can see that the Apostle Paul was very concerned about perseverance, even in a time of affliction of Godly leaders as Paul was an example for believers. Satan tempts also by afflicting and suffering to weaken the faith of others. We can see this in 1 Thessalonians 3:1-5. If we look at verses 4-5 of this passage we can see that the Apostle Paul is very concerned that the saints would become fearful and lose heart. In other words, falling away from the true faith.

For indeed when we were with you, we kept telling you in advance that we were going to suffer affliction; and so it came to pass, as you know.

For this reason, when I could endure it no longer, I also sent to find out about your faith, for fear that the temper might have tempted you, and our labor would be in vain.1 Thessalonians 3:4-5

ALL TRUE BELIEVERS MUST PERSEVER IN THEIR FAITH!

These are just a few ways that Satan tempts mankind to go against a HOLY LOVING GOD!

He is The Deceiver

The word deceive is the opposite of decent. To deceive someone means to act upon misleading someone, whereas decently is to be respectfully adequate. The book of Revelation tells us that Satan is the deceiver of the entire world:

> And the great dragon was thrown down, the serpent of old who is called the devil and Satan, who deceives the whole world; he was thrown down to earth, and his angels were thrown down with him. (Revelation 12:9)

As the deceiver, he is responsible for all the falsehood of lying in such as the so-called false unbiblical facts, theories and of course lying in general. He even attacks believers with the deception of compromising the Good News of the Gospel. The Gospel is simple, but man tries to subtract or add to it, to blind a person to some other way of thinking. The true Gospel is the liberty of living in the Grace of God through the Word of God. When someone is trying to hedge a believer away from the Good News of God, it is this hedging that is not of God, but from Satan. It is every believer's responsibility to know the truth about the Word of God and to stand and strongly hold to it.

In the book of Galatians (1:3-7), we see the Apostle Paul telling the saints of Galatia that it was by God's grace, which is God's unmerited, undeserved gift because of the Lord Jesus who voluntarily died on the cross for their sins, that they are given a new life that is everlasting. Yet they are abandoning Christ and are headed for a wasteland of some other false gospel that is not true, right, real, or good and above all, not from God (Galatians 1:6).

Paul put this matter under a microscope. Why? Because no distortions are to be made to the Gospel of Christ, not even in the slightest. Then he says that the Gospel is actually not different but that some others have taught it to you differently, and the outcome is that they (those hearing it) are intruded upon and their hearts are troubled. But it goes further than this. Because the deceptive work by Satan works through the falseness of those teachers, it appears to be a different Gospel and the Grace of God is maligned. Believers are not to allow Satan to deceive them at all; they are to hold fast to the true grace of the Gospel of Jesus Christ! Here is the verse that backs this up not to accept a different Gospel:

> …which is really not another; only there are some who are disturbing you and want to distort the gospel of Christ. Galatians 1:7

So, we can see by all this that Satan can deceive by using so-called religious men to trap you into thinking in an unchristian way by putting aside the Grace of God.

He Is a Tormentor

The words "to torment" can vary in meaning from harassing, which can be very disturbing and destructive, to the point of very painful torture, near to the point of death.

Satan Torments Mankind by Suffering and Sickness

He does this for a number of reasons, such as he wants mankind distracted away from glorifying God. He wants God to get the blame for sickness and death. Sometimes it is not the person who is suffering the torment that fails God, but it is those that are around the tormented one that Satan has the goal of distracting away from God. Such as them saying things like, "I can't handle caring for this sick family member and where is God?" Or there are some that say "thank God I am not like that person." Satan distracts mankind away from God by despair or pride in some form. All because he is a tormentor and because he knows mankind has a nature to sin. In the book of Acts (10:38), we see the Apostle Peter stating that Jesus Christ was from God and that proves that He (Jesus) had the power of God by the Holy Spirit, because He healed many that were tormented by Satan.

Jesus Christ did heal many from the torment of the devil and in the Gospel of Luke (13:10-16), we see one incidence in that He healed a woman with an oppressing spirit. This was not a bad backache, because if it was a bad backache we would see something in the Scripture telling us about her pain. Even though she was bent in two, she could still walk to Jesus. When the unclean spirit was released, she was able to stand straight immediately without Jesus ever touching her. Yet Satan was still doing his evil work, because those in the synagogue wanted their control over God and His Messiah. This is what Jesus said to them:

And this women, a daughter of Abraham as She is, whom Satan has bound for eighteen long years, should she not have been released from this bond on the Sabbath day? Luke 13:16

God sometimes allows something to come into our life in the area of ill health to keep us humble, so we do not become prideful in our own self. God allows Satan just enough rope to accomplish God's goal and plan. This can be seen in 2 Corinthians 12:7-9. We can see this in verse 7. The Apostle Paul understood this because he was given an extraordinary vision from God in the highest third heaven. Here he explains this to us:

Because of the surpassing greatness of the revelations, for this reason, to keep me from exalting myself, there was given me a thorn in the flesh, a messenger of Satan to torment me—to keep me from exalting myself! 2 Corinthians 12:7

In verse 8, we can see that Paul prayed three separate times to remove this thorn of torment. No one really knows what the thorn was: bad eyes, pain in the hand etc., no one knows. But in verse 9, we can see God's answer to Paul's three prayers for the torment removal. God basically told Paul that His grace is all he needs and that God's power is made perfect in working through human weakness! This is why God allows for human weakness, so that God's power can be exalted through us!

Another Way That Satan is a Tormenter is That He Tempts Believers to Deny Christ and His Saving Work

We can see this in the case of Simon Peter and his denial of the Lord Jesus in Luke 22:31-62. Within this passage, we can see how Satan tries to break a believer down to the point of denial of Christ as Lord and God. In verse 31 of this passage, Satan makes a demand toward Simon (also called Peter) to destroy his faith. In verse 32, we see Jesus telling Peter He has prayed for him, and after Simon Peter goes through this ordeal and he still has faith, then he is to strengthen his believing brothers in their faith in Christ.

Jesus said that the rooster would crow after Simon Peter denied Him three times. In verse 61, we see Jesus turn to Peter and then he (Peter) remembered what Jesus told him. We can see Peter's response to this torment in the below verse:

And he went out and wept bitterly. Luke 22:62

Another Way Satan Torments is That He is the Instigator of Persecution

Why persecution? Because it can bring fear, poverty, suffering and disgrace. Persecution gives a feeling of not knowing what to expect next, with the full intent of hatred behind it for one's loved ones or for oneself. One always wants to hold to their faith and not be injured, yet there are some whose faith will turn into disbelief if persecution is allowed. But God will reward those that have lack of physical strength and it is God who will supply assurance in their faith to the point of beyond this life. He will supply assurance to the point of glorifying Himself, who is a true One who rewards those that gave their life for their Christian faith. God knows full and well who the instigator of tormenting persecution is. This next verse will show us that. This is Jesus Christ speaking:

Do not fear what you are about to suffer.
Behold, the devil is about to cast some of you into prison, so that you will be tested, and you will have tribulation for ten days. Be faithful until death, and I will give you the crown of life. Revelation 2:10

In this verse there are two things that need to be clarified. The number ten (as in the days) of the Bible is a number of completeness; meaning don't lose your faith, follow it through to the point of giving your life. Next, Jesus is telling us that the one that loses their life because they stood up to the torment of persecution to the point of giving their life for their faith in Him (Jesus Christ), that He (Jesus) would literally reward them for their faith by crowning them because they overcame the tormentor.

Satan also Torments Because He Has the Power of Death

Every time you see a cemetery of any type, this is not the work of God, but of the tormenting power of death from Satan. Satan enjoys hurting people; therefore, he has no partiality to who he torments by death. The death of an unborn child, child, parent, grandparent, spouse or friend, makes no difference to Satan. This is his work and not God's work. But he brings torment to this life so people will put the blame on God and not on themselves through their own nature to sin against God. This is because Satan tries to put every man in the ultimate place of torment. This ultimate place of torment is the Lake of Fire, which is where Satan is also going (Revelation 20:10). This is the reason why Jesus Christ the God-Man had to take on a human body of flesh and shed His blood to the point of death, so He would make Satan powerless in this way and take away the sting of death to those that believe in Him, Jesus Christ as Lord. But to those who reject Jesus Christ as their Lord and

Savior, they give Satan what he wants and that is to be with him in eternal torment, which is Hell. The Word of God tells us that the torment Satan has is the power of death. This next verse tells us how Jesus Christ took this power of torment and death away for each of Christ's true believers.

Therefore, since the children share in flesh and blood, He Himself likewise also partook of the same, that through death He might render powerless him who had the power of death, that is, the devil. Hebrews 2:14

24

THE MASTER TEACHING OR DOCTRINE OF THE CHRISTIAN CHURCH

———❧❧❧———

To Be a True Church, It Must Be a Biblical Church As Christ Intended.

The Bible is to be the sole authority and doctrine of the true church. The Bible is for the guidance of one's practical life because it is truly God breathed (Inspired) and without error.

> ...and that from childhood you have known the sacred writings which are able to give you the wisdom that leads to salvation through faith which is in Christ Jesus.

All Scripture is inspired by God and is profitable for teaching, for reproof, for correction, for training in righteousness. 2 Timothy 3:15-16

Also look up 2 Peter 1:20-21, because in these verses you will see there are not many interpretations of Scripture but ONLY ONE! GOD'S WAY, not our way! All true believers must believe Christ as their Lord and Savior. Therefore, He is to be their only mediator and advocate between God and themselves. Why? Because Jesus Christ is 100% God, and 100% sinless Man! He is the only true way and access to God.

For there is one God, and one mediator also between God and men, the man Christ Jesus, 1Timothy 2:5

Here are other verses showing that Jesus Christ is to always have preeminence at all times: John 14:6; Acts 4:12; Hebrews 9:15. All true believers in Christ have access to God in prayer and do not, again as the Scripture says, do not need anyone else such as a priest, parent or other person, etc., to speak or pray to God for them. Why is this? It is because Christ Jesus the God-Man is the bridge from man to God and the Word of God the Bible is completed.

The Bible is God's path or way for the Christian. The Bible teaches that all true believers have a priesthood. This is called the priesthood of believers. In case you may be thinking some church leaders are priests, I'm sorry to say that the New Testament in the Bible tells us that the church leaders today are to have leader titles such as "Bishops", who are those that oversee a small number of churches, then Pastors, then Deacons (1 Timothy 3:1-7; Titus 1:5-7). There is no mention of one going to their church leaders called "Priest", not even one time. But there is great news! All true believers are in the priesthood of believers because Christ Jesus is the ultimate Priest and Savior of all believers. As the priest in the Old Testament had access to God, Jesus Christ was and is the ultimate and perfect sacrifice for believers on the altar of the cross. The sacrifice of Christ's crucifixion was and is perfect, and it was by this that believers have access to God. Therefore, a true believer must understand that Christ is the only Mediator between them and God. Not any other man with any title at all, ONLY CHRIST!

...and He has made us to be a kingdom, priests to His God and Father-to Him be the glory and dominion forever and ever. Amen. Revelation 1:6

Here are other verses that show us about the priesthood of believers: Revelation 20:6; Exodus 19:6; 1 Peter 2:5; Isaiah 61:6.

The meaning of the word church in the New Testament means a group, and the church is a group out of the ways of the world. Therefore, the true Christian church is an organized assembly of believers who are indwelled with the Holy Spirit.

But if the Spirit of Him who raised Jesus from the dead dwells in you, He who raised Christ Jesus from the dead will also give life to your mortal bodies through His Spirit who dwells in you. Romans 8:11

Here are some other verses about the distinctiveness of God's true church.

1) The church as a body (Romans 12:1-16), the body of Christ.
2) Christ is the head (1 Corinthians 12:12-27) of all believers which is His body that has many members.

The Nature of the Church

There are two aspects of the nature of the true Christian Church. First, there is the Invisible Universal Church. This is the mystical body of all true Christian believers here on earth, as well as in glory from all over the world and from all generations. They are the true Christian believers that lived here on earth, from the first true believer in the Messiah Jesus Christ, to the very last believer that will be before He (Jesus) comes to meet His bride the church at His second coming. We can see this marriage of Christ as the Groom and the perfect sacrifice as Christ is the Lamb in the book of Revelation (19:6-9).

In (Revelation 19:6) we see all His believers in a state of blissful rejoicing.

In (Revelation 19:8) Christ will prepare His true church in all purity. Because of their faith and acts of faith in Him.

In (Revelation 19:7 and 9) it shows us the marriage of Christ the Lamb, who also is the Groom to His bride, who is also the body of Christ. Christ is the Head and the church is His Body, which is one reason why it is called His universal church.

"Let us rejoice and be glad and give the glory to Him, for the marriage of the Lamb has come and His bride has made herself ready."

Then he said to me, "Write, Blessed are those who are invited to the marriage supper of the Lamb.'" And he said to me, "These are true words of God." Revelation 19:7; 9

Other verses that are related to the purity of the universal church are Ephesians 5:27. Then we have Revelation 21:9 explaining that Christ is the Lamb for His church and that the Lord Jesus Christ is also the Groom to be married to His bride the universal church. In Revelation 21:8, it tells us who are not part of the universal church and who in turn is not a member of the bride of Christ. This is a strong warning that needs to be heeded!

The Visible Local Church

The local Christian church is the institution of God that is responsible for carrying out all of the principles, precepts and commands of the Word of God in this present age of Grace. All true local Christian churches are to work in a united way to glorify the Lord Jesus Christ with compassion, one with another, because this is desirous and because all true members are of the body of Christ. Here is how the Apostle Paul addresses some of the true local individual churches in the Scriptures:

Where	Addressed as	Verse
In Rome	"the church"	Romans 16:1,5
In Corinth	"the church of God"	1 Corinthians 1:2
In Galatia	"the churches of Galatia"	Galatians 1:2
In Colossae (notice as saints)	"the saints and faithful brethren"	Colossians 1:2
In Thessalonica	"the church"	1 and 2 Thessalonians 1:1

Jesus Christ spoke to all the seven churches in Asia Minor collectively. The reason for this is because one of the titles and names for Jesus Christ is Guardian or Bishop of souls of His people (1 Peter 2:25). Christ is the Bishop over all His local churches. This is what He said:

He who has an ear, let him hear what the Spirit says to the churches. He who overcomes will not be hurt by the second death. Revelation 2:11

Then the Apostle Paul tells us in the First Letter to Timothy, how all local churches are to believe and give forth the great testimony of the One living true God! We can see this in 1 Timothy 3:15-16. Here is the common testimony all true local churches are to believe and live by, no exceptions.

By common confession, great is the mystery of godliness:
He who was revealed in the flesh,
Was vindicated in the Spirit,
Seen by angels,
Proclaimed among the nations,
Believed on in the world,
Taken up in glory. 1 Timothy 3:16

The Purpose and Functions of the Church is to Worship God

Mankind was created to worship the true God. It is very unfortunate that people worship other people and also false gods or things. Some are spiritual, some are material and others are related to human power, but the true Christian church is a place to worship the true God of the Holy Bible only, with no additions at all. This worship is to be done with the new, circumcised heart that God has given to each true believer from the Spirit of truth:

...for we are the true circumcision, who worship in the Spirit of God and glory in Christ Jesus and put no confidence in the flesh. Philippians 3:3

Here are some other verses about worship: Acts 20:7; Hebrews 10:25.

Worship also by singing spiritual songs and hymns (Ephesians 5:19).

To Love God

The church is a place where all true believers are to be free to express their love for God. Believers are not to bring into the church the ways that the world thinks. Believers are to be loving-hearted, not tyrannical, competitive or political because these ways of thinking are not of God.

Do not love the world, nor the things in the world. If anyone loves the world, the love of the Father is not in him. 1 John 2:15

Another good verse to look up is Romans 2:4. Every believer must understand that love for God is the first focus, not the worshiper or worshipers.

The Church Is To Be In Fellowship

All believers in the true church are to be companions and brothers, not competing with one another or being political. All believers in the true church are to be loving and non-manipulative, not trying to get their own way because God's way is to be the only right way in and through the church. This is what the Apostle John said about this:

> ...but if we walk in the Light as He Himself is in the Light, we have fellowship with one another, and the blood of Jesus His Son cleanses us from all sin. 1 John 1:7

The Church Is To Glorify God

The word glorify is similar to worship but glorify also means to honor. In other words, one must not try to appease God, but must honor Him in respect and not be so overly emotional to the point that it leads to an outright show. To glorify God is to honor a loving God from a pure heart. Why do we need to and why should we? Because believers have not been bought with a cheap price, believers have been bought back to God by the perfect sinless, shed blood of Christ Jesus. That is why all believers are to glorify God!

> For you have been bought with a price: therefore glorify God in your body. 1 Corinthians 6:20

Here are two other verses about the church glorifying God: Acts 4:21; Romans 15:9.

The Church Is To Be Good To All

The Gospel of the Apostle John tells us that God loved the world so much that He sent Jesus to save us (John 3:16). Therefore, it is logical as well as proper that a church of true Christian believers are to do the right and kind thing to all people. The Apostle Paul tells us this, but he also says to be this way particularly that the church should do right and be kind to all true Christian believers. Paul said this so all people who assemble together would glorify God and also feel safe and encouraged. Here is how he said it:

> So then, while we have opportunity, let us do good to all people, and especially to those who are of the household of faith. Galatians 6:10

The Church Is To Preach and Teach the Word of God as the Only Authority

Preaching is different than teaching. Whereas teaching is primarily spiritual and intellectual, true preaching of the Holy Bible involves the Spirit of God working through the preacher in bringing forth the truths of God's Word, yet utilizing the whole being of the preacher. By this I mean the preacher's will and his intellect and his emotions. This is greater in fervor and urgency to motivate greater understanding of God's Word. The Word of God commands both the preaching and teaching to take place in the church. One interesting point about preaching is that preaching also proclaims and encourages an overall spiritual message of God. Whereas teaching gives us all facts. Here is the priority the Apostle Paul has commanded for the preaching of the Word of God and where he gave advice to Timothy as a young pastor:

> I solemnly charge you in the presence of God and of Christ Jesus, who is to judge the living and the dead, and by His appearing and His kingdom: preach the word; be ready in season and out of season; reprove, rebuke, exhort, with great patience and instruction. 2 Timothy 4:1-2

Strong words from the great Apostle Paul. It is very unfortunate that many churches are teaching facts, but are not preaching the truths of God's Word. Here are other verses about preaching God's Word: Matthew 4:17; Mark 1:4; Romans 10:4; 2 Peter 2:5. Here are verses that also show us of the importance of teaching: Matthew 11:1; Mack 4:2; Ephesians 4:11; 1 Timothy 2:7.

The Church Is To Evangelize the World

Evangelizing is the act of bringing the Good News of the saving Gospel of Jesus Christ to one or a group of people that have never heard the Good News. This also applies to those who may have heard the Gospel in the past but have not yet made a decision in accepting Jesus as their Lord and Savior. A great example of this is found in the book of Acts in chapter 8. In this chapter we see Philip evangelizing the Ethiopian eunuch using the Old Testament book of Isaiah.

All true believers are not gifted with the gift of evangelism, but Jesus has commanded all true Christians from His church to evangelize and make other disciples. This is to be done worldwide. Here is Jesus Christ after He arose from the dead and is preaching to His disciples what is called The Great Commission. It is a command that tells all true believers that they have a responsibility to evangelize the world in bringing others into the church by discipling them.

Here is Jesus Christ giving the Great Commission:

> Go therefore and make disciples of all the nations, baptizing them in the name of the Father and of the Son and of the Holy Spirit, teaching them to observe all that I commanded you; and lo, I am with you always, even to the end of the age. Matthew 28:19-20

All true believers are to be evangelizing, not some believers. This is why it is called the Great Commission, because all disciples of Jesus Christ are commanded in this great mission of making disciples. Also, this tells the church to be involved in some form of this mission outside the church. Here are some verses about evangelism and the mission that all believers need to apply to their life: Acts 21:8; 2 Timothy 4:5. Here is a verse that shows us how the purity of the Good News is to be brought to others:

> For Christ did not send me to baptize, but to preach the gospel, not in cleverness of speech, so that the cross of Christ would not be made void. 1 Corinthians 1:17

Here are some verses in the Scripture that need to be looked up and read on mission outreach: Acts 13:1-3, 15:36-41.

The Church Is To Pray and Give Testimony

Prayer is an important form of worship. It is basically blessing God. As Christians are God's children, they are to talk to God and ask for their needs to be met. This is to be done in faith, and believers are to give testimony to others of God's answers from their prayer to glorify and thank Him. A perfect example of prayer and the attitude of it is the Lord's Prayer found in Luke 11:1-13. The Apostle Paul, in writing to the church in Thessalonica in his first letter to them, said that they need to be joyful at all times, and then he says to always pray and never stop. Here is the famous short prayer verse:

> …pray without ceasing. 1 Thessalonians 5:17

Paul tells all believers the same thing. All true believers are God's universal church and we always should be praying non-stop. Other verses about prayer are Philippians 1:4, which says we should always offer prayer with joyfulness, and Philippians 4:6 which tells us that all things should be prayed for.

The Church Is to Observe the Ordinances of Baptism and the Lord's Supper, also called Communion. Every true Christian church is to practice these two ordinances regularly.

Baptism

Baptism, to be correct and Biblical, is to be performed by totally immersing the person's body under a place of water, such as a baptismal or tank or pool or even a river. This new believer is to be immersed only one time, not two or three times. Baptism is for only a person that has accepted Christ as their Savior by faith alone. Once a person is baptized in this correct form, there is no reason for that person to ever be baptized again, ever! Sprinkling and pouring is just not biblically correct. Baptism is commanded to the church to be taught about and performed, yet one must understand that it is a person's faith in Christ that saves them, and in no way is it that it is the act of baptism that saves the individual. Therefore, infant baptism is very unscriptural. So why is the church commanded to baptize those who are committed and have accepted Christ as Lord and Savior? The reason is that baptism by immersion symbolizes an outward act that demonstrates the inward work of Christ in that person's life. It is God's commanded way of symbolizing Christ's death, burial and resurrection. This is also an outward testimony for others to observe about that person's faith in Christ. Here are two verses to show you this:

> Go therefore and make disciples of all nations, baptizing them in the name of the Father and of the Son and of the Holy Spirit. Matthew 28:19

Then we read:

> ...having been buried with Him in baptism, in which you were also raised up with Him through faith in the working of God, who raised Him from the dead. Colossians 2:12

Other verses on baptism are: Mark 16:15-16; Acts 2:41.

The Lord's Supper (Communion)

The Lord's Supper was instituted and established by Jesus Christ. This Holy Supper is to be partaken of (and only by) believers and on a regular basis. The elements of un-yeasted bread and a cup of grape juice (juice of the vine) are used to symbolize the body and blood of the Lord Jesus Christ. This is to commemorate the Lord's death until He comes back from His throne in Heaven. Therefore, the Lord's Supper should be taken very respectfully and seriously. We can read about the first Lord's Supper in the Gospel of Luke (22:1-23). Here are the key verses in this passage.

And when He had taken some bread and given thanks, He broke it and gave it to them, saying, "This is My body which is given for you; do this in remembrance of Me." And in the same way He took the cup after they had eaten, saying "This cup which is poured out for you is the new covenant in My blood." Luke 22:19-20

Here are other verses within the Bible about the Lord's Supper or Communion: 1 Corinthians 10:16-17; 11:20-34.

The Church Is To Discipline Believers

The word discipline comes from, and is very similar to, the word disciple. A disciple is one who is to be learning. Therefore, the word discipline in the primary meaning means to train to develop and to grow correctly. Unfortunately, this is something that is lacking in the church today, but yet it should still be done. It is also very unfortunate that many times when it is done today, it is not done correctly, but in fact it is done in a very disgraceful and harmful way. Church discipline is to first be done with love, and the steps and process in Scripture must be taken and adhered to, just as the Scripture tells the church of believers. One other thing is that church discipline is not for the unbeliever, but for the true believer. It is a right to the believer for the process of church discipline to be done according to the Scripture. This is how the believer can know that this discipline is of God and that the believer is given the full, loving option to repent (change their mind) and stop their sin that they are in. Jesus gave the correct steps in Matthew 18:15-17. The first verse says this.

If your brother sins, go and show him his fault in private; if he listens to you, you have won your brother. Matthew 18:15

In verse 16, Jesus instructs that if the person doesn't care to listen to the offended person who went out of their way to talk to the one who sinned, they are to bring one or two believers of the church with them who will be witnesses of the person who continues their sinful way of thinking. Then in verse 17, Jesus said if the person refuses to understand, then tell those in the gathering of the church and if he still refuses to understand, then just treat him as an unbeliever.

The Apostle Paul also tells us that Scripture needs to be practiced and he even shows us a very immoral incident that happened in the church of Corinth in 1 Corinthians 5:1-13. Then in his second epistle to the Corinthians, after the discipline was properly carried out, Paul basically tells the church to reinstate the repentant believer to the church in love. This can be found in 2 Corinthians 2:1-11.

The Officers of the Church for Today

The biblical church group of officers are to be bishops and pastors. They are considered overseers. The bishop is one who oversees a group of churches. Some may call this a superintendent of churches. Unfortunately today, there are some that may be considered in this type of position and may have an enormous amount of churches to oversee. In this case, the overseeing of churches may only go to the most prosperous churches, or the churches that are in trouble of closing down. But at any rate, these churches are not really getting the spiritual oversight they may need due to the overwhelming numbers of churches they are responsible for. Sometimes, they are responsible for anywhere from 50-150 churches. This is way too many churches for any person to handle. Even the Apostle John was considered the Bishop of the seven churches in the book of Revelation (1:1-11). The biblical bishop is to be a pastor to pastors. He is to give oversight and protection to the pastor and the congregation in the most biblical way. But what does this mean? The doctrines in this book that you are currently reading are what a Bishop and a Pastor are to be preaching and teaching. Why? Because it is the Doctrine of Christ.

By now all of you have read that Jesus Christ was born of a virgin. The Bible teaches this, and it is a "must" for one as a Christian never to deny that Jesus Christ was born of a virgin because the Bible states this point blank! There is no way around this, even if it is scientifically impossible. If God states it in His Word, He made it possible and it truly happened. So what am I leading up to? If a pastor somehow may have said he believed in the virgin birth of Christ and then for some reason is swayed and corrupted to disbelieve this, that pastor needs to be removed from his office as pastor. This also goes for bishops, deacons and deaconesses as well. All offices and officials are to be knowledgeable of the biblical Doctrines of the church and must be under the Doctrine of the Word, who is Christ Jesus the Lord. Another thing that the Bishop is to do is to protect the Pastor and the congregation in the matter of doctrinal error from one or some that come into the church to corrupt it. In other words, if one of the members of the church, or a person who is not a member of the church, come in and trouble the church with false teaching of the Word of God, the Bishop is to show support for the Pastor and those in the congregation that hold to the true biblical Doctrine. The Bishop is also to facilitate the Pastor in any type of church discipline. Most people know that a Pastor is to be the overseer of his flock, but the Bishops are to also be loving examples to all their churches as a whole. The Pastor is to put his family first and then his flock. Why his family first? Because they are his first flock. Their needs are to be met and they are to be safe at all times. The Pastor is to love his flock and the flock is to love the pastor and his family. One thing that needs to be mentioned is that it is very unfortunate, and unfortunate indeed, that some churches do not have pastors but they have priests. This is not from the New Testament Bible and it is again very unfortunate. No church today is to have a priest. Why is this? The answer is very simple. It is because Jesus Christ is the only High Priest, whose sacrifice of His blood on the cross is the only sacrifice needed for salvation. You see the priests in the Old Testament were responsible by God for the sacrifices of the people. In the New Testament, Jesus Christ is that ultimate sacrifice, as He gave of Himself with the shedding of His blood on the cross. This is why there is no need for priests today. We can go directly to our living High Priest, Jesus, in prayer. For one to take His place in any way (such as an official way) as an example of Christ is a very unbiblical official title for today, and therefore is unchristian. This is what the Bible tells us about Jesus Christ being the only High Priest that we see in Hebrews 3:1-19, and no one has any right to take glory away from Christ. This is what the first verse of this passage says:

Therefore, holy brethren, partakers of a heavenly calling, consider Jesus, the Apostle and High Priest of our confession. Hebrews 3:1

It is very unfortunate that the true office of a Pastor has become transferred to the unbiblical New Testament office of priest. All glory is to go to one High Priest and that is Jesus Christ only. As Christians, the Bible also states that as true believers, we are all in the priesthood of God (1 Peter 2:9). But we are not to look up to any human, so-called priest whose position takes glory away from Christ. One other thing is that Jesus Christ always glorified His Father in heaven to the point where He made this statement:

Do not call anyone on earth your father; for One is your Father, He who is in heaven. Matthew 23:9

If you look at this whole passage of Scripture in Matthew (23:1-12), Jesus is basically saying that, yes, we all have human fathers, but God is the only one to be called our spiritual Father, teacher and leader who is Christ Himself. So why is it today that so many types of churches put themselves in such unbiblical authority, to the point of calling a pope or priest, "father"? This passage of Scripture blatantly tells us this is not of God. There is only one spiritual Father who is God. This is why there are to be pastors and not priests who are looked up to as in the place of God. To look up to a man and call him Father in this way is very de-glorifying to God that created both of them.

But What Are the Qualifications of Bishop and Pastors?

These qualifications are found in 1 Timothy 3:1-7, 5:17 and Titus 1:5-9. In the first verse we read that to have a proper desire to be a pastor or bishop is to be considered a very good and honorable thing to do:

It is a trustworthy statement: if any man aspires to the office of overseer, it is a fine work he desires to do. 1Timothy 3:1

Then in the next verses of the same passage, we basically see the type of person he is to be:

Verse 2, One needs to be in good standing and eager to guide.

Verse 3, Not to live in a worldly way but a God-respecting way.

Verse 4, He is to be the loving leader of his family.

Verse 5, If he is not able to lead his family how can he lead the church?

Verse 6, He is not to be a new Christian and then think he can teach unbiblical, unsound doctrine, promoting lies like Satan.

Verse 7, His life must be good out of the church so the unsaved can't rightly accuse him of being a crook, liar, drunkard, etc., and give him a bad reputation.

Just a note: These are conditions that must be understood in the proper light, such as in

1 Timothy 3:2 and Titus 1:6. Many people think that if one with this office is divorced once, he is no longer to be in the ministry. The minister is responsible to be the best spiritual leader, but if his wife is adulterous or she rebels in a traitorous way against her very important position in the pastor's life and divorce occurs, the pastor can re-marry and still serve the Lord. These passages in the original writing meant to be married to only one wife at a time! In other words, one is not to be married to two women at once, as this is not of God. As to the actions of the overseer as pastor or bishop, here is a list of some:

He is to be an example to all (1 Corinthians 4:15-16, 11:1).

He is to administer the ordinances (1 Corinthians 11:20-34; Matthew 28:19-20).

He is to be a man of responsibility and prayer (1Timothy 2:15, 3:16-17, 4:2).

He is to rebuke and encourage (1 Thessalonians 5:12).

He is to oversee souls (Acts 20:28-31).

He is to feed and lead his flock (1 Peter 5:2).

He is to evangelize in the church, but also out of the church even if it brings hardship (2 Timothy 4:5).

Just a note: Many pastors don't evangelize today and many evangelize only in a church with altar calls, etc., but the true pastor is not to be hidden by four walls. He is to go to the unsaved/ lost and bring them to faith (2 Timothy 4:5).

Deacons

The qualifications of deacons are similar to those of the pastor. We can see this in 1 Timothy 3:8-13. One thing is to be said upfront, and that is that the word "deacon" has a meaning of a servant. This means the congregation is to respect the office of deacon but the more important thing is that the deacon is not to usurp the pastor's spiritual leadership in any way. A deacon is not a pastor; a deacon is to be a servant to the pastor, as well as the church.

Basic Deacon Responsibilities

The deacon is to help administer the church ordinances as directed by the pastor. He is to help the pastor in the act of visiting the sick and those with spiritual problems (James 5:14). He is to exercise church discipline as instructed in Matthew 18:15-17; 1 Corinthians 5:1-13; and Romans 16:17-18. The greatest example of a deacon was Stephen. He was a true servant of the church; nothing was too low for him to do. Sometimes deacons want to preach the Word of God, but they are not to usurp the pastor. The pastor has the bishop to answer to. Deacons are not to be a threat to the pastor in any way, ever. If a deacon or any man needs to witness or preach, God will open the doors for Him. We can see that God opened a great door for Stephen and many others. The church is not to be held in by four walls. I encourage you to read about this great servant of God and take a good look at his all-encompassing boldness and love for the Lord Jesus Christ, even to the point of his own death. You can read about Stephen in Acts 6:1-15 and 7:1-60.

Final words about the doctrine and major teaching of the church

The church is to be under the authority of the Word of God by living in the truth, love and doctrine of the Word of God. Just look at 2 John 1-13, which is the reason for John's whole second letter. In this letter you will see a perfect balance of living according to God's Word and you will again see words like truth, love, and doctrine or teaching interchangeably. These are the words of balance. If one of these is not upheld, there is danger, pain and deception to follow. The church and each individual needs to live according to God's Word because the Lord Jesus Christ is the only Head of His Church, not any denomination or individual group. There is to be no other so-called Head of the church in any other considerable way. By this, I mean not even the State. The State is to have no dictate over the church, as well as the church is not to dictate to the State. They are to be separate by nature, yet both are ordained institutions of God and needed for their separate work (Matthew 16:18, 22:15-21; Mark 12:17; Romans 13:1). In closing, these are to be the basics of the true Christian churches based on the Bible, truly as God intended. These basics need to be believed by Christians because of the simple reason that this Doctrine of the church is from the Inspired (God Breathed) Word of God the Bible, and not man's idea.

25

THE MASTER TEACHING OR DOCTRINE OF FUTURE EVENTS ALSO CALLED ESCHATOLOGY

―――~~~――

There Are Five Exciting Basic Parts to Future Biblical Events They are:

1) THE RAPTURE OF THE CHURCH
2) THE GREAT TRIBULATION
3) THE MILLENIUM
4) THE GREAT WHITE THRONE JUDGEMENT
5) ETERNITY FUTURE

These future events listed above are all in chronological order.

The Rapture of the True Universal Church

The word "rapture" is a Latin word which is an expression that is equated to words such as "to be snatched up" or "caught up" found in (1 Thessalonians 4:17). Jesus Christ first mentions this Great Event of being taken up with Him to be with Him in heaven in John 14:3. Jesus will come from heaven and with the shout of His voice and His trumpet, those believers who have been dead from the beginning will arise to Christ and go to Him first. Then the living believers on the earth will also be taken up to meet Christ in the clouds, to be with Jesus for everlasting life (1 Thessalonians 4:16-17).

Here is verse 17.

> Then we who are alive and remain will be caught up together with them in the clouds to meet the Lord in the air, and so we shall always be with the Lord. 1 Thessalonians 4:17

One question each person professing to be a believer in Christ must ask themselves is "Am I ready to meet Jesus now?" How do I know that the time is close, as so many true Christians believe today? For this to be answered, one must read the whole chapter of Matthew 24. There are many signs in Matthew that are happening today and the others are on the way. The Apostle Paul tells us that the rapture of the church is a true mystery of God and that those who are alive at the time of the rapture will truly be given an eternal body from a perishable body. That is the mystery.

> Behold, I tell you a mystery; we will not all sleep, but we will all be changed. 1 Corinthians 15:51

As mentioned earlier, all of the true believers in Jesus Christ who have died—or another way of putting this in a kinder form is, those that are sleeping—will first be resurrected and then raptured before the living, walking, talking believers on the earth. We see this in 1 Thessalonians 4:13-16. Here is the last verse:

> For this we say to you by the word of the Lord, that we who are alive and remain until the coming of the Lord, will not precede those who have fallen asleep. 1 Thessalonians 4:15

All believers are taken up and all will be given a glorified body. A brand new body, not a fixed-up body. A brand new and eternal body without a sin nature, without the ability to ever sin against God. What a great gift, I can't wait! Being in a perfect body and meeting Jesus my perfecter with all His other perfect children (1 Corinthians 15:53-58)! The time of the rapture is a time of mystery and also a time of great blessing. Yet with all the special effects and with the ignorance-producing evil that people read about, and watch on television and the movie theaters, this mystery may appear to be scary to some. The Apostle Paul actually tells us that it is a time of blessing, in the sense that this event is to be one of comfort. This is what he says about our attitude looking forward to the rapture:

Therefore comfort one another with these words. 1 Thessalonians 4:18

The whole event of the rapture is to be a comfort to all believers and they are not to fear anything related to the rapture, because God has it all covered and has taken care of all of it even down to the last detail. Believers are also to be comforted even further knowing that the receiving of a new glorified body will not take any span of notable time. After all, it takes nine months to give birth to an average child, but this is not the case with our new glorified bodies. This will take place in such a rapid amount of time that one will be startled at how short the time will be. So how long will it take for the rapture of one's body and to be given an imperishable glorified body? This will all take place in the speed of the twinkle of one's eye. How fast is that? It's less then a split second, that's how fast!

Then as the believers are with Christ in heaven, all believers will have to stand before Him in His Judgment Seat, The Judgment Seat of Christ. But as it was said before in this book, the believer's sins have been judged on the cross of Christ as one puts their faith in Christ. This judgment (the Judgment Seat of Christ) is not for the believer's sin that has already been taken care of by forgiveness, this judgment is for the believer's works. We can do nothing to save our selves from our sins, but after our salvation, each and every believer is created for good works in Christ. But what is the reason for good works? The main reason for good works is to receive a reward from Christ. But I've even heard Christians say, "But I don't want rewards." My response is, why not? Christ is to reward our good works and we will have the great honor of laying our reward(s) at the feet of the Lord to glorify and exalt Him further. This is the greatest and best reason of all, wouldn't you say!

There are ground rules for rewards. The Apostle Paul tells us about these ground rules in 1 Corinthians 3:10-15. This needs to be read straight from the Bible passages mentioned.

Here is a brief description of 1 Corinthians 3:10-15.

Verse 10. The Apostle Paul tells us that he was chosen by God to lay the most accurate foundation, which is to know the Doctrine of Christ; each person must carefully build on this precious and precise foundation.

Verse 11. The foundation is complete which is Christ and all other foundations are not recognized by God.

Verse 12. The person that builds, must build on the foundation with eternity in view and with the greatest value of love for the truth, which comes only from His Word which is the completed Holy Bible.

Verse 13. The reason for this is that God will test a person's work as fire burns out impurities in the refining process of gold, silver, etc.

Verse 14. After God tests the works of a person that has built on the perfect foundation of God's Holy Word and it stands God's test, that person will get an eternal reward from God.

Verse 15. But if the person's work is totally consumed by the refining process and there is nothing left, that person will not receive a reward but that person will still be saved, but like one who has been through the loss of a fire. God is a loving God but one must also understand that God is a Holy God! All believers will be judged for their works by the Lord Jesus Christ.

For we must all appear before the judgment seat of Christ, so that each one may be recompensed for his deeds in the body, according to what he has done, whether good or bad. 2 Corinthians 5:10

The Great Tribulation

The Great Tribulation is a seven-year period that immediately follows the rapture of the true believing Christian church. We can see reference to this in Daniel 12:1-2, Matthew 24:21 and Revelation 7:14. One must realize that now that the church has been raptured and is in heaven with Christ the Lord, the earth will be a very different place to live on because of all the confusion and the lack of a true church presence on the earth. It will be a time of severe persecution and evil on the earth. We can see this in the whole chapter of Matthew 24, then in 2 Thessalonians 2:3-9 and also in Revelation 6:1-17, the last book of the Bible.

In the whole chapter of Revelation 13, it tells us about the mark of the beast. As said earlier, the tribulation will be for seven years. These are the events of the seven years and many will take place simultaneously moving forward, rather than one after the other. There will be a great deal of trouble on the earth. This is what Jesus said:

For nation will rise against nation, and kingdom against kingdom, and in various places there will be famines and earthquakes. Matthew 24:7

There will be an antichrist that will appear and he will make an agreement with Israel through the false prophet for seven years. He (the antichrist) will claim to protect Israel, but after three and a half years he will break the agreement.

This will leave Israel very vulnerable after their defenses were encouraged to be very relaxed. There will be many judgments that God will send upon the earth through the tribulation, such as the seven seal judgments and six bowl judgments. To get a better understanding of these, the whole book of Revelation needs to be read and understood. There are no inaccuracies within the Word of God and it must be the authority of one's faith in the true God.

The big picture is that Israel will be betrayed. This will be God's way of judging the nation of Israel, due to the fact of their rejecting their true Messiah Jesus Christ (Jeremiah 30:7; Daniel 12:1-4). One also needs to grasp that Satan is the energizer of the antichrist, false prophet and the beast. It is Satan who is the one who doesn't want God's plan to succeed, even after the church has been raptured up. Even at this time of the great tribulation, if one does not accept the mark of the beast (666) from the anti-christ, energized by Satan as explained in Revelation 13, and they accept Jesus as their Savior and Lord, they may even have to die for their faith. But Christ Jesus will still at this point save them and give them everlasting life. This can be seen in Revelation 13:8-10; 20:4-5. NO ONE should ever accept the mark of the beast because it is a true sentence of eternal Hell. As for all the gentile nations (all those nations that are non-Jewish) God will also use the tribulation to judge these nations for their rejection of the Lord and Savior Jesus Christ, who is the God and Messiah of Israel. This judgment includes the gentile nation's sins against Israel as a nation and their people.

> For behold, the LORD is about to come out
> from His place
> To punish the inhabitants of the earth for their iniquity;
> And the earth will reveal her bloodshed
> And will no longer cover her slain. Isaiah 26:21

So as one can see, the whole world in the tribulation period truly is in a great mess. Earthquakes, famines, pestilences, death, wars and lawlessness of all sorts. It will be a time of trouble never experienced before. But who will be blamed for all of this? Israel, the Jewish nation, of course! We have seen this all through history. At this point the antichrist will gather all the nations of the earth together (Zechariah 14:1-4). They will all gather against Israel with the goal of totally annihilating the nation that God gave to the Jewish people:

For I will gather all the nations against Jerusalem to battle, and the city will be captured... Zechariah 14:2a

This will take place at the second half of the tribulation, which is in the last three and a half years of it. Just at the point of the total annihilation of Israel, the Savior and the Messiah that Israel rejected, who is Jesus Christ the Lord, will return to Israel with His believers, who are called His saints during the time of the famous battle of Armageddon to eliminate the anti-Christ and his worldwide armies. This is to be known and understood by all Christians. The best references in the Bible for this topic are 2 Thessalonians chapter 2 and Revelation Chapter 19.

Then that lawless one will be revealed whom the Lord will slay with the breath of His mouth and bring to an end by the appearance of His coming. 2 Thessalonians 2:8

The Millennium

After the Great Tribulation, Christ comes to earth with His saints to set up His kingdom. This will be for a period of one thousand years and this is why it is called the Millennium, meaning a thousand. It is at this time that Christ will rule the earth in all holy righteousness and justice. This will be a time that will be the fulfillment of the prophecies to the Jews. We can see this in Zechariah 14:9 and Revelation 20:1-7.

And the LORD will be king over all the earth; in that day the LORD will be the only one, and His name the only one. Zechariah 14:9

This next verse mentions the tribulation saints resurrected, as well as the one thousand year reign of Christ.

Then I saw thrones, and they sat on them, and judgment was given to them. And I saw the souls of those who had been beheaded because of their testimony of Jesus and because of the word of God, and those who had not worshiped the beast or his image, and had not received the mark on the forehead and on their hand; and they came to life and reigned with Christ for a thousand years. Revelation 20:4

Another one of the purposes of the Millennium is that God will reward the saints who are the true believers. The Bible says that the saints are to reign on the earth as Christ has made His saints priests to God for His kingdom. All believers will rule and govern with the Lord as part of His reward to His children. This can be seen in Revelation 5:6-10. Here is the key verse to this topic:

You have made them to be a kingdom and priests to our God; and they will reign upon the earth. Revelation 5:10

And men will say, "Surely there is a reward for the righteous;

Surely there is a God who judges on earth!" Psalm 58:11 Here are some other verses for the topic: Psalm 9:7-8, Proverbs 11:18.

The time of the Millennium is also a time when God can set His creation free again. Because of sin entering into the world, suffering also came along with it. God's plan for the human race was to live a life of glory with Him. That is why God gave man a free will. But man overstepped a boundary that God gave, and this was the reason why God subjected the world to frustration. To turn humanity back away from the slavery of sin with the future purpose of turning humanity back to Him (Romans 8:18-23). The Millennium is for creation to be set free because the believer will not have a nature to sin any more. Therefore, God will set all creation free. The book of Isaiah makes reference to this and how free and safe all creation will truly be (Isaiah 11:1-9).

The Apostle Paul gives us a much greater understanding about this in the book of Romans (8:18-23). Here is a brief overview of these verses.

Verse 18. Paul tells believers that suffering here on this earth is of no comparison to the wondrous glory and bliss each believer will be living in eternity.

Verse 19. Creation is in a state of impatient yearning for God's true children, because creation was made for them to give God glory.

Verse 20. Then Paul goes on to say that creation was stopped in the way that it's harmony was removed to show man that his way is ineffective, but that God's way is the only hope that man would turn to God, through His Son.

Verse 21. This is the only way true freedom for creation can take place from the enslavement of sin and death, and to be free as God intended for His born again children to live and live in His Glory.

Verse 22. Paul tells us in this verse that everyone knows that creation is in a current painful suffering state, just as a woman who is about to give birth.

Verse 23. The true believer must realize that we, as the children of the true God, are now spiritually alive and have produced fruit by the Holy Spirit (Galatians 5:22-23) and yet we are still struggling internally, looking and watching for Christ to take us homeward to heaven, and also to receive a glorified body that we will get from Christ when He comes to get us. Here is how the Apostle Paul said it.

And not only this, but also we ourselves, having the first fruits of the Spirit, even we ourselves groan within ourselves, waiting eagerly for our adoption as sons, the redemption of our body. Romans 8:23

Here again, is just a glimpse of what life will be like:

The nursing child will play by the hole of the cobra,
And the weaned child will put his hand on the viper's den. Isaiah 11:6-8

One more thing! You may be thinking, "so who, from the beginning of time, will be the citizens of this Godly millennium?" They are as follows, those from:

Pre-Judaism	Faith as Credit
From the time of Adam until Judaism, started by Abraham	All those people from the Gentile and the Jew from the beginning of time who put their faith in the true God and Savior.

The Time of Judaism	Faith as Credit
Jew and Gentile	All those who put their faith in the promised Messiah, who is from God, who is Jesus Christ.

The time of the New Testament	Faith unto Salvation and looking to His second Coming
The Church	The Jew or Gentile who put their faith in the Messiah and Savior as Lord and God because of His death, burial and resurrection and His ascension.

Believers in the tribulation	Faith as to the Savior and Messiah
Those that accept Christ as Savior, Messiah and Lord, not accepting the antichrist, false prophet and the mark of the beast (666). They may be martyred for their faith.	Those looking for the second coming.

Elect Holy Angels	Holy, sinless, faithful to God.
	Those that stayed true in all matters to their wonderful position given to them by God and never rebelled against God.

All five of these groups are, and will be, citizens of the eternal kingdom starting with the Millennium.

One's citizenship is not based on one's earthly heritage, such as this next verse will show us, and citizenship is not by one's own way, but only God's way.

Yet your fellow citizens say, "The way of the Lord is not right; when it is their own way that is not right. When the righteous turns from his righteousness and commits iniquity, then he shall die in it." Ezekiel 33:17-18

Salvation and citizenship, in God's understanding, is not by heritage or ritual but only by faith in His Word, which is the Doctrine of Jesus Christ as the only true Savior. On a positive note, this is what the Apostle Paul tells us in the Word of God about a true Bible-believing Christian.

So then you are no longer strangers and aliens, but you are fellow citizens with the saints, and are of God's household, having been built on the foundation of the apostles and prophets, Christ Jesus Himself being the cornerstone. Ephesians 2:19-20

By these verses we can see that once a person truly puts their faith in the Lord Jesus Christ of the Holy Bible, they are true citizens and children of God. Never to be a stranger or even alienated by God, ever!

During the Millennium, the enemy Satan will be bound up and thrown into the bottomless pit, also known as the abyss. He will be there for the length of the Millennium. At the end of the thousand years he will be released for a little while. We can see this in Revelation 20:1-3. At this point in time, during the Millennium, now that Satan is in the abyss, Christ Jesus will raise up those tribulation saints (believers) that lost their life because of the tribulation, which was the worst time in history on the earth of the saints. Here is what the Bible says about Christ raising up those tribulation saints and how He blesses them (Revelation 20:4-6). Let us look at the first verse in this passage again:

Then I saw thrones, and they sat on them, and judgment was given to them. And I saw the souls of those who had been beheaded because of their testimony of Jesus and because of the word of God, and those who had not worshiped the beast or his image, and had not received the mark on their forehead and on their hand; and they came to life and reigned with Christ for a thousand years. Revelation 20:4

Let me make it very clear. Those who have been dead since the beginning of man, who have not accepted Jesus Christ as Messiah or Savior to come, and those who did not accept Him as their Messiah, Savior and Lord after He came to earth and have rejected Him, are considered unsaved and are of the enemy Satan. These Christ Jesus will raise later on to condemn them to eternal hell.

The rest of the dead did not come to life until the thousand years were completed. This is the first resurrection. Revelation 20:5

Those people who are in the tribulation and would not worship the beast nor accept the mark of the beast (666), but accepted Christ as Lord under the worst conditions in all of history and who would have died for their faith in Christ, these are the blessed that will be of the First Resurrection. They will reign and be priests unto the Lord Jesus Christ our God, for the full length of the Millennium. We can see this in the next verse:

Blessed and holy is the one who has a part in the First Resurrection; over these the second death has no power, but they will be priests of God and of Christ and will reign with Him for a thousand years. Revelation 20:6

At the end of the 1000 years, Satan will be loosed. This is stated in Revelation 20:7. Next, Satan will start to stir up his evil trouble throughout the nations at that time going to the furthest parts of the world, and utilize those from the gradual rebellious to those of the most rebellious. Satan will then gather a countless, enormous number of rebels deceived by him (Satan) for war. We see this stated in Revelation 20:7-8. Then this enormous number that is deceived by Satan's evil armies goes to surround Christ's kingdom, the Holy City of Jerusalem and home of the saints, and then at that point God will send heavenly fire down to consume those armies to destroy them with a total consumption. We can see this in the next verse:

And they came up on the broad plain of the earth and surrounded the camp of the saints and the beloved city, and fire came down from heaven and devoured them. Revelation 20:9

The last statement about the one who has tempted, instigated, troubled and is responsible for all types of evil, wickedness, corruption, illness and death, but above all the dishonor of the one and only true God. Then this enemy Satan who is also known as the devil, will then face not his end, but his beginning of eternal suffering and constant torment without any degree of ceasing throughout all eternity future.

322

This is seen in the Apostle John's statement in Revelation 20:10. This place of eternal suffering is called the lake of fire where the beast and false prophet have also been deposited Revelation 20:10.

> And the devil who deceived them was thrown into the lake of fire and brimstone, where the beast and the false prophet are also; and they will be tormented day and night forever and ever. Revelation 20:10

And who will do this? The King above all kings and the Lord of all lords, Jesus Christ Himself will throw His enemy into the Lake of Fire.

Because He is the...

KING OF KINGS AND LORD OF LORDS. Revelation 19:16b

The Lord Jesus Christ is the only one who can, and will, put an end to Satan and all his corrupt systems.

The Great White Throne Judgment

Christ is not yet finished. He has one more fearful judgment to perform. The Great White Throne Judgment! This is found in (Revelation 20:11-15). Jesus Christ was given all authority by God the Father to perform all judgment and He will perform this final judgment and it will take place from His throne and is called the Great White Throne Judgment (John 5:27). Here is another verse that tells us about Jesus Christ's power to judge:

> For not even the Father Judges anyone, but He has given all judgment to the Son. John 5:22

There you have it! All in this judgment will have to face the Lord Jesus Christ. God the Father raised His Son Jesus Christ on day three from His death and was visibly seen by a great many credible witnesses (Acts 10:40). This is the main reason why Jesus Christ must be preached about even today, because God the Father appointed His Son, who is the second person and member of the God-head, to judge all the living and all the dead (Acts 10:42). Another verse to backup that Jesus Christ will be the Judge of all times, nations, races, etc., is this verse that the Apostle Paul wrote to a young evangelist:

> I solemnly charge you in the presence of God and of Christ Jesus, who is to judge the living and the dead, and by His appearing and His kingdom. 2 Timothy 4:1

Christ is the Righteous Judge, no one else. This is the way it is! It is so important to accept Him as the loving, life-giving Lord that He is!

So you may ask what this Great White Throne Judgment is anyway. Again, this is the last and final judgment that will be performed. Now for what it is, this is the judgment of those who rejected the Lord Jesus Christ as their One who could save them from all their wrongdoing, which is called sin. Only He is the Messiah, Savior, Lord and God who can save and give eternal life. There is no one else! Some may say, "yes, I believe in Jesus." But many times this superficial attitude and way of just saying they believe in Jesus, means they believe Him like some historical figure just like Julius Caesar or George Washington. Jesus Christ must be accepted as the Lord and Savior of one's life—which also means that He, Jesus Christ, as the second person of the Godhead—is truly God to them. There is no other way around this.

In this judgment, Jesus Christ will raise all those from the dead because He is the God of the resurrection. But this judgment is only for those who rejected Him and hated Him, those that hated His believers and those that did not care and enjoyed doing evil. But not only those individuals will receive judgment, even those who were religious, who didn't want to open their eyes to the fact that they were worshiping false gods, will be judged. This judgment goes even as far as those who say they believe in Jesus or God and make all types of clamor and rich celebration and have little or no faith in God's Word, the Holy Bible. I mean those who teach and believe that God's Word, the Bible, is not the final authority. Those that add their feelings over the true faith in the Old and New Testaments. The Holy Bible is to be the only authority of anyone's true faith in the Only God. This is God's way, not my way or any other man's way.

So, the outcome of this Great White Throne Judgment will be if you have accepted Jesus Christ as your Lord and Savior, then you are 100% safe. If you have not, you are 100%, according to the Word of God, judged already. Christ Jesus will have no problem placing anyone who has not made Him Lord of their life into the Lake of Fire to stay throughout all eternity. What does this mean? This means eternal suffering in every possible way, but mostly separation from God. It amazes me why ignorant jokes are said about Hell or the eternal Lake of Fire. But it really amazes me even more why a person would ignore, reject or even hate Christ or His true followers. Especially after this Great Judge Jesus Christ was crucified for them so that they would receive everlasting life from this only great Savior. Here are some verses in the Holy Bible that will show you that God means real business at the Great White Throne Judgment for those that are not His. These are the unsaved; those that are not born again, unbelievers, one or all of the above will put a person in the Lake of Fire. NO JOKE! Let's see what the Apostle Paul said under the inspiration of the Holy Spirit, the third person of the Godhead, to believers:

For after all it is only just for God to repay with affliction those who afflict you, and to give relief to you who are afflicted and to us as well when the Lord Jesus will be revealed from heaven with His mighty angels in flaming fire, dealing out retribution to those who do not know God and to those who do not obey the gospel of our Lord Jesus.

These will pay the penalty of eternal destruction, away from the presence of the Lord and from the glory of His power, when He comes to be glorified in His saints on that day, and to be marveled at among all who have believed — for our testimony to you was believed. 2 Thessalonians 1:6-10

I know this is strong language, but it is from God and all need to know and understand it. Next we have the passages of the book of Revelation that were written by the Apostle John, under the inspiration of the Holy Spirit about the Great White Throne Judgment:

Then I saw a great white throne and Him who sat upon it, from whose presence earth and heaven fled away, and no place was found for them.

And I saw the dead, the great and the small, standing before the throne, and books were opened; and another book was opened, which is the book of life; and the dead were judged from the things which were written in the books, according to their deeds.

And the sea gave up the dead which were in it, and death and Hades gave up the dead which were in them; and they were judged, every one of them according to their deeds.

Then death and Hades were thrown into the lake of fire. This is the second death, the lake of fire.

And if anyone's name was not found written in the book of life, he was thrown into the lake of life. Revelation 20:11-15

Then there is the final rebuke to those who have stubbornly rejected Christ. And the final, loving encouragement from Jesus Christ, the righteous judge, who has showed sinful mankind from the very beginning to the very end of this creation His way, His truth and His life all through His patient love. Notice this balance of eternal rebuke for the unjust and eternal love for those justified for their sin through Him.

Then He said to me, "It is done. I am the Alpha and the Omega, the beginning and the end. I will give to the one who thirsts from the spring of the water of life without cost.

"He who overcomes will inherit these things, and I will be his God and he will be My son.

"But for the cowardly and unbelieving and abominable and murders and immoral persons and sorcerers and idolaters and all liars, their part will be in the lake that burns with fire and brimstone, which is the second death!" Revelation 21:6-8

Then there is the finalized statement of Jesus Christ's final Great White Throne Judgment. In this verse we can see that not one bit of impurity will ever enter the new creation of heaven and earth. All those that were condemned to the Lake of Fire will never be released or will ever be able to escape. All those who are God's true children through Jesus Christ will always be in a state of bliss and in His safety. Here is the verse:

> ...and nothing unclean, and no one who practices abomination and lying, shall ever come into it, but only those whose names are written in the Lamb's book of life. Revelation 21:27

Eternity Future the New Heaven and the New Earth

Following the Rapture of the church, the Great Tribulation, the Millennium and then the Great White Throne Judgment, it is then that eternity future will take place. Jesus Christ will be the establisher of a completely New Heaven as well as a newly-created earth which will never end, but will be ever-lasting without even the thought of an end. All believers who are established from all times and ages past will dwell with the Lord and God, Jesus the Messiah and Christ. We can see this in the next verses:

> Then I saw a new heaven and a new earth; for the first heaven and the first earth passed away, and there is no longer any sea. And I saw the holy city, new Jerusalem, coming down out of heaven from God, made ready as a bride adorned for her husband. And I heard a loud voice from the throne, saying, "Behold, the tabernacle of God is among men, and He will dwell among them, and they shall be His people, and God Himself will be among them." Revelation 21:1-3

The above three verses are somewhat of an outline of events. In verse 1, it stands alone in telling us that everything will truly be new and wonderful from that point to eternity future. Verse 2, points to the new enormous, awesome city of God, the heavenly New Jerusalem where the Lamb of God who is also the Alpha, the beginning and the Omega who is the end will rule. The beauty of this heavenly city, the New Jerusalem, will be its enormous size (1,500 miles by 1,500 miles by 1,500 miles high) with twelve layers of gorgeous precious stone that the light of Christ will shine through. With Christ's light shining through each layer, there is no need for a sun to give light because the Son of God will provide a more glorious light. This is what the Lord Jesus Christ has waiting for His children. I pray and hope to see you there! These are the corresponding verses that tell us about this new heavenly Jerusalem, that need to be read straight from the Bible in Revelation 21:5-27.

The third verse of the first three verses in Revelation chapter 21 also correspond with the fourth verse. It tells us of the glorified, blissful life every child of God will have with the Holy, Loving, Lord Jesus Christ and how there will be such a high quality of life; Christ Himself will have removed all of those negative emotions, thoughts and fears and give us totality of healing to all of His beloved children.

...and He will wipe away every tear from their eyes; and there will no longer be any death; there will no longer be any mourning, or crying, or pain; the first things have passed away. Revelation 21:4

Looking at Revelation 22:1-5, it gives us a greater visual understanding of what it will look like inside the truly eternal city of the New Jerusalem.

Then he showed me a river of the water of life, clear as crystal, coming from the throne of God and of the Lamb. Revelation 22:1

In this verse, an angel shows the Apostle John a river that is the living water of God. So clear and so pure that it will continually be refreshing and eternally healing without any type of contaminates even in the slightest. The origin of this living water will be God the Father, the Son, and the Holy Spirit—but with the emphasis on the Lamb of God who is Christ. The reason is that Jesus Christ was the slain blood sacrifice for His children.

> ...in the middle of its street. On either side of the river was the tree of life, bearing twelve kinds of fruit, yielding its fruit every month; and the leaves of the tree were for the healing of the nations. Revelation 22:2

The Apostle John tells us that in the middle of the path of the river (translated as the middle path of the river; like a street has a path, so does a river have a path) that this river flows on both sides, meaning through the tree. Look up Psalm 1:3; as in this verse, you will see that the tree is firmly planted and that its roots are healthy and it produces fruit, because it is healthy and strong. But this tree in the New Heavenly Jerusalem will have water on both sides of it and through it to produce all twelve different types of fruit, symbolizing the blessing of God's nourishment and our dependence on God in our life eternal.

By this "each month", meaning each cycle, it seems to be that there may be time in all eternity. But John may be speaking about different cycles in heaven, just as we have in our life today—such as the Sun rises and sets, and also the cycle of spring, summer, fall and winter. Also, one other thing is that in that time period some cultures went according to lunar cycles for time, rather then the solar cycles adding up to a year. So I believe the Apostle John is talking about twelve continuous, exhilarating, amazing, totally blissful cycles in eternity. This verse also talks about leaves on this magnificent awesome tree for the healing, so nations can be healed.

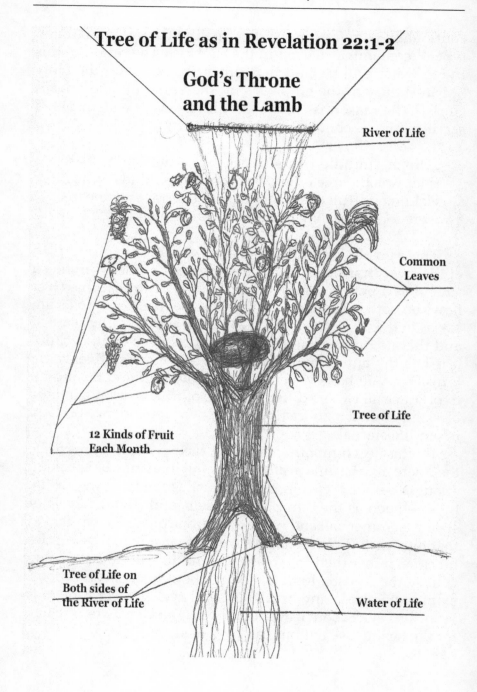

Tree of Life as in Revelation 22:1-2

God's Throne and the Lamb

River of Life

Common Leaves

Tree of Life

12 Kinds of Fruit Each Month

Tree of Life on Both sides of the River of Life

Water of Life

But are the nations sick at this time, after John tells us in the first four verses of Revelation 21 that there is a completely new heaven, as well as a new earth, and all brand-new creation? So are the nations sick NOW? AGAIN! The answer is absolutely "NO."

We can all see the most common part of this tree, and all trees for that matter, are their leaves. Now, mind you, everything is in a sinless state. These leaves are for wellness by preventing any type of illness. All of God's children will love each other no matter what experiences happened in the past to them in and on the old earth. The leaves are like a common vitamin; let's say vitamin C. All people need vitamin C for good health, whether we get it in vegetables, fruit or even if their source is pine needles, as is the source for some in Asia today. We all need vitamin C for good health to prevent a disease called scurvy, and many other diseases and problems. So these leaves that John is talking about are for God's children to prevent any kind of illness in eternity. This healing is similar to and like preventive nutrition, rather then a medical need. All needs will be understood, to the greatest point of harmony that has never been experienced, to all the Glory of God through the Lamb.

> There will no longer be any curse; and the throne of God and of the Lamb will be in it, and His bond-servants will serve Him. Revelation 22:3

The Apostle John in this verse is telling us that all blessing to the fullest will take place, always! The term curse here is not as we know it in the western part of the world, such as bad or dirty evil language, because this is considered course jesting described in Ephesians 5:4. One needs to know that the meaning of cursing in this verse, means having a wish, or to have a strong desire for bad and evil to happen to someone. The Apostle John said this new eternal future state will be so pure that it will not even have a possibility of even a bad wish anywhere in it. John also mentions that the presence of God and His Son the Lamb will be so knowingly present, that He

(God) will always be in all our thoughts and desires and wishes and so on. Just think about it, the great bliss and comfort of knowing that we could never do wrong, be wronged or be wrong in any way ever again! As the verse goes on to tell us, all will be serving God and only God!

> ...they will see His face, and His name will be on their foreheads. Revelation 22:4

In this verse, we see the closeness of God and how His children will have great initiative of willful desire as well as knowledge, along with great happiness in this eternal bliss. And yet still with a free will! Because His children will never feel separated or lonely. Because His children will always see the loving face of God and all of His children will always have His (God's) assurance of belonging to the Greatest Most Holy, Loving being through all eternity. Even to the point that God's name will be placed on their forehead. All of God's true children will be marked for true eternal greatness, not in the human sense of the word, but in a godly sense of the word because, again, all the glory goes to God throughout eternity.

And there will no longer be any night; and they will not have need of the light of a lamp nor the light of the sun, because the Lord God will illumine them; and they will reign forever and ever. Revelation 22:5

The Apostle John in this verse is making us aware that God's true children, who have put their trust and faith in the Lamb, will in no way be limited in eternity future. There will always be light and this light will not be daylight that we can only see, feel, and keep healthy. But this is the kind of light that will go way beyond any other type of light, that will also be an internal source and the source will be from God. This light given by God to each of His children will not just be from within, but God will also be providing His light from without.

The degree of total bliss can never be understood in this life but as John ends this statement in this verse, he tells us that all of us who are God's true children will continue to grow in great godliness, power, love, beauty, wisdom, understanding, knowledge and anything else that is within the will of our All Holy, Loving, Sovereign God. But there will never be an end because this will truly be everlasting. This is the great eternal life that the Lord Jesus Christ has waiting for all those that have accepted Him as their Lord and Savior, starting with this life. A great unmerited gift, beyond all measure, comprehension or imagination. In conclusion, I want to leave you with two more verses from God's Word.

He who overcomes will inherit these things, and I will be his God and he will be My son. Revelation 21:7

And

Blessed are those who wash their robes, so that they may have the right to the tree of life, and may enter by the gates into the city. Revelation 22:14

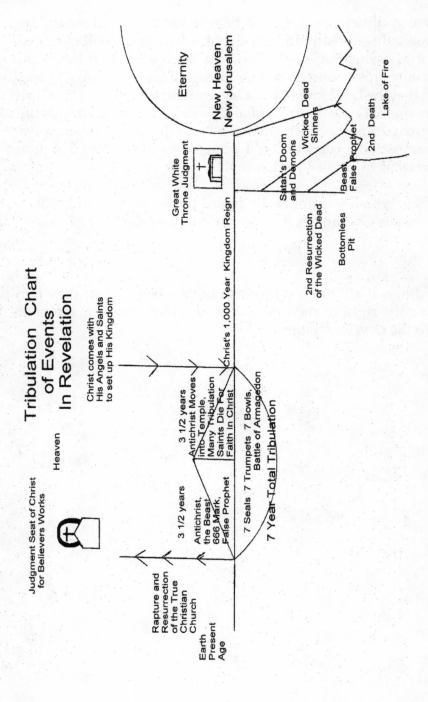

Tribulation Chart
of Events
In Revelation

Judgment Seat of Christ
for Believers Works

Heaven

Christ comes with
His Angels and Saints
to set up His Kingdom

Rapture and
Resurrection
of the True
Christian
Church

Earth
Present
Age

3 1/2 years

Antichrist,
the Beast,
666 Mark,
False Prophet

3 1/2 years

Antichrist Moves
into Temple,
Many Tribulation
Saints Die For
Faith in Christ

7 Seals 7 Trumpets 7 Bowls,
Battle of Armageddon

7 Year Total Tribulation

Christ's 1,000 Year Kingdom Reign

Great White
Throne Judgment

Eternity

New Heaven
New Jerusalem

Satan's Doom
and Demons

Wicked Dead
Sinners

Beast
False Prophet

2nd Death

Lake of Fire

Bottomless
Pit

2nd Resurrection
of the Wicked Dead

26

PROPHECIES OF JESUS CHRIST FROM THE OLD TESTAMENT COMPARED TO THE NEW TESTAMENT

—⟨⟨⟨⟩⟩⟩—

Some have said there are many interpretations of Scripture. The Bible says this is not true in any way. There is only one way to interpret and understand Scripture because it is from God. The leader of the Apostles, who is Peter, says it this way from the Scripture:

So we have the prophetic word made more sure, to which you do well to pay attention as to a lamp shining in a dark place, until the day dawns and the morning star, arises in your hearts.

But know this first of all, that no prophecy of Scripture is a matter of one's own interpretation, for no prophecy was ever made by an act of human will, but men moved by the Holy Spirit spoke from God. 2 Peter 1:19-21

Here are Fifty Fulfilled Prophecies about Jesus Christ (There are many more).

Old Testament	Jesus Christ	New Testament
Genesis 3:15	Born from a woman	Galatians 4:4
Genesis 12:3 Genesis 22:12	Descendant through Abraham	Matthew 1:1 Acts 3:25
Genesis 17:19 Genesis 21:12	Descended from Isaac	Luke 3:35
Genesis 28:14 Numbers 24:17	Descended from Jacob	Matthew 1:2 Luke 3:23-24
Genesis 49:10	Out of the tribe of Judah	Luke 3:23-33
Isaiah 9:6-7	Descended of King David	Luke 3:23-31
Ezekiel 37:24	Is a Shepherd to His people	Matthew 2:6
Isaiah 9:7	Heir to King David's throne	Luke 1:32-33
Micah 5:2	Pre-existence of Jesus the Son of God	Colossians 1:17
Psalm 45:6-7	Christ and Messiah anointed and eternal	Hebrews 1:8-12
Psalm 110:1	To be called Lord	Matthew 22:43-45
Micah 5:2	He was born in Bethlehem	Matthew 2:1 Luke 2:4-5
Isaiah 7:14	Born of a virgin	Luke 1:26-27,30-31
Daniel 9:25	The time of His birth	Luke 2:1-2
Psalm 72:9	Shepherds worshipped Him	Luke 2:8-15
Jeremiah 31:15	The slaughtering of children	Matthew 2:16-18
Hosea 11:1	Flight by night to Egypt	Matthew 2:14-15
Isaiah 40:3 Malachi 3:1	Preparing the way by the forerunner	Matthew 3:1-3

Malachi 4:5-6	Christ preceded by Elijah	Matthew 11:13-14
Psalm 2:7	Declared the Son	Matthew 3:17
Proverbs 30:4	The coming of the Son of God	Luke 3:3-6
Isaiah 9:1-2	His ministry in Galilee	Matthew 4:13-16
Psalm 78:2-4	He was to speak in parables	Matthew 13:34-35
Isaiah 11:2 Psalm 45:8	He was anointed by the Holy Spirit	Matthew 3:16 John 3:34
Deuteronomy 18:15	Christ is the Prophet	Acts 3:20,22
Jeremiah 7:11	The temple that is the house of prayer is abused by being a place of merchandising	Matthew 21:13
Isaiah 61:1-2	Binding the broken hearted	Luke 4:18-19
Isaiah 35:5-6	Heals the blind, deaf and lame	Luke 7:22
Isaiah 53:3	Rejected by the Jews who are His own people	John 1:11 Luke 23:18
Psalm 110:4	A Priest after the order of Melchizedek	Hebrews 5:5-6
Isaiah 53:9	He was sinless and had no guile	1 Peter 2:22
Psalm 118:22	Betrayed by Jewish leaders	John 7:48
Zechariah 9:9	His Triumphal entry on a donkey	Luke 19:35-38
Psalm 8:2	Worshipped by infants	Matthew 21:15-16
Isaiah 53:1	He was not believed	John 12:37-38
Zechariah 13:7	The Shepherd's sheep are scattered	Matthew 26:31 Mark 14:50

Psalm 41:9,55:13-14	Betrayed by a close friend	Matthew 10:4 Luke 22:47-48
Zechariah 11:12	Betrayed for thirty pieces of silver	Matthew 26:14-15
Isaiah 53:7	Silent before His accusers	Mark 15:4-5
Isaiah 50:6	Spat upon and beaten	Matthew 26:67
Psalm 35:19	Hated for no reason	John 15:24-25
Isaiah 53:5	Sacrifice for others	Romans 5:5-8
Isaiah 53:12	Crucified with criminals	Mark 15:27-28
Zechariah 12:10	His hands and feet were pierced	John 20:27
Psalm 109:4	He prayed for His enemies	Luke 23:34
Psalm 22:17-18	Lots were cast for His clothing	Matthew 27:35-36
Psalm 34:20	None of His bones were broken	John 19:32-33,36
Zechariah 12:10	They pierced His side	John 19:34
Isaiah 53:9	Buried in a rich man's tomb	Matthew 27:57-61
Psalm 16:10 Psalm 49:15	He was physically resurrected	Mark 16:6-9 John 20:11-31
Hosea 6:2 (Third day)	Resurrected on the third day	1 Corinthians 15:4 (Third day)
Psalm 68:18	The ascension of Christ, to be seated at God the Father's right hand	Mark 16:19 Acts 1:9 Ephesians 4:8

27

130 STATEMENTS AND STANDARDS BASED UPON TRUE BIBLICAL DOCTRINE WITHOUT HUMAN BIAS

———〜〜〜———

1) Unbelievers will be in the Lake of Fire because they have rejected the true, loving God who provided faith for salvation for them.

2) Christians should be baptized and have communion. Christians should know that baptism is a commandment of God by Christ, but one must know and believe that it is faith in Christ that saves them, not the act of baptism or communion. These are to be done because of their love for Christ, but in no way can these give you eternal life. Only Christ alone is the giver of eternal life.

3) Christ was not a vegetarian and you don't need to be one, but you're allowed to be one according to the Word of God.

4) Christians are not to be in the occult in any way, which means no Ouija boards, horoscopes, palm reading, psychics, etc.

5) Christians are not to continue to sin because they are forgiven.

6) Christians are not to take drugs such as marijuana (pot), heroin, LSD, etc. No drug abuse, including the abuse of prescription drugs.

7) Some Christians may drink alcohol, but are not allowed to get drunk.

8) Some Christians may smoke cigarettes, a pipe or cigars but it is an addiction and does not glorify God. Therefore, it would be better to quit or never to start smoking at all.

9) Christians are not to use God's name in vain, such as saying G_d D__n it! This is sin and there is no way a person is to justify making this okay in any way. It is sin and it needs to be called sin, just as all other sin.

10) Christians are not to lie or give false witness in court or anywhere else for that matter.

11) Christians are not to be homosexuals. Some people may be tempted in this way, but in this case it is not the temptation, it is the act that is sin. God commands all Christians to be heterosexual.

12) Christians are not to hate a person who is practicing homosexuality, but they are to hate the sin and still love the sinner.

13) Christians are to know and believe that there is a Hell. Otherwise, why would Christ have to die on the cross and shed His blood for the sins of the world?

14) Believers are to know and believe that there is an enemy, the devil, and his demons (fallen angels).

15) Christians are to know that there are holy angels of God, but they are not to be worshipped. Worship is for God only.

16) Christians cannot be demon-possessed because God, the Holy Spirit, indwells them. But believers can be oppressed by demons.

17) Believers can experience sickness, poverty, etc. These circumstances do not in any way mean that God doesn't love them. God always loves His true children in Christ.

18) Believers are to know and believe that the Bible (the Holy Scriptures) is the inspired Word of God and is perfect in all ways.

19) The Christian Church is not to be competitive, as this is not of God and also because the true church (the Universal Christian Church) is the Bride of Christ; it is foolish and contrary for a body to compete against itself.

20) True believers are to know that the Bible does not contradict itself at all.

21) Jesus Christ was and is Jewish and is still the King of the Jews and always will be. Therefore, the Gentile believer is to love the Jew as well as the Jewish believer. Both types of Jewish and Gentile believers are to love the unsaved as well, and be a witness for Jesus Christ the Messiah.

22) God hates all sin but loves the sinner onto salvation.

23) Hatred, abortion, adultery, murder, idolatry and lying are all sin, even if modern society seems to justify these sins as normal for today.

24) Destructive anger is sin.

25) Productive, loving anger is not sin.

26) Believers are to know that Christ will raise and rapture the dead believers first and then rapture the living believers after them.

27) Jesus Christ is the only One. Again, He is the only One who can forgive sin, no one else. No priest, no pastor and no other being, human or false god, can forgive sin. Therefore, one must go only to Jesus Christ in prayer to receive forgiveness of their sin(s).

28) Christians are not to pray for the dead.

29) Christians are not to pray to Mary or any so-called patron saint. Not even those that are the major apostles such as Peter, Paul or John. Not only is this insulting to God, it is wrong and foolish; it is sin.

30) Yahweh (Jehovah) the "I AM", is the only God and He is the only true God of the Bible. No one else.

31) Christ can forgive ANY sin.

32) Sin is sin, not as some like to say, "I made a mistake."

33) Christians are to believe that Christ died on the cross for the forgiveness of the sins of the world.

34) Christians must know that God is One in three persons:
The Father is God
The Son is God
The Holy Spirit is God
All three Persons are One God.

35) Christians must know and believe that God's grace is a totally unmerited favor of God to forgive sin.

36) Believers are to know and believe that it is only by the saving work of Christ that they will be going to Heaven (John 3:16).

37) A believer's good deeds cannot ever get them into heaven. Only true faith in Jesus Christ can save them and get them into heaven.

38) Jesus Christ is not a separate God. He is one with the Father and the Holy Spirit.

39) Jesus Christ, the son of God, is not and never was, and never will be, a brother to Lucifer as a false, so-called Christian religion claims.

40) Jesus Christ never sinned.

41) Jesus Christ obeyed His Father always.

42) Believers are to pray for the sick, their wife or husband, children, family, church, world, enemies, etc., to glorify God the Father, the Son and the Holy Spirit.

43) Believers are to be led by God through His Word, not by willfulness from self or others.

44) Christ is seated at the right hand of the Father, which is the hand of authority.

45) Jesus is the only way, truth and life-giver.

46) True Christians are to first love God above all.

47) True Christians are to then love man (his brother). But who is his brother? They are men and women of all nations and races.

48) True believers know that they can do nothing to save themselves and that it is only Jesus Christ who can save them. Only by faith in Him.

49) True believers love the truth of God's loving Word, the Bible, and share it and to not repress others and hold back the Word from others.

50) True Christians have an attitude to forgive others.

51) True Christians know that even though they have power over sin given to them by the Holy Spirit, at times they may sin. Then, it is the Holy Spirit who convicts them of sin and then the believer is to go to the Lord Jesus Christ in prayer, and ask forgiveness for their sin to continue to have fellowship with Him. They are to realize that they are always saved. God's love is not conditional to His children.

52) Christians are to always love their spouse and children and have no favorites.

53) Christians don't need to be rich to please God, as the world teaches today. Even though many would like to think that an abundance of money and riches may appear as being in God's blessing, this is not the truth in God's Word.

54) As believers, we all need money to live for food, clothing and shelter. But we are not to have a love for money!

55) A Christian is to be true to God and himself as well.

56) A Christian is to be a responsible person.

57) Christians are to love their parents even if they were abused by them as children. They are to hate the sin and love the sinner.

58) Christians are to love Jews.

59) Christians are to give to the church in some way such as time, money, etc.

60) Christians are not to lie, steal or hate anyone.

61) Christians are to witness to others about the Lord and Savior Jesus Christ.

62) Christians are to be disciples (learners) of Christ and His Word.

63) Christians are to pray for their enemies.

64) Christians are to forgive their enemies.

65) True Christians believe and teach that Christ was born of a virgin.

66) True Christians believe that Christ arose from the dead in body on the third day and that He will come again.

67) True Christians know that Jesus Christ truly loves them and forgave their sin at the cross.

68) Christians are to obey the law of the land, but not to go against God's Word, the Bible.

69) Christians are not to encourage abortion, but they are to help the person in need with unwanted pregnancies.

70) Christians are not to hate a woman because she had an abortion. Christ still wants her to know Him and become His daughter.

71) Christians are not to bomb abortion clinics.

72) Christians are to pray for non-Christians that are ignorant and hard-hearted about sinning.

73) Christians are to pray for their leaders; even if they are not doing God's will and are not in agreement with them.

74) Christians are not to divorce except for unfaithfulness. This can mean sexual, breaking the law and abuse of a spouse or child.

75) Christians are not to abuse or neglect their family, spouse or children.

76) Christians are not to commit incest.

77) Christians are to be married to one spouse at a time.

78) The Old and New Testament is the only valid Bible and is complete. No other book is God's Word.

79) Christians are to read their Bible daily.

80) Christians know that there is no one equal to Christ. Not Moses, Mohammed, Buddha, etc. No one.

81) No Christian is to predict the day or hour of Christ's coming, but all Christians are to know that we are in the last days and we should be looking forward to His coming for us.

82) Christians are to know that all true Christians will be in heaven and non-Christians will be placed in Hell.

83) The true Christian and non-Christian are to know that after this life there is only Heaven or Hell, and that there is no purgatory or limbo. There is no place in between, only one or the other.

84) There is only one level of Heaven. Unfortunately, there is a false teaching that there are three levels in Heaven and all people go to one of them. This is a teaching not from God and is a lie.

85) Christ, because He is God, never had the ability to sin and therefore, never will. So, He is true to His Word.

86) God is immutable which means that He is unchangeable.

87) God is true to His Word the Bible.

88) Christians are not to believe that baptism saves an infant or an adult. Why? Because it is only simple faith in Jesus Christ that saves a person from their sins.

89) There is no power in water, but again, it is faith in Jesus Christ that saves a person. Christ does command that baptism is only to be for knowing believers as an outward testimony. Therefore, it is not to be performed with the idea that baptism saves a person.

90) Christians need to know that the Gospel message revolves around three major words in the Bible. These words are Death, Burial and Resurrection of Jesus Christ.

91) A Christian must believe that Jesus Christ arose from the dead physically and not as some cults have taught in the past that He only arose in spirit only.

92) Faith in the shed blood of Christ is a MUST for the forgiveness of sins.

93) Christians are to know that Jesus Christ has three major titles. They are Prophet, Priest and King. There is no one greater than Christ in these titles.

94) It is okay for a woman to wear pants or slacks to church. Some church leaders and men in the church may not like this, but Christ looks upon the heart and not cosmetic looks of any person.

95) Church tradition and the way things were done in the church for many years is never to surpass the authority of the Scripture.

96) Christ looks at your heart, not your family heritage, whether good or bad. Christians are to see others this same way also.

97) Christians are not to be prejudiced, but they are to understand and even encourage the positives of each culture. They shouldn't expect others to fit into their own, more-dominant-in-number culture.

98) Many intellectuals will look at the Bible and say it contradicts itself. They believe this because they try to study the Bible as a book of history, science or art, which it is not. The Bible is a spiritual book and should be studied as such. When these people try to understand the Bible by theory and hypothesis the way they would study a history or science book, they run into trouble. A person needs to study the Bible as truly from the Creator, and it is only then that they will understand and learn that there are not any contradictions in the Word of God.

99) There is no such thing as a sinless Christian. Only Christ is always and in every way totally sinless.

100) Christians must not get involved with drug abuse at all, as this is considered witchcraft in the Bible.

101) Christians are not to get involved with any sort of witchcraft or vampires, etc. There are no good witches. Not even white witches as depicted in fairy tales. None!

102) Because each person has received their soul from and through their parents at conception, and each living person is to worship God, abortion is sin and murder. Women don't own their bodies and men don't own the woman's body. Therefore, no one else has a right to abort a child even though science likes to depersonalize it and call it an embryo. It is God who owns our bodies. Not humans, male or female. God owns humanity; humanity does not own itself.

103) Some do not preach or teach about the Gospel message which is the Death, Burial and Resurrection of Jesus Christ, and its main focus, which is the total work of the Son of God that is for our salvation and knowing that salvation is not by any of our works. It doesn't matter how much you love your church. If your church is preaching the wrong gospel you should leave. There can only be salvation from God's way. It must be God's Gospel, not ours!

104) Some people believe that Hell doesn't exist. Some people even joke about it and say they will have a lot of fun there or that it's ok, because all their friends will be there. They should understand that Hell will be a place of great torment. Every true believer must believe that Hell is a real place because Jesus Christ said many times that it does exist, and He is the One and only God-man and because He is God. He never lies.

105) Some Christians will eat meat and some will eat vegetables. The Bible says that it didn't matter in the time of the New Testament. Even Jesus Christ ate meat so it is a matter of conscience and no one is to judge the other, just because one may feel that it is odd or wrong (Romans 14:1-4,6).

106) Christians are to pray for their government leaders and not speak in a put-down manner toward them (Romans 13:1-7).

107) Most Christians worship on Sunday (the Lord's Day) and some on the Saturday called the Sabbath. Some don't have much concern for the day! The key is that it's a matter of worshipping God in truth and any day is fine. It is not the day that is a major concern. We can see this in Romans 14:4-8.

108) The Bible is a true book and it has scientific and historical true facts, in that it cannot be refuted by secular science or history even today. It must be understood and realized that the Bible is the only book of Divine Spiritual Truth from God.

109) Sin is not a mistake, or a genetic pre-disposition, or because of bad health, mental or physical. It is not considered okay in fighting for one's honor. Being passive is the sin of transgression, and being too aggressive is the sin of trespassing. All are sin, not mistakes. Sin is based on willful envy, lying, hate and pride, and so on. Sin is against God and it is the rejection of God.

110) Jesus Christ is the God-Man which means that He is fully God and fully man. He could never, and will never sin, because He was never born with a nature to sin. Therefore, from the time He took on humanity (became a human), He could never sin. Here is an important verse to look up, showing us the overshadowing of Mary's sin nature in the conception of Christ Jesus, in conceiving Him with a Holy nature not a sin nature (Luke 1:35).

111) Christians are to know that Christ is God and He is a person in the Triune God. He is not some extraterrestrial being that got here from a UFO.

112) Christians are to know that there is only one world and not many worlds, and no other creatures. The reason for this is because the Bible teaches that God gave His only Son to the world, not the worlds (John 3:16).

113) Jesus Christ as God the Son has performed the greatest miracle of all time past, present and future. He arose from the dead. No one in all of history ever or will ever be able to do this. No one! And no one in any other faith or religion will ever come close because Jesus Christ is truly God and the only true God-Man!

114) Christians should study Bible prophecies knowing that it is the Bible that is to be the focus of prophecy, not history books or other books nor false prophets, etc. It is the Bible that has the final word and authority, nothing else.

115) All true prophecy is only of Christ. All other so-called prophecy is not of Christ, but is of an adverse evil; one of many evil types used to try to take away glory from

God and to deceive undiscerning people, to distract them from the true faith in Christ which is the one true faith in the One true God.

116) True Christians believe that all races came from Adam and Eve, and God inspired (breathed life) into Adam.

117) Some think that the races came from outer space and this is false and is a lie of the devil because God made the races, and it is only through Jesus Christ that any person of any race can be saved only through Jesus Christ.

118) If a person does not believe in Christ as their Savior, God will send them to Hell. This is not because God is a God of fear or hate, it is because God gives all men the faith to know and believe in the One and Only true God. It is God's gift to all men to exercise their faith in the true Creator through their free will, but if their heart is hardened, God will place them in Hell because of their rejection of the true God. God is Holy and deserves His honor even in the knowledge of His creation. So, one must believe in the truth and love of God and live in the intent to worship Him in truth, and standing strong in God's great reward of future blissful, everlasting life.

119) Atheists say there is no God. The question I have for them is where did this world come from? Their answer will be from _____. And my response to them is where did _____ come from? And again my response would be and where did _____ come from, and so on; this could happen one time or many times. In the end, there will always be a greater being and Creator and His name is God.

120) One must realize that atheists are blind to the reality they live in. You may have even heard the very human saying that love is blind. But if one looks at this, it is to be real, true love in a relationship that cannot be one-sided. For the atheist it is a blind hate for God and love for self only! But this love for self is sad and

foolish because the Bible (God's Word) says that only a fool does not believe there is a God (Psalm 14:1) and that a fool doesn't desire to have understanding, but is more concerned about telling others what he thinks (Proverbs 18:2).

121) Those who claim they are agnostic say they believe in some sort of greater being. Most also think it is okay to just live a decent life and they need not be concerned to pursue knowledge in understanding the true loving Creator. The reason for this is because those who think this way think that if there is a God, He must reveal Himself their way, not God's way (through the Bible). Agnostics believe they are not sure if there is a God. They deny God and do not think He is the One who created them and gave them life and all the good of life. One other important thing about this word "agnostic" is that many people who really think they are smart, and think that in taking this label it makes them appear as mental giants. But in fact, the Greek meaning of the word agnostic is a word that implies ignorance, not intelligence.

122) Atheists and agnostics are people of pride and deny reality. They believe in their own world and that is a world of foolishness. And yet, they go as far as to think that all is well.

123) If a church says that they are a Bible-believing church and they are preaching very little about the death, burial and resurrection of Jesus Christ and are also not mentioning sin, that church has lost its focus and needs to get back on track, or the people of the church need to find a true Bible-believing church to worship at.

124) Teaching and preaching in churches is to be centered on Jesus Christ, not tradition, not denominations and not politics.

125) All the major teaching of Christ's doctrines are very important. They are like joints. If one joint is out of place, then it is dangerously dysfunctional. The

doctrines must be taught and believed or eternal damage is being done.

126) Just because you have worked or are working in the church, doesn't mean you are a Christian. Even if you are an organist, Sunday school teacher, pastor, etc. You must believe the Gospel in order to receive salvation.

127) Without one understanding that the blood of Christ was shed for the forgiveness of sin, there can be no salvation. If one rejects this and claims to be a Christian, they are either ignorant or not a true Christian.

128) Christian churches should have a total worship service together. This means worship time and Sunday school should be close knit. For instance, worship time is to be for husband and wife and children (including teens), singles, etc. All together, not separated. Sunday school should be husbands and wives, as well as singles, in one class and the children in other classes from grades 1-2, 3-4, 5-6, 7-8, 9-10 and 11-12. College students are old enough to be in adult classes. A system like this breeds maturity and comfort in spiritual growth in Christ Jesus, because all are to be examples to each other.

129) All music played or performed in the church is to be done in such a way that all the words in the songs, hymns and melodies need to be heard. The style of the music is not to have priority over the being able to hear the words or the sound of the music. Ever! The reason being is so the words can and should be discerned at all times to protect all believers in their growth.

130) The church needs to be united, not divided, to promote community, family and true unity. The understanding of this is for the overall Christian church to promote family unity, not the husbands in this group, and the wives in another group, or the children in yet another group. Husbands and wives divided and children divided in church breeds weak, divided families and their children suffer the most (Galatians 3:28).

CPSIA information can be obtained
at www.ICGtesting.com
Printed in the USA
BVHW082053310720
585160BV00001B/70

9 781628 714807